DATE DUE		
MAR 19 1997			

GLOBALISATION AND INTERDEPENDENCE IN THE INTERNATIONAL POLITICAL ECONOMY

To Stephanie, for her forbearance, constant support and companionship in times both good and bad

GLOBALISATION AND INTERDEPENDENCE IN THE INTERNATIONAL POLITICAL ECONOMY
Rhetoric and Reality

R.J. BARRY JONES

PINTER PUBLISHERS
London & New York

Distributed in the USA & Canada by St. Martin's Press Inc.

Pinter Publishers
25 Floral Street, Covent Garden, London, WC2E 9DS, United Kingdom

First published in Great Britain 1995

Distributed exclusively in the USA and Canada by St. Martin's Press, Inc., Room 400, 175 Fifth Avenue, New York, NY10010, USA

R.J. Barry Jones is hereby identified as the author of this work as provided under Section 77 of the Copyright, Designs and Patents Act 1988.

British Library Cataloguing in Publication Data
A CIP catalogue record for this book is available from the British Library

ISBN 1 85567 057 7

Library of Congress Cataloging-in-Publication Data

Jones, R.J. Barry
Globalisation and interdependence in the international political economy : rhetoric and reality/R.J. Barry Jones.
p. cm.
Includes bibliographical references and index.
ISBN 1-85567-057-7
1. International trade. 2. International economic relations.
I. Title.
HF 1379.J66 1994 94-18162
337—dc20 CIP

Typeset by Saxon Graphics Ltd
Printed and bound in Great Britain

Contents

Preface

My interest in international interdependence was crystallised by the attainment of fashionable status by the concept during the mid-1970s. Many of the contemporary invocations of the term remained vague and imprecise. Too many usages also implied a cosy and straightforward world that had little in common with the turbulent complexity of the world as experienced by many people. The pioneering work on international interdependence of the Contemporary International Relations Theory Research Group was then undertaken within such a critical spirit.

Little has changed since the publication of *Interdependence on Trial* (London: Pinter Publishers, 1984, edited by R. J. Barry Jones and Peter Willetts). The term interdependence continues to be used, and abused, with casual abandon. Moreover, the related notion of globalisation has emerged to reinforce, and partly substitute for, many earlier references to international interdependence. The concept of globalisation, however, raised many of the same difficulties encountered by that of international interdependence. Both terms continue to refer to important conditions and developments within contemporary international relations. A critical review of both notions thus appears to be both timely and desirable.

R. J. Barry Jones
Reading, March 1994

Section 1

INTERNATIONAL INTERDEPENDENCE AND GLOBALISATION: DEFINITIONS AND ISSUES

CHAPTER 1

Introduction: interdependence and globalisation in the contemporary international system-dispositions and definitions

Central problems

Interdependence and globalisation have become two of the most potent ideas about the contemporary world. They are also amongst the most abused and misused terms in popular usage. Ambiguous in usage, and vague in referent, interdependence and globalisation mean many quite different things to different people.

The idea of globalisation has assumed much of the role played by the concept of interdependence in the study of international relations and the international political economy in the late 1980s and early 1990s. Indeed, as will be seen subsequently, some of the more far-reaching interpretations of interdependence have evolved, almost unaltered, into contemporary notions of globalisation. However, many of the definitional, theoretical and empirical problems encountered by earlier ideas of interdependence continue to be shared by notions of globalisation.

The proliferation of contrasting usages and definitions of the term 'interdependence' has been such as to persuade some observers to advocate the abandonment of the term.[1] However, interdependence continues to remain both an evocative and an analytically important term, particularly when applied to the contemporary world. Many basic processes and conditions, affecting economic stability in the industrialised world and survival and developmental prospects in the Less Developed Countries, are characterised by features best captured by the term 'interdependence', or, in some instances, by its successor concept of globalisation. While repudiation may not be the most attractive option, considerable care and caution must, however, be exercised if the ideas of interdependence and globalisation are to be rescued from confusion and restored to a fruitful role in the study of the contemporary human condition.

The problems with the notions of interdependence and globalisation are not only that their empirical referent has been defined in quite different ways, but that divergent usages of the terms also reflect contrasting views of the way in which the world works, and ought to work. Apparently simple questions about whether interdependence in world affairs is increasing soon collide with a range of theoretical disputes and attendant technical controversies. Second-order questions, about whether any growth of interdependence and globalisation in world affairs is to be judged as desirable or undesirable, revive and compound the analytical and normative differences engendered by apparently simpler questions about empirical 'realities'.

Contrasting implications of interdependence and globalisation

The definitional issues concerning the terms interdependence and globalisation do not apply to the terms in isolation. The term 'interdependence' is often accompanied by significant adjectives: 'human'; 'global'; or 'international'. Globalisation carries its own implications of referent and significance. Many of these adjectives, and implications of significance, are applied with the same measure of linguistic and conceptual profligacy with which the term interdependence, itself, has often been used. The significance of these adjectives, and implications, may, however, be considerable.

'Human interdependence' is a term often employed to emphasise the degree to which individual human beings do not, and cannot, live in isolation from their fellows. Implying, as it does, the degree to which each individual in the modern world depends upon others and the extent to which others are, in turn, affected by the individual's actions, the notion of human interdependence contrasts with an excessively individualistic view of the human condition. Human interdependence thus embraces a set of assumptions about the social nature of humanity, and ethical propositions about considerate and responsive conduct. A normative commitment to sociability and responsibility towards others is thus often inherent in doctrines of human interdependence.

'International interdependence' evokes a very special realm of activity and ideas. The term 'international' is generally employed as a synonym for interstate. 'International interdependence' thus embraces those forms of interdependence that arise amongst, and only amongst, properly constituted states ('national' or otherwise). Much of the substance, and distinctiveness, of 'international interdependence' derives from the fragmentary effects of a world divided into politically and legally autonomous entities, each jealous of its 'sovereignty' and concerned to maintain the myriad manifestations of competence and independence. Thus, as much of the subsequent discussion will indicate, the interdependencies associated with economic exchanges *within* established states thus differ in a number of important respects from those attaching to *international* trade. Moreover, the general ease of reference to international interdependence reflects a high level of accommodation to the assumptions, and expectations, of a politically fragmented world and, in many cases, an unquestioning acceptance of the implications of such *embedded statism*.

'Global interdependence' proceeds beyond the world of interstate relations to a vision of a world community, however undeveloped that community may be at the current stage of human evolution. Minimally, such global conceptions of interdependence invoke no more than a recognition of the measure of common fate to which all inhabitants of the planet earth are subject. Maximally, the idea of global interdependence embraces far-reaching notions of moral commonalty and mutual impact. Notions of global interdependence elevate the concept of human interdependence to the global level, while cross-cutting with international interdependence in a complex, and often discordant, manner. The apparent moralism and idealism of those who emphasise global interdependence reflects the challenge to the dominant practices and principles of statism that is inherent in the priorities signalled by such a global perspective.[2] Contemporary conceptions of globalisation straddle this tension in an uncomfortable manner.

A distinct perspective upon the international political economy, developed by Robert Keohane and Joseph Nye, Jr., moved from an emphasis upon the significance of *transnational relations* in the modern international system[3] to a conception of the contemporary world in terms of *complex interdependence.* This latter notion turned upon the proposition that the growth and deepening of associations amongst nominally independent states would eventually generate a world characterised by: multiple channels of connection amongst societies, or their members; the ending of any clear hierarchy amongst the issues of salience to governments, with, in particular, the decline of security issues as the dominant concern; and, finally, the diminishing use, or utility, of force in those relations amongst states within which complex interdependence prevails.[4]

The contextual conditions envisaged in the notion of complex interdependence are echoed in A. G. McGrew's conception of globalisation in terms of the 'multiplicity of linkages and interconnections between the states and societies which make up the modern world system' and the processes through which 'events, decisions, and activities in one part of the world can come to have significant consequences for individuals and communities in quite distant parts of the globe'.[5]

Competing definitions of interdependence

Notions of interdependence, and their modern resonances in concepts of globalisation, thus highlight features of, and processes within, the contemporary international system that are of clear, potential importance. Each term, however, requires further scrutiny before it can be deployed with confidence and effect.

The term interdependence often finds its most substantial expression within composite concepts, of the kind considered in the preceding discussion. However, it requires examination in its own right, for different definitions vary as to the essential characteristics of any relationship of interdependence. Definitional approaches to interdependence have divided along two basic axes: the first, that of interconnectedness versus mutual dependence;[6] and the second, that of atomistic versus holistic views of interdependence.[7]

Interdependence has often been equated with patterns of transactions[8] and interconnections amongst actors of various kinds:[9] a view of interdependence that draws close to some conceptions of globalisation. In international economic relations, evidence for such interconnectedness is to be found in shipments of commodities and goods, financial flows, communications and sympathetic movements in the values of a variety of such economic indicators as interest rates, wages, employment rates and prices. Data on such indicators is readily available and easily processed by modern computers. Patterns of such transactions and interconnectedness are therefore relatively easy to identify. A definition of interdependence in terms of such patterns is thus methodologically attractive, if substantively contested.[10]

Quantitative technicalities aside, aggregate data about interstate commercial flows, or cross-border sensitivities, do not, in themselves, demonstrate the importance of the associations revealed. In common parlance the term interdependence, as applied to international relationships, generally denotes something of weight and substance. This element of qualitative significance is submerged by definitions that equate interdependence with patterns of transactions and interconnectedness, and by the corresponding quantitative measures. Something important must be at stake for interdependence, as it is commonly viewed, to be involved. Alternative approaches to interdependence thus seek to clarify the substantive essence of such relationships and build them into useful definitions of the phenomenon.

Definitions of interdependence that embrace the importance of the stakes involved emphasise the notions of dependence and mutuality. Dependence suggests the reliance of an actor upon some other; mutuality implies that all the actors involved in some relationship, or set of relationships, are dependent upon one another in one, or more, important respects. Such a definition of interdependence as mutual dependence is, in David Baldwin's view, the traditional usage of the term.[11] This basic judgement does not, however, resolve serious questions about the direction, duration, seriousness and balance of the dependencies involved in any relationship(s) or interdependence.

Definitions of dependence and interdependence that satisfy the minimal criteria of significance for the participant(s) can thus be constructed:

> *Dependence* exists for any actor when a satisfactory outcome on any matter of significance for that actor requires an appropriate situation or development elsewhere.

thence:

> *Interdependence* exists for a grouping of two or more actors when each is dependent upon at least one other member of group for satisfactory outcomes on any issue(s) of concern.[12]

Such basic definitions do not, however, settle the range of questions raised by notions of interdependence. A valiant attempt to clarify and resolve some of the questions concerning the nature of dependencies involved in interdependence relationships was made by Robert Keohane and Joseph Nye, in their seminal work, *Power and Interdependence: World Politics in Transition*.[13] Keohane and Nye sought to establish a clear qualitative distinction between two conditions: sensitivity and vulnerability. This distinction is initially clear and cogent:

> Sensitivity involves degrees of responsiveness within a policy framework — how quickly do changes in one country bring costly changes in another and how great are the costly effects.[14]

> Vulnerability can be defined as an actor's liability to suffer costs imposed by external events even after policies have been altered.[15]

There are, however, a number of unresolved difficulties and persisting ambiguities in the notions, as deployed by Keohane and Nye. Sensitivity is the least problematical of the two concepts. It successfully achieves the objective of differentiating between trivial patterns of interconnectedness and substantive dependencies, and interdependencies,[16] by emphasising the costliness of the changes induced in one country by changes elsewhere. The only serious shortcoming with this view of sensitivity is its neglect of the subjective dimension of the response of governments and peoples to perceived, or actual, dependencies. Subjective sensitivity of this kind is of considerable importance in practical politics and policy-making, and is clearly implied by popular usage of the term sensitivity. It is not, however, directly addressed in Keohane and Nye's discussion of the term.[17]

The notion of vulnerability poses far more taxing difficulties than does that of sensitivity. These are indicated by a further account of the condition by Keohane and Nye in which they argue that:

> The vulnerability dimension of interdependence rests on the relative availability and costliness of the alternatives that various actors face.[18]

The difficulty here is that the apparent clarity of the first definition of vulnerability has been surrendered. That definition could be restated as the simple unavailability of a policy option that would protect an actor from any future costs generated by the given external event. The second account, however, takes the question of 'vulnerability' into a realm of double variability: the variability of the relative availability of policy options; and the relative costliness of those options and the conditions that they might create.

The translation of 'vulnerability' from absolute condition to a variable quality is a wholly realistic development. However, it erodes the simple distinction between sensitivity and vulnerability, if that distinction is to be drawn in terms of costs. Time and relative costs are now the variables that define a two-dimensional area within which any situation of depen-

	Short-term	long-term
high costs	high sensitivity	high vulnerability
low/zero costs	low sensitivity	low vulnerability

Figure 1.1 The sensitivity/vulnerability spectra in international interdependence

dence will be located. Figure 1.1 illustrates such a two-dimensional area and reduces the range of possibilities in the sensitivity-vulnerability spectra to four polar forms.

Reference to *dependencies* in the above discussion has been no mere casual departure from the use of the terms 'sensitivity interdependence' and 'vulnerability interdependence' in Keohane and Nye's work. Interdependencies are, indeed, instances of mutual dependencies, but the significance of these to the participants in the relationship may vary markedly. Indeed, it is possible for one bilateral relationship to involve a relatively trivial sensitivity dependence in one direction, but a critical dependence, of high vulnerability, in the other. The asymmetry and imbalance characterising such a pattern of 'interdependence' may have very serious implications for the relationship. Asymmetry and imbalance could be particularly pertinent to the potential for relative power and influence between the participants. Such asymmetry and imbalances are, moreover, prevalent within the contemporary international system. Reference to sensitivities, or vulnerabilities, in terms of *dependencies* thus serves as a continuing reminder of the inequalities of capability and condition affecting contemporary states and their interrelationships. It also provides a corrective to loose associations between international interdependence and mutual benefit.

Methodological and theoretical questions

Technical, definitional and theoretical issues are also involved in the question of whether interdependencies are discrete to the specific international relationships within which they can be identified, or are conditioned components of wider complexes of processes and relationships. These issues are central to the question of the utility, and even the legitimacy, of ideas about growing globalisation within the international political economy.

The issue here can be defined, simply, by the question as to whether analysis must be confined to those entities, and relationships, that can be observed directly and unproblematically; or whether analysis may legitimately evoke factors and forces that are not immediately manifest in the world of day-to-day observation. In the realms of interdependence and globalisation, three positions can be identified on this issue: a purely *atomistic* perspective; a form of *empirically-based holism*; and range of theoretically more ambitious approaches that share a common *realist holism*.

Atomistic approaches to interdependence are content to construct descriptions of contemporary interdependencies from the wealth of data on international economic flows, and correlated movements in the values of various indicators of economic activity, or other patterns of association in non-economic areas.[19] Models of world-wide interdependence are then constructed through simple conjunction of the profusion of bilateral interdependencies.

Holistic approaches to interdependence, or globalisation, can be developed in one of two possible ways: through descriptive aggregation or deduction from prior theoretical foundations.

Descriptive aggregation, involving extensive empirical observations of international interrelationships, and their characteristic consequences, can be undertaken for two purposes. The first is to construct a simplified model of the complex set of relationships and interdependencies that highlights their most important aspects. The second is to develop a persuasive argument that the complexity of the overall set of relationships and interdependencies is such as to generate its own influence on the developments within that complex system: that the *whole* of the set of international interactions has become more than the mere sum of the individual parts. The density and complexity of mutually 'supportive' interrelationships is the key concept of the empirical-holistic perspective. The international system is viewed as a set of 'billiard balls' of such intense and durable interconnections as to mould the actions and reactions of each individual occupant of a place on the table-top.[20]

The identification of a self-sustaining pattern of complexity amongst observable actors, and their interrelationships, is thus at the heart of an empirical-holistic model of contemporary international interdependence and globalisation. Some analysts, however, favour holistic models of the contemporary international political economy that make claims for the existence, and substantial effect, of factors and forces that are not, and cannot be, directly observable. The analogy of Noam Chomsky's theory of the deep-structural sources of human speech serves to illustrate the nature of such approaches. This asserts, not merely that human languages are highly complex sets of interrelated words and grammatical rules, but that language, in all its day-to-day complexity, is actually governed by a deep-structure in the human brain, which cannot, as yet, be observed directly but only adduced from the common characteristics of observable human languages.[21]

Realist-holistic approaches to the construction of models of contemporary interdependence and globalisation share these presumptions of structural linguistics and hence contrast sharply with the atomistic approaches. The latter reflect the empiricist and positivist orientations that were popular in Western 'social science' during the 1950s, and 1960s. Realist holism also echoes, as has been suggested, the 'Platonic realism'[22] of the kinds of structural theories that became more fashionable from the late 1960s onwards[23] and the various 'Marxisms' that have remained attractive throughout the twentieth century.[24] Such approaches emphasise the critical difference between the 'realities' of day-to-day appearances and the more basic 'realities' that are supposed to underlie those superficial experiences. Empirical holism marks something of a compromise between pure atomism, with its denial that international interdependencies exhibit holistic characteristics, and the realist holism of many Structuralist and neo-Marxist approaches.

The methodological and philosophical issues involved in competing approaches to modelling interdependence and globalisation thus raise serious analytical and practical questions, that go to the heart of the nature, and possibility, of 'social science'. The problem is that of the increasing theory-dependence of analysis as the approach moves from that of simple atomism through empirical holism and on to realist holism. The former approach is content to work with the international interactions and interdependencies that *appear* to present themselves naturally in the world of immediate observations. As the approach becomes more holistic, however, the significance of any empirical interaction, association or interdependence is increasingly established, a priori, by the theoretically-based, holistic model, itself. The possibility of a self-justifying and self-sustaining analytical syndrome thus becomes a serious danger in such approaches. While such a danger does not justify the automatic rejection of such approaches, it does raise issues of considerable significance and complexity.

Holistic approaches to interdependence and globalisation also illustrate the difficulty of sustaining, in practice, the analytically neat distinction between 'top-down' and 'bottom-up' approaches to international relations.[25] Atomistic conceptions of interdependence clearly represent a form of 'bottom-up' analysis. The problem comes, however, with holistic conceptions of interdependence and globalisation. Realist holism evades the issue by relying upon a priori assertions about the status and role of unobservable phenomena operating at the macro-level. The acceptability of this solution to the 'level of analysis' problem remains, however, dependent upon the acceptability of such central reliance upon the 'existence' and role of non-observable phenomena in human affairs. The problem for many analysts of international relations, however, arises with the adoption of an empirical-holistic approach. The procedure here progresses from a 'bottom-up' form of aggregative analysis to 'top-down' propositions about the conditioning effect of a dense and complex system of interactions upon the subsequent behaviour of the actors on the international stage. Attempts to overcome this problem of switching focus lie at the heart of works like Kenneth Waltz's *Theory of International Politics*,[26] but have been widely criticised as a seriously flawed enterprise.[27]

Contrasting conceptions of globalisation

The popular notion of globalisation encounters many of the methodological issues raised by the contrast between atomistic and holistic approaches to international interdependence, as did the earlier notion of *complex interdependence.*[28] A.G. McGrew's definition, quoted earlier, remained largely agnostic as to the atomistic or holistic character of the globalisation. However, while acknowledging the unevenness of the extent and effect of globalisation in various dimensions of international life, McGrew does emphasise the contemporary intensification of a number of salient patterns of interconnectedness and interdependence, within the international political economy.[29] Such developments might entail no more than the spread and deepening of atomistic interdependencies, but do suggest that holistic features, whether empirical or realist, may be on the advance.

The ambiguities in the popular notion of globalisation thus reflect the ambiguities manifest in the more ambitious conceptions of interdependence. Some progress can be made here if a number of analytically distinct, though often empirically associated, meanings of the term can be identified. Increasing reference to globalisation could be little more than a symptom of a growing sensitivity, within the ranks of social and political analysts, to the global context within which a range of pertinent developments takes place. As such, it might denote little more than a timely expansion of analytical horizons. It is also possible that references to globalisation signify little more than fashionable semantics. The entitling of an interesting collection of seminal essays on international interdependence by Ray Maghoori and Bennett Ramberg as *Globalism Versus Realism*[30] provided an early illustration of the way in which evolving fashion could encourage the replacement of one term — interdependence — by a close relative of globalisation — globalism. Globalisation may therefore be little more than the relabelling of phenomena that have already been addressed via the more wide-ranging conceptions of international interdependence.

Semantic manoeuvres aside, the idea of globalisation is also suggestive of a number of analytically distinct phenomena and developments within the international system. A number of contemporary conditions hint at the increasing significance of the external context for issues that were formerly deemed to be 'national' in character or amenable to local resolution. However, these conditions range considerably in their nature, implications and potential development. Moreover, it is often unclear whether the term globalisation is being used to denote a condition that has already been attained or to highlight tendencies within the international political economy that will eventually generate a 'globalised' world order.

One element of possible globalisation is the growth of direct linkages amongst nominally separate societies and/or associated actors. The scale and significance of progress in such forms of association is, however, a complex issue requiring both discriminating empirical identification and theoretical interrogation. The issue, here, is akin to that of international interconnectedness under another name, with the same problems of translating raw data on patterns of association into persuasive claims of real, and abiding, significance. The ultimate significance of many contemporary developments is highly debatable, as is their possible reversibility. Thus, there is uncertainty about the significance of the growth of Transnational Corporations' transnationally integrated systems of supply and production. The complex repercussions of the Stock Exchange crashes of 19 October 1987 raised important questions about the extent, and ultimate significance, of global financial interconnectedness and 'integration'.[31] The considerable emphasis that some observers place upon rising levels of international conference participation by academics, and similar forms of personal, transnational association, is also a matter of debate and some scepticism.

Growing exposure to the competitive pressures exerted by an increasingly open international trade system might constitute a further form of globalisation. The pressures experienced by any one society, in this respect, need not come from those societies with which it trades directly. It may be sufficient to know that a given export market is threatened by another competitor, for effects to be felt in an exporting economy. However, many of the most severe pressures will be experienced through direct challenges from local producers within established export markets, and from growing import penetration of home markets. Globalisation, by this measure, is a direct function of the growth of competition in an international free-trade system.

The wider and more rapid diffusion of technology, advanced capital equipment and general know-how, may further intensify the potential pressures exerted by an increasingly open trade system. The lead enjoyed by the more technologically advanced economies will be subject to ever growing threat, as they face the reduction of the time-lag before innovative advantages are eroded and economies with lower wage levels are able to supplement basic cost advantages with increasing technological sophistication.

The effects of the globalisation, generated by the combination of a free-trade system and the acceleration of technological diffusion, may not be confined to those economies that have traditionally enjoyed a lead over the majority of their fellows, however. The pressures exerted by such an evolving system will also create a set of increasingly common constraints for all societies that pursue rapid economic growth and substantial levels of prosperity. Moreover, the practical ability of societies to 'choose' not to conform to the apparent dictates of a globalised economy might be reduced, substantially, by the supposed globalisation of culture and aspirational patterns, stimulated by the global spread of 'Western' material and cultural products.

The general question then arises as to whether the simultaneous growth of a number of these patterns of association and influence has a significance that is greater than the mere sum of the growth of each, viewed separately. Such a question takes the issue directly to the effects of the increasing density of international interactions and, where there are significant cross-linkages, the consequences of growing complexity. Globalisation would thus be a function of the qualitative effects, on the patterns of constraints and opportunities facing actors, of the increase in the density and complexity of international interactions.

The rhetoric of contemporary globalisation thus highlights a number of developments that may be intensifying within the contemporary international political economy. However, propositions concerning the steady increase, and central salience, of such developments need to be interrogated carefully if unwarranted conclusions about contemporary 'realities' are to be avoided. The human record is replete with reversals of apparently well-established trends and of overconfidence in ephemeral truths and 'realities'. The only real certainty about the future is the constancy of change. Moreover, the nature and significance of change is often a function of the tempo with which contributory developments occur: a development that takes decades to crystallise may have quite different social, economic and political consequences from a similar development that takes only a few years, or even months. The disruptive effects of rapid liberalisation in the Russian economy have provided dramatic demonstration of the significance of time and tempo in many central developments.

One critical source of the uncertainties that must always attach to the shape and significance of any patterns of association amongst human beings is the susceptibility of those patterns to intentional change by the actors involved. The 'social' realm may not be external to human consciousness, in the same sense as are the planetary systems. If the relationship between the human 'observer' and the human behaviour that is the object of that observation is inherently complex and analytically problematical, then the significance, and durability, of any patterns of interconnectedness, interdependence or globalisation are open to serious questions.

The construction of interdependence and globalisation

Many of the established approaches to the study of social, economic and political life treat their subject matter as if it were akin to, though not identical with, the phenomena of the natural world.[32] Dissatisfaction with such an approach to human studies has, however, been both varied and vigorous; it ranges from Peter Winch's emphasis upon the linguistic bases of cultural specificity,[33] through Thomas Kuhn's paradigmatic view of 'science'[34] and Lakatos's notions of 'research programmes',[35] to the recent enthusiasm for 'critical' approaches, stimulated by the Frankfurt School.[36]

Such issues are particularly relevant to the study of contemporary interdependence and globalisation. Much discussion of interdependence and globalisation, its development and its effects, has a deterministic flavour. Many views of these phenomena convey, as will be seen subsequently, the impression that irresistible forces within an 'objective' economic realm are driving global economic interdependence, and even integration, forward inexorably. Moreover, the effects of any growth of interdependence and globalisation upon individual states, international political relations and human life, in general, are assumed to be simple and automatic. The picture thus presented of central developments in the contemporary human condition is both simplistic and misleading. An alternative, and more discriminating, perspective would therefore be most helpful.

The contrast is between the simplistic approach of many traditional views of interdependence and globalisation and that offered by the 'critical' theories that have become popular in recent years. An emphasis upon the linguistic, and ideational, foundations of the human condition are taken to an extreme in some critical theories.[37] Their ultimate implication is an extreme form of voluntaristic idealism in which the reader is invited to accept that no individual's view of 'reality' has more substance than any other's and that by implication, 'reality' may be imagined, or reimagined, at the will of the thinker/writer.[38]

An approach to the study of human affairs that avoids both the positivism of much traditional 'social science' and the extreme voluntarism of 'critical' perspectives, is possible through a *constructionist* approach to human action and institutions. Such an approach emphasises the foundation of human actions and institutions in shared values, beliefs, understandings and expectations of the participants in any economic, social or political order, while acknowledging that the complex of interacting and mutually reinforcing behaviour thus generated constitutes a 'reality' of considerable force, pattern and durability.[39] This is particularly appropriate to the study of contemporary interdependence and globalisation, for it encourages attention to the practical processes, and the uneven historical record, through which the patterns of contemporary interdependence, and their institutional foundations, have been established.

Methodologically such an approach has a clear starting-point on the *reflective* side of Robert Keohane's distinction between *reflective* (or *cognitive) and rationalistic* approaches to the study of international relations and the international political economy.[40] However, the central role that is also ascribed to the 'realities' that are generated through the complex sets of self-reinforcing intersubjectivities of the members of societies, economies and polities, readmits those empirical complexities that may generate the kinds of unintended outcomes and unexpected consequences that require a form of analysis that comes close to that of the rationalistic approach, while not necessarily accepting the ontological presumptions of its more extreme forms. The simple distinction between reflective and rationalistic approaches to international relations may thus not be that easy to sustain in practice, if analysis is not to be unduly restricted by a priori methodological constraints, or confined to the 'understanding' side of the understanding/explanation divide in 'social science'.[41]

A major theme within the subsequent discussion will thus be the central role of political purposes and processes in the generation of contemporary international interdependence and globalisation. Far from being automatic and self-generating conditions, most instances of interdependence and globalisation have arisen as a result of the patterning of the modern world into sovereign states and the uneven manner in which these states have then acted and interacted. Interdependence and globalisation are, it will be argued, always changeable, as well as manipulable, conditions; and it is in the realms of the 'political' that the immediate sources of such change or manipulation are to be found.

The political sources of much of contemporary international interdependence and globalisation are the subject of the next chapter, Chapter 2. The implications of such phenomena for the political and moral life of the contemporary world are then explored in Chapters 3 and 4. The four chapters of Section 3 start, in Chapter 5, with a review of the definition of interdependence, globalisation and proximate concepts. Chapter 6 surveys the varied range of dependencies and interdependencies that characterise the contemporary international political economy. The discussion in Chapters 7, 8 and 9 then turns to the complex issues surrounding the sources, scale, consequences and likely future developments of international economic interdependence and globalisation. Chapter 10 then presents an overview and concluding discussion of the many issues generated by interdependence and globalisation in the modern world and its study.

Key issues within this discussion will be those of the degree to which interdependence and globalisation are the automatic consequences, or causes, of other central developments in the international political economy and the extent to which the development of interdependence and globalisation has benign or malign, and ultimately conflictful, implications.

The primary conclusions of the discussion will be that patterns of interdependence within the contemporary international system are highly varied, frequently asymmetrical and commonly imbalanced. Globalisation will, moreover, be seen to be a seriously simplistic conception of an international political economy that is, in reality, composed of multiple layers of differing patterns of action and interaction. A 'layer cake' world of diversity both within and amongst its distinct, albeit ultimately interconnected, 'layers' is far from that envisaged by the simpler models of international interdependence and globalisation.

Notes and references

1. P. A. Reynolds and R. D. McKinlay, 'The concept of interdependence: its uses and misuses', in K. Goldmann and G. Sjostedt (eds.), *Power, Capabilities, Interdependence: Problems in the Study of International Influence* (Beverly Hills: Sage, 1979).
2. For an example of such a general perspective see: J. W. Burton, *World Society* (Cambridge: Cambridge University Press, 1972).

3. See: R. O. Keohane and Joseph S. Nye, Jr. (eds.), *Transnational Relations and World Politics* (Cambridge, Mass.: Harvard University Press, 1972).
4. Robert O. Keohane and Joseph S. Nye, Jr., *Power and Interdependence: World Politics in Transition* (Boston: Little, Brown, 1977), esp. pp. 24-9.
5. A. G. McGrew, 'Conceptualizing global politics', pp. 1-28 in A. G. McGrew and P. G. Lewis (eds.), *Global Politics: Globalization and the Nation-State* (Cambridge: Polity Press, 1992), p. 23.
6. See, in particular, the discussion of D. Baldwin, 'Interdependence and power: a conceptual analysis', *International Organization*, Vol. 34 (Autumn, 1980), pp. 471-506.
7. See: R. J. Barry Jones, 'The definition and identification of interdependence', in R. J. Barry Jones and P. Willetts (eds.), *Interdependence on Trial: Studies in the Theory and Reality of Contemporary Interdependence* (London: Pinter Publishers, 1984), esp. pp. 30-3.
8. On the supposed significance of which for creating 'integrated' communities see Karl Deutsch, *Nationalism and Social Communication* (Cambridge, Mass.: MIT Press, 1953).
9. See the discussions in: R. Rosecrance and A. Stein, 'Interdependence, myth or reality', *World Politics*, Vol. 26, No. 1. (October 1973), pp. 1-27; R. Rosecrance, *et al.*, 'Whither interdependence', *International Organization*, Vol. 31, No. 3 (Summer 1977), pp. 425-45; and R. Rosecrance and W. Gutowitz, 'Measuring interdependence: a rejoinder', *International Organization*, Vol. 35, No. 3 (Summer 1981), pp. 553-7.
10. See, for instance, Mary Ann Tetreault, 'Measuring interdependence', *International Organization*, Vol. 34, No. 3 (Summer 1980) pp. 429-43; and Mary Ann Tetreault, 'Measuring interdependence: a response', *International Organization*, Vol. 35 (1981), pp. 557-60.
11. Baldwin, 'Interdependence and power', pp. 471-506.
12. This is a slight development of the definitions offered in Jones and Willetts, *Interdependence on Trial*, p. 8.
13. R.O. Keohane and J.S. Nye, Jr., *Power and Interdependence: World Politics in Transition* (Boston: Little, Brown, 1977).
14. Ibid., p. 12.
15. Ibid., p. 13.
16. As intended by Keohane and Nye, ibid., p. 9.
17. For a further discussion see, R.J. Barry Jones, 'The definition and identification of interdependence', pp. 23-5.
18. Keohane and Nye, *Power and Interdependence*, p. 13.
19. See, for example, the work of Richard Rosecrance and various associates, quoted above.
20. For an account in this vein see Section 1 of B. Buzan, C. Jones and R. Little, *The Logic of Anarchy: Neorealism to Structural Realism* (New York: Columbia University Press, 1993).
21. For one of the earliest elaborations of this approach see Noam Chomsky's seminal review of B.F. Skinner's book, *Verbal Behavior*, in the journal *Language*, Vol. 35, No. 1 (1959), pp. 26-58.
22. For a discussion of 'Platonic realism', see J. Cottingham, *Rationalism* (London: Paladin, 1984), esp. pp. 13-18.
23. Of which Keohane and Nye's notion of 'complex interdependence' is a partial example. See Keohane and Nye, *Power and Interdependence*, esp. Ch. 2.
24. For examples see John Maclean, 'Marxist epistemology, explanations of "Change" and the study of international relations', in B. Buzan and R. J. Barry Jones (eds.), *Change and the Study of International Relations: The Evaded*

Dimension (London: Pinter Publishers, 1981), pp. 46-67; and S. Gill and D. Law, *The Global Political Economy: Perspectives, Problems and Policies* (Hemel Hempstead: Harvester/Wheatsheaf, 1988).

25. On which see M. Hollis and S. Smith, *Explaining and Understanding International Relations* (Oxford: Clarendon Press, 1991), esp. pp. 7-9 and Ch. 5.
26. Kenneth Waltz, *Theory of International Politics* (Reading, Mass.: Addison-Wesley, 1979).
27. See, in particular: Richard K. Ashley, 'The poverty of Neo-Realism', (*International Organization*, Vol. 38, No. 2 (Spring, 1984), pp. 225-61) reprinted in R.O. Keohane (ed.), *Neo-Realism and Its Critics* (New York: Columbia University Press, 1986); and R. J. Barry Jones, 'Concepts and models of change', in B. Buzan and R. J. Barry Jones (eds.), *Change and the Study of International Relations: The Evaded Dimension* (London: Frances Pinter Ltd., 1981), pp. 11-29.
28. Keohane and Nye, *Power and Interdependence*, esp. pp. 24-37.
29. McGrew, 'Conceptualizing global politics'.
30. Ray Maghoori and Bennett Ramberg, *Globalism Versus Realism: International Relations' Third Debate* (Boulder, Colo; Westview Press, 1982).
31. For reports revealing the extent of the anxieties and uncertainties aroused by that episode see reports in the magazine, *The Economist*, 24 October 1987.
32. For critical accounts of such approaches to 'social science' see the discussions in: Alan Ryan, *The Philosophy of the Social Sciences* (London: Macmillan, 1970); R. S. Rudner, *Philosophy of Social Sciences* (Englewood Cliffs, N. J. Prentice-Hall, 1966).
33. Peter Winch, *The Idea of a Social Science and its Relation to Philosophy* (London: Routledge and Kegan Paul, 1958).
34. Thomas Kuhn, *The Structure of Scientific Revolutions*, expanded edn. (Chicago: University of Chicago Press, 1970).
35. Imre Lakatos, 'Falsification and the method of scientific research programmes', in Imre Lakatos and Alan Musgrove (eds.), *Criticism and the Growth of Knowledge* (Cambridge: Cambridge University Press, 1970).
36. For reviews of these approaches and their implications, see Michael T. Gibbons (ed.), *Interpreting Politics* (Oxford: Basil Blackwell, 1987); and Mark Hoffman, 'Critical theory and the inter-paradigm debate', *Millennium*, Vol. 16, No. 2, (1987) pp. 231-49.
37. Other variants are essentially partially disguised neo-Marxism. See, for instance, the work of W. A. Cox, 'Social forces, states and world orders: beyond international relations theory', *Millennium*, Vol. 10, No. 2 (Summer, 1981), pp. 126-55 (reprinted in R.O. Keohane, *Neo-Realism and Its Critics* (New York: Columbia University Press, 1986).
38. Derrida stands as one of the extreme exponents of this view; see David Wood (ed.), *Derrida: a Critical Reader* (Oxford: Basil Blackwell, 1992); C. Norris: *Derrida* (London: Fontana, 1987); and G. B. Madison (ed.), *Working through Derrida*, (Evanston, Ill.: Northwestern University Press, 1993).
39. See Peter L. Berger and Thomas Luckmann, *The Social Construction of Reality: A Treatise in the Sociology of Knowledge* (Harmondsworth: Allen Lane, The Penguin Press, 1966); and, for a more recent development of this approach, see Anthony Giddens, *The Constitution of Society: Outline of the Theory of Structuration* (Cambridge: Polity Press, 1984).
40. Robert O. Keohane, 'International institutions: two approaches', *International Studies Quarterly*, Vol. 32 (1988), pp. 379-96.
41. See M. Hollis and S. Smith, *Explaining and Understanding International Relations* (Oxford: Clarendon Press, 1991).

CHAPTER 2

International interdependence and globalisation: the political-economic interface

The sources and consequences of international interdependence and globalisation involve questions of some complexity and embrace contending perspectives upon human affairs. The key question here concerns that of the direction of influence between the political and the economic. This question, itself, involves the separability of economics and politics and thence the extent that such separability is admissible analytically, and the weight and direction of the influences between these two central dimensions of human activity.

The relationship between the political and the economic is an issue that has separated the major perspectives upon 'political economy': 'liberal', Marxist, and Economic Realist.[1] Economic liberalism, while appearing to offer clear prescriptions of the optimal relationship between politics and economics is, as will be seen below, somewhat more elusive in the view offered of their causal interconnections. Classical Marxism and Marxism-Leninism rejected any simple division between the economic and the political. Any distinction between the economic and political aspects of any politico-economic era was, rather, a matter of level and preponderant influence. The 'political', and other, components of the *superstructure* of any society were seen to be the ultimate product of the 'economic' *infrastructure.* Economic Realism, in contrast, identifies a complex interaction between the political and economic aspects of any society, but assigns a potentially decisive influence over long-term developments to political authorities and communities.

Economic liberalism, the politico-economic relationship, interdependence and globalisation

The view of the relationship between politics and economics maintained by Economic liberalism is of paramount significance given its authoritative position within the modern, Western-dominated, international order. Moreover, it offers a clear interpretation of the sources and consequences of international economic interdependence, and the implications of increasing globalisation. The liberal view of the political-economic relationship is often depicted as one of maximum separation. This, however, is an oversimplification and the prescription of no more than a relatively small group of ultra-liberals.

The existence of a distinctive *liberal* perspective upon the political economy is, itself, a matter of some controversy. The range and diversity of work that falls under this general heading is so great as to question the existence of one, cohesive school of thought. However, there are a number of assumptions and preferences that are common to a wide range of writers and practitioners and that identify their work, broadly, with the classical liberal tradition.[2]

Classical liberalism was the child of the Enlightenment in its fundamental beliefs in individuality and rationality. In extreme formulations, the individual human being is deemed to be existentially, and morally, prior to any community within which he or she is located. Such an ontological and ethical primacy of the individual permeates the subsequent judgements and interpretations of the liberal perspective.

The key to individual happiness and 'social' well-being, within the classical liberal paradigm, lies in the assumption of rational self-interest. A rational individual will be able to determine the best deployment of his, or her, productive capabilities, given the pattern of rewards for productive efforts. Equally rational judgements will be possible about the best patterns of consumption that are possible from available funds. Rational, self-interested individuals will also require, and provide the ingredients for, well-functioning liberal democratic systems.

The relationship between a *laissez-faire*, private enterprise economic system and a liberal democratic polity is central to classical liberalism; the survival of the one is ultimately dependent upon the survival of the other. Free markets provide individuals with the signals necessary for rational consumption decisions and the freedom to choose what, and from whom, they will secure the necessities of life. Free markets also allow producers to commit their productive resources to the most fruitful areas of production and then sell their products, with no let or hindrance, on the most favourable terms. When free markets are reinforced by the sanctity of property rights, then individuals are truly free to enjoy freedom and assert their liberties publicly: there can be no threat of arbitrary dispossession of the basics of livelihood in retaliation against officially disfavoured forms of behaviour. Free markets and property rights are thus believed to provide a necessary foundation for individual freedom and a viable liberal democratic political system.

In a similar vein, a liberal democratic system will remain under the ultimate control of a community of rational, self-interested individuals. The wish to preserve their liberties, free markets and property rights will ensure that such rational, self-interested individuals will deploy democratic influences to constrain governments from any attack upon free markets, or property rights. The liberal democratic order and the *laissez-faire* economic system are thus mutually necessary for, and supportive of, one another.[3]

Despite their emphasis upon the individual, classical liberals recognised, unlike some later ultra-liberals, the essentially social character of the human condition. More recent explorations of the implications of rational, self-interested behaviour have concluded that such behaviour encounters a fatal paradox *of rationality*, with free-riding individuals acting in such a way as to sabotage effective collaborative activities for any community, where such collaboration is voluntary.[4] Classical liberalism was not, however, confounded by this problem, for it remained an essentially *rationalist* perspective on the human condition; inspired by the belief that human beings were moving from the shadows of the primitive towards the light of reason. The new, enlightened human being would spontaneously acknowledge the requirements of the good life, including those features of conviviality and communality that made life bearable for all members of any society. Narrowly selfish behaviour would thus be abjured by individuals equipped with *enlightened* self-interest, and such enlightenment would sustain orderly and productive democratic politics, as much as it would generate any necessary collective endeavours. The bedrock of interconnections amongst human beings thus embraced substantial political and moral interdependencies.

Classical liberalism also envisaged a powerful and promising relationship between many developments at the international level. Here, the imperative was for governments to minimise their interference in trade relations. If all states adopted such a minimalist stance, then free trade would flourish and interconnections proliferate and deepen. Free trade would extend consumption opportunities, while providing producers with additional incentives for specialising in areas of production in which they enjoyed a relative international advantage. Global efficiency would thus be promoted, as consumers increased their levels of satisfaction and productive resources were deployed with maximum effectiveness.

Efficiency was not, however, the only contribution of an international free-trade system, as envisaged by classical liberals. Such efficiency was also seen to have benign political effects. The opportunities provided by the international market would stimulate a new level of interdependence in economic exchanges and the promotion of a mutuality of interests. A competitive international market would change the international division of labour and the location of production. Societies would withdraw from areas of production in which they found themselves to be internationally uncompetitive, to be redeployed in directions in which competitive advantages could be identified. The evolving pattern of productive specialisation would make all societies increasingly dependent upon imports of those goods and services that they no longer produced. They would also become more heavily dependent upon the continued accessibility of the export markets for the goods and services in which they had decided to specialise.

The effects of such a growth of objective international economic dependence were seen to be twofold. First, it was believed that increased dependence would deter societies from those forms of international behaviour that threatened to disrupt regular supplies of imported goods and services. Indeed, in the extreme case sustained military activity might become a practical impossibility for societies that had become dependent upon foreign sources of basic military supplies. Second, it was also believed that international antagonisms would progressively dissolve as societies increasingly recognised the mutuality of benefits and interests arising from the new international division of labour.[5]

Not all those of a generally 'liberal' orientation have, however, been equally optimistic about the benign effects of the unfettered free market. 'Compensatory liberals', as they have been dubbed by R. D. McKinlay and R. Little, doubt the equity of outcomes generated by such a system and, in some cases, its efficiency and even self-sustainability.[6] A greater emphasis upon community, and upon authoritative guidance of the market, has been the response of such compensatory liberals to the complexities of the modern economy. Comparable doubts about the self-sustaining, and self-regulating, character of a liberal international economy are also shared by the 'regime liberals' that will be discussed later in the section on Economic Realism.

The optimistic rationalism of classical liberals, however, underlay the belief that the package of benefits generated by an international free-trade system, intensifying interconnectedness, a new international division of labour and ever growing interdependence, would so commend itself to all those involved as to become virtually self-generating and self-sustaining. This belief was particularly appealing to liberal opinion during the prosperous and peaceful period of late nineteenth and early twentieth-century European history.[7] The predictions of a new era of benign interdependence had every appearance of imminent fulfilment. Confidence in such a simplistic view of a complex realm of human activity was, however, to be rudely shattered by the cataclysm of the First World War.

One line of continuing controversy, however, has focused on the role of non-democratic states, and their ruling regimes, in undermining the positive, and pacifying, effects of an international free-trade system and its supposedly benign patterns of interdependence. Such notions, which were much popularised by President Woodrow Wilson of the USA, have crystallised in the modern proposition that democratic states do not make war on one another. This doctrine, however, requires a rather selective definition of democracies, given the variety of historical evidence and experience.

The shock of the First World War thus failed to deliver a death-blow to doctrines of benign interdependence. Much of the classical liberal interpretation of the sources and consequences of expanded international trade, and growing economic association amongst societies, was to be revived by debates about the character of the post-Second World War revival of the world economy and moves towards the integration of European economies, as will be seen in later discussions.

Marxist perspectives on politics, economics, interdependence and globalisation

Marxist approaches to politics, economics and the patterns of interdependence in the modern world can be difficult to pin down with precision, given the variety of 'Marxisms' that have emerged during the long, and often turbulent, evolution of this determinedly radical approach to human affairs. The problem is further complicated by the concentration of Karl Marx himself on the domestic political-economy of capitalist societies. All versions of Marxism do, however, differ sharply from classical liberalism in their view of the nature of economic activity in a 'capitalist' world, the relationship between economics and politics, the viability and acceptability of *laissez-faire* economic systems,[8] the nature of contemporary interdependencies and the significance of globalisation.

It is possible to distil a form of 'classical Marxism' from the writings of Marx himself, that were widely read before the 1960s, and a range of 'traditional' interpretations of 'Marxism'. For such 'classical Marxism', human history had passed through a series of successive phases, marked by specific *modes of production*. Each mode of production was characterised by a peculiar combination of productive techniques with distinct *relations of production*. The techniques of industrial production might thus be wedded to differing relations of production: industrial capitalism, where capitalistic relations of production held sway; communist industrialism, where communal ownership and collective self-determination prevailed.

The prevailing mode of production formed the core, or *infrastructure,* of any society, or historical stage. Popular values and beliefs, the substance and form of the legal system, the shape and character of the political system, all constituted the derivative, or *superstructural* features of that historical stage of social development. Early interpretation of Marx's writings also saw the state and its functioning, both internal and external, as a function of the needs and interests of the dominant economic groups within any society .

Classical Marxist theory was also based upon the doctrine of the *labour theory of value.* This identified the *real* value of any goods or services as being a product, wholly, of the human labour that had been invested in their production. Within a capitalist system, the owners of capital were able to take advantage of their pivotal position within the productive system. The conditions determining the prices of goods and services were, in the short term, distinct from those determining the wages and salaries that had to be paid to workers. Capitalists, as the owners of the means of production, employers of labour and sellers of the goods and services produced, were thus in a position to pay their workers less than the market prices secured for their products. Such a regular, and necessary, extraction of 'surplus value' was the essence of the systematic pattern of *exploitation* that lay at the heart of the capitalist mode of production. However, the need of capitalists to extract surplus value was also the key to its eventual self-destruction.

The source of cycles of boom and bust within capitalism, and the long-term secular decline of profitability, lay in the combined consequences of labour's role in the generation of value and the dynamics of capitalist competition. Competitive pressures forces within each industry forced capitalists to invest in new productive technologies; not to do so would result in a progressive loss of competitiveness. However, the new productive technologies were invariably costly to introduce and more capital intensive than their predecessors. New investment thus resulted in the shedding of labour within each enterprise individually, and throughout industry generally. Increasing unemployment reduced the effective market for the products of the capitalist system at the very time that a healthy, if not expanding, market was required to absorb the increased output of the new, ever more productive and costly, machinery.

In the medium term, the paradox of increasing production with increasing unemployment resulted in cycles of boom and bust: boom when new investment was buoyant; bust when the problems of selling the product of that investment, and meeting its capital costs, were then confronted. In the longer term, the progressive reduction of the labour force would fuel a steady fall in the rate of realisable profit within the capitalist society and generate an inexorable slide into crisis, collapse and revolution.

The systematic extension of his political economy to the international sphere was to constitute the substance of Marx's unfinished last section of *Capital.* Many of his followers could not, however, evade the twin issues of the international dynamics of the capitalist order and the apparent failure of capitalism to collapse within a reasonable time-span. The two issues were resolved by developments in Marxist analysis during the latter years of the nineteenth century. The central element of this emergent perspective was that of imperialism: its sources, nature and role.

Late nineteenth-century Marxists gradually developed an answer to the puzzling non-occurrence of the expected collapse of advanced capitalist societies. The resurgent imperialism of the latter part of the century was identified, by Marxist analysts like Hilferding,[9] as the prime escape mechanism of mature capitalism. Drawing upon such insights, Lenin then formulated the full Marxist-Leninist theory of imperialism as the 'highest stage of capitalism'; and its last! [10]

Lenin's interpretation of 'capitalist imperialism' drew upon classical Marxist sources. The labour theory of value and the doctrine of the 'law' of the falling rate of profits were both accepted and incorporated. In the world thus envisaged, the competitive struggle within, and amongst, advanced capitalist countries would become increasingly intense. Two further developments in the progress of capitalism were, however, now emphasised: the increasing concentration of capital, ultimately into the new form of *finance capital;* and the significance of increased overseas investment and, with it, a reinvigoration of Western *imperialism.*

Finance capital emerged from the steady replacement of owner-managers, as the dominant form of capitalist enterprise, by ownership by large financial institutions. These institutions had been created by two processes: the first, that of the steady emergence of powerful financial service institutions, owning an increasing proportion of the industry that they previously serviced; the second, the growth, diversification and financial expansion of industrial enterprises to a point of transformation into 'arms-length', rather than close-quarters, owners and managers of productive enterprises. Whatever their origins, finance capitalists enjoyed, and practised, greater flexibility and international mobility than their more modest, and geographically rooted, predecessors. They were, in particular, well placed to pursue profitable overseas investment opportunities when promised greater returns than could be obtained from continued investment in their countries of origin.

Given the predicted contraction of profitability within the advanced capitalist economies, the Marxist-Leninist theory of *capitalist imperialism* envisaged the overseas flight of mobile financial capital. International economic development was, it was acknowledged, always an uneven process. Such *uneven development* meant that many areas remained relatively undeveloped and therefore available for potentially more profitable investments. The higher rates of return from such overseas investments would boost the flagging profits of major capitalist institutions and provide the capitalist system with a welcome reprieve from inevitable collapse. Overseas investments also brought with them the additional advantages of new, cheap sources of raw materials for industry; plentiful supplies of a widening range of foodstuffs to feed the metropolitan work-forces; and an expanded market for the output of the ever more productive industries of the capitalist economies.[11] However, investments of such profitability, and value, had to be protected. Where local conditions proved unacceptably unstable, political authority had to be established and, if necessary, imposed by the investors' parent countries. The revival of imperial acquisitions of the later nineteenth century flowed, according to this Marxist-Leninist theory of capitalist imperialism, from just such considerations and impulses.

The patterns of this revitalised imperialism also had significant implications for the interrelationships of the advanced capitalist countries, in the view of Marxism-Leninism . While profitable opportunities for investment and imperial acquisition continued to exist within the less developed parts of the world, the competitive tensions amongst the advanced capitalist societies could be maintained within tolerable limits. Once, however, imperial opportunities were exhausted, the advanced capitalist countries would turn upon one another, generating the kinds of tensions and antagonisms that were ultimately to explode in the First World War.

In his emphasis upon ultimate conflict amongst the great capitalist metropoles, Lenin differed sharply from another influential 'Marxist' of the age – Karl Kautsky. Kautsky highlighted the possibility of collaboration amongst the advanced capitalist powers to underpin the continued profitability of the institutions of finance capitalism. Special patterns of 'interlocking interdependencies' were thus envisaged in this concept of *ultra-imperialism.*[12] Workers and employers would continue to be related through an essentially exploitative relationship of capitalist 'interdependence', while all 'benefiting' from a new, imperialistic 'interdependence' with the less developed sectors of the world economy. Major capitalists remained interdependent with their representative governments. The governments of the leading capitalist powers, in their turn, were interdependent in their mutual need to sustain an environment suitable for the continued profitability of their capitalist enterprises. The 'layer cake' of resultant interdependencies thus exhibited many of the complex, exploitative interconnections identified by critical analysts of contemporary globalisation.

The elaboration of the full Marxist-Leninist critique of advanced capitalism and capitalist imperialism clearly prioritised economic forces and identified a range of economic and political interconnections that incorporated critical interdependencies. At the heart of all productive relationships within capitalism was that, definitionally exploitative, interdependence between the owners of capital and their employees. Internationally, capitalist imperialism had instituted a massive expansion of interdependencies, in which the continued prosperity of the capitalist metropoles, and the moderation of their internecine tensions, was dependent upon profitable investments and markets in, and primary products drawn from, their colonies . In their turn, the colonies received the products of the capitalist countries' burgeoning industries. Moreover, traditional Marxist-Leninists also shared Marx's own view that imperialism would prove to be a major modernising influence upon the Less Developed Countries which would, eventually, be equipped with the preconditions for their own industrial development.[13]

A number of the major experiences of the twentieth century have, however, confronted classical Marxism-Leninism with serious challenges. The recovery of the capitalist-imperialist world from the cataclysm of the First World War and its survival, however tenuously, of the Great Depression of the late 1920s and early 1930s stimulated many second thoughts about, and adaptations of, the revolutionary optimism of Lenin's writings. Major shocks to the doctrinal core of Marxism-Leninism were, however, avoided until the period that ran from the phase of decolonisation through to the collapse of communist control in the former Soviet Union. Such major challenges to the propositions, and expectations, at the core of Marxist-Leninist teachings fragmented radical political economy and propelled it in a number of revisionist directions, ranging from a repudiation of the labour theory of value,[14] through to an acknowledgement of the relative autonomy of the state in modern societies.[15] The voluntaristic spirit of much of the radicalism of the 1960s and early 1970s was also a significant source of support for a lessening of enthusiasm for a form of deterministic political economy that was already subject to increasing strain by developments in the 'real world'.

A number of attempts have been made to combine several of the central themes of 'traditional' Marxism, with the less deterministic spirit of contemporary analysis. The notion of a world capitalist system, that interrelates the experiences of all economies, within a global capitalist structure and dynamic, has thus persisted in the work of a number of influential theorists. Immanuel Wallerstein's studies of the emergence of the modern capitalist world rest upon, and sustain, such a perspective.[16] Much of the same outlook informs Robert Cox's studies of the contemporary international capitalist political economy.[17] While often seeking to accommodate insights from such work on the 'objective' character of the world capitalist system, neo-Gramscian perspectives go further in a voluntaristic direction by emphasising the centrality of hegemonic ideologies in the management, and dominant interpretations, of the international political economy.[18]

Despite the many set-backs and revisions to which they have been exposed over the decades, Marxist-Leninist interpretations of imperialism, and its central interdependencies, have retained a place in radical political economy. A major difference between modern and pre-war variants of Marxism, however, lies in the later abandonment of a positive view of the impact of imperialism upon the colonial territories. All modern forms of Marxist political economy stress the central salience of imperialist dominance for the advanced capitalist economies, differing only in the particular significance attributed. Increasingly, however, capitalist imperialism has been condemned as the source of many of the major ills experienced by today's Less Developed Countries.

Capitalist imperialism has, in neo-Marxist demonology, assumed varied forms and had profound effects. The term 'imperialism' has been stretched far beyond its traditional meaning of the superimposition upon one territory of governance by, or at the direct behest of, another state or political system. Neo-Marxist interpretations of contemporary international politico-economic relations deem them to be inherently 'imperialistic', given the supposed needs, and structural impact, of contemporary capitalism. 'Imperialism' may thus be identified in relationships, and interconnections, across state frontiers in which there is no formal political subordination of one state by any other. The concept of *neo-colonialism* captured much of this stretched notion of imperialism and found specific application in neo-Marxist interpretations of the circumstances of former colonial territories.[19] The formal political independence of such societies was contrasted sharply with their continuing economic subordination to the needs and interests of their former imperial masters. Multinational corporations, based in the metropolitan state but continuing to operate in the former colonies, were seen to be a major source of continuing economic domination and political interference.

The development of neo-Marxism was not, however, to rest with the concept of neo-colonialism. The view of modern 'imperialism' as a primarily economic relationship, albeit with profound political consequences, also permitted the retrospective reinterpretation of the historical experience of many societies that had not been colonised during the latter half of the nineteenth century. Much of Latin America had thrown off the yokes of Spanish and Portuguese colonialism well before the maturity of modern capitalism. Large areas of Asia had also escaped the direct control of Western powers during this period. Neo-Marxist interpretations identified the invasive influence of the dominant capitalist powers within an increasingly interconnected world economy, which drew the more vulnerable of such societies, remorselessly, into patterns of *informal empire.* Informal empire had comparable effects to formal colonialism: subordinating, and distorting the patterns of development of, the economies thus incorporated.

Critical concepts of neo-colonialism and informal empire contributed directly to the full elaboration of an analysis of the relationships between the advanced capitalist world and the Less Developed Countries. This was now deemed to be a fundamentally antagonistic form of interdependence: a view of that thus reverses the benign connotations often associated with the term. *Dependency Theory* (or Dependencia Theory), as it became widely known, envisaged an intimate historical association between the development of the Advanced Capitalist Societies and the positive underdevelopment of the Less Developed Societies with which they came into contact.[20]

Dependency Theory thus goes beyond both conventional liberal development theory and classical Marxism in rejecting the view that the 'undeveloped' condition of the Less Developed Countries resulted from a simple process of falling behind the progress of the more dynamic Advanced Capitalist Societies. Rather, as advanced capitalist countries impacted upon the less developed areas of the world they were seen to have subordinated the economic, social and political structures of the latter to their own economic needs, irrespective of the formal nature of the political relationship between the dominant and subordinate economies. Raw materials were extracted where discovered; new sources of basic foodstuffs were developed where feasible; local markets for manufactures were exploited everywhere, at the expense of local craft industries.

Such formative Dependency is seen to have generated many distorting effects within the subordinate economy. The economy was converted from a high level of self-sufficiency to over-concentration on a narrow range of export commodities. The affected economy thus became dependent upon imports of many staples, and such imports had to be paid for from earnings generated by exports of primary commodities to the capitalist metropoles. Tribal communities and peasant farmers were dispossessed of their land. New, heavily exploited, work-forces were recruited for the new mines, oil wells and plantations. Enlarged towns and cities exerted a growing attraction to an aspirant, and sometimes desperate, rural population. The local economy was thus destabilised and a perverse, and inherently damaging, form of economic interdependence had been born.

Such exploitative interdependence also spawned a large, dependent 'class' within the dependent society. Owners of land, employees in banks, shipping agents and a host of those in other service industries, all found their well-being and fortunes associated with the interests of the foreign capitalist enterprises that operated in their countries. Dispossessed farmers and poor shanty town dwellers also provided an abundant source of cheap labour for home and work-place alike. Local social, and ultimately political, power thus rested in the hands of well-rewarded groups that identified primarily with the external sources of their prosperity.

From such sources sprang, in the view of Dependency Theorists, the classic characteristics of Dependency: distorted, monoculture economies, with an overdependence upon inherently unreliable primary commodity markets; distorted social structures; rural depletion and sprawling shanty towns; political and military power effectively monopolised by a self-regarding urban elite of servants of foreign capitalist interests. Cycles of prosperity and slump, with corresponding cycles of democracy and authoritarian rule, then resulted as favoured groups have sought to preserve their advantages in the face of deteriorating economic conditions and consequential unrest amongst the socially and economically disadvantaged. Many of the characteristic political ills of such societies are thus attributed directly to their relationships of dependency with the advanced capitalist economies.

Dependency Theory provides a distinctive vision of international interconnectedness as a form of interdependence that is essentially exploitative of, and fundamentally distorting for, the subordinate economies involved. It also identifies a clear causal connection amongst political conditions and developments within Dependent societies, and the economic relationship between those societies and foreign advanced capitalist countries. There is a hint of determinism in this picture, which suggests that a relationship of Dependency has clear and unavoidable consequences for all Dependent societies. Only disengagement from economic relations with the Advanced Capitalist Societies can, therefore, permit an escape from Dependency, genuine and sustainable economic development and progress towards stable democratic forms of government. International networks of Dependency cannot be reformed; only abolished.

Strong echoes of the Dependency model are also to be found in the studies of the historical evolution of the 'world system of capitalism' of such analysts as Immanuel Wallerstein. With its emphasis on the structural differentiation of the emergent world capitalist system into core, semi-core and periphery, Wallerstein's analysis emphasises the centrality of unequal exchange, economically, and subordination politically.[21] Further echoes can also be detected in the critical writings of Robert Cox, with his attempts to rescue and nurture a lightly *materialistic,* but profoundly *historicist* analysis of the modern international political economy.[22]

The view provided by Dependency Theory, and like perspectives, is not, however, unchallenged by radical theorists of the contemporary world political economy. Dependency Theorists place a far greater emphasis upon the supposedly vital contribution made to the capitalist industrialisation of the imperial powers by the surplus extracted from the subordinated territories than was true for classical Marxists and Marxist-Leninists.[23] Indeed, the surplus derived from exploitative relations with subordinated economies is believed by the more extreme of Dependency Theorists to have been the critical precipitant of the dramatic emergence of industrial capitalism within the eighteenth and nineteenth centuries.

Dependency Theorists also deem all economic relations between Advanced Capitalist Societies and Less Developed Countries to be inherently far more damaging to the latter than is true of either traditional 'Marxists', like Bill Warren,[24] or 'post-Sraffian' analysts of the structural problems confronting Less Developed Countries.[25] The simple determination of state forms and governmental behaviour, envisaged in Dependency Theory, has also been challenged by the revisionist theories of some neo-Marxists, about the nature and role of the state.[26] The Gramscian emphasis upon the role of hegemonic ideologies, and the peculiar interdependencies thus suggested, is also discordant with the more economistic perspective of Dependency Theory.[27] This will be considered further in the next chapter.

'Marxist' approaches to contemporary interdependence in the international political economy are thus various and varied. The issues raised by such approaches, and the critical questions highlighted by the debates amongst the competing variants, lead into a consideration of the contribution of a quite different perspective on contemporary interdependence and globalisation – that of Economic 'Realism'.

Economic Realist and Structuralist approaches to international interdependence and globalisation.

Economic Realism

Economic Realism claims its 'Realist' credentials from two central propositions: that of the critical role of inequalities of 'power' and influence within the contemporary political economy; and that of the centrality of states within the prevailing international order. There are, however, serious questions about the degree to which many contemporary Economic Realists share the deterministic tendencies evident within some of the leading proponents of political realism and 'neorealism'.[28]

The mantle of 'Realism' sits slightly uneasily on the shoulders of Economic Realism over the issue of determinism. Much of traditional *political realism* shares the form of determinism that permeates Hans Morgenthau's views of the universal principles of political and international conduct.[29] The 'given' character of the international political system and structure is taken even further in Kenneth Waltz's neorealism.[30] Such a 'deterministic' view of the inevitability of power-oriented states accords with Economic Realism to the extent that the role and primacy of the state in the prevailing international order is taken as a given. However, much of the interest of Economic Realists in the possibility of purposeful action to alter, or transform, prevailing patterns of economic capability and advantage, echoes of a rather more voluntaristic view of political activity and the sources of significant changes in the international political economy than is true certainly for most variants of Marxism and probably some versions of liberal political economy. Thus, while patterns of international interconnectedness may signify real interdependencies, a more possibilistic perspective cautions that such a connection can rarely be assumed a priori.

The task for Economic Realism, then, is to develop a discerning analysis of any international economic relationships to identify the sources, and consequences, of disparities of wealth, industrial strength, technological capacity, economic organisation and general politico-military capability and influence. Given the constraints of location, and resource base, many of these central conditions are the products of human action, often under the direction of authoritative leadership. Moreover, such conditions influence, in their turn, the extent of, and limitations upon, the capacity of governments for effective action in many spheres. One of the critical questions, here, concerns the nature and strength of the relationship between individual political economies and the wider system. Developments may not be technically predetermined, but they may be highly constrained by the prevailing structures of power and influence in the international political economy.

Economic Realism thus locates the character of the contemporary international political economy firmly within its historical origins and context. The emergence of industrial capitalism within Western Europe provides a major starting-point for analysis,[31] as will be shown at greater length in Chapter 3. From that historical well-spring has grown the industrialism of the modern world, the dynamic role of the capitalist order and the political primacy of the 'nation-state'.[32] Prevalent patterns of economic strength and weakness, of advantage and disadvantage, also find their roots in that seminal experience.

Historical experiences are thus the source of the ordering principles within the international political economy, the general 'culture' that sustains that order, the structural features of the international political economy and the primary characteristics of its component economies. International structures and domestic structures are intimately interrelated. The product is a complex pattern of interconnectedness, and frequent interdependencies, within and amongst the discrete economies that together make up the contemporary international political economy.

States may thus be pivotal to economic developments nationally and internationally in both the short and longer terms, as will be seen at some length in the next chapter. Not only do state authorities lead and direct substantial programmes of domestic economic and industrial development, for both economic and political purposes, they also seek to influence international economic relations for political and strategic purposes. Classical mercantilism was founded upon the accumulation of reserves of precious metals in national treasuries and war chests, and the pursuit, where possible, of a combination of national self-sufficiency coupled with the development of dependencies amongst others upon the home state. Modern forms of 'neo-mercantilism' have extended the range of economic objectives thought proper for state action. The manipulation of economic relations for political and strategic purposes has also maintained its appeal to modern statesmen, whether as a means of enforcing United Nations edicts or disciplining threatening, or troublesome, adversaries.[33]

Economic Realism thus envisages the political exploitation of existing dependencies. Moreover, existing patterns of international interconnectedness could, with time and determined effort, be converted into significant dependencies, that progressively render the dependent societies vulnerable to the influence, and even dictates, of the dominant partner. Power thus remains the primary focus of Economic Realism: the sources of economic strength; the economic sources of political and military strength; and the effective deployment of economic strength and influence in relations in both interstate relations and dealings with all manner of other actors on the international economic stage.

Structuralist perspectives

Economic Realist and Structuralist analyses are not always closely associated in the literature on the contemporary international political economy. Indeed, Structuralist interpretations are often associated with those approaches, such as Dependency Theory, that have an affinity with contemporary forms of Marxist theory. However, the emphases upon the characteristics of 'national' economies and the prospects for, and limitations upon, state action in Economic Realism are echoed by its distant Structuralist cousin. The latter approach focuses on the way in which the structural characteristics of 'national' economies underpin an imbalanced pattern of international 'interdependence' between the rich, industrial societies and their less developed 'partners'[34] and, hence, projects a vision of a damaging form of globalisation.

Structuralist models of the modern international political economy thus summarise the characteristic features of an inherently imbalanced pattern of international interdependence. The Advanced Industrial Countries (AICs) export advanced goods and services to economies of all types, but predominantly to other AICs; generate very high standards of living for their populations; and exert a dominant influence upon the international political economy. The Less Developed Countries (LDCs), in contrast, export primary commodities, or highly standardised manufactured goods, mainly to Advanced Industrial Countries; generate low standards of living for their populations; and exert, with notable exceptions, negligible levels of positive influence upon basic developments within the international political economy. LDCs import advanced goods and services overwhelmingly from Advanced Industrial Countries.

Within 'national' political economies, a range of interrelated features constitute the sources, respectively, of general economic strength and weakness. The historical development of a diverse economy; a strong industrial base; high levels, and wide diffusion, of technological competence; and well-developed financial institutions, are closely associated with a well-paid and highly skilled work-force; good social and economic conditions; and the ability to establish influence and project substantial military force internationally. Such societies characteristically export a wide range of goods and services and have a strong presence in those markets for high value-added products that exhibit high income-elasticities of demand. The growth of general income in the world economy thus generates increasing proportional demand for the more developed economies' products. Technical advances do not threaten the prices of most of their products or returns to either capital or labour. The complex of social, economic and political conditions that has been established in the Advanced Industrial Countries allows, thus far, the preservation of margins and, in consequence, high returns to all those still engaged with the more prosperous sectors of their economies.

In marked contrast, societies that are significantly 'less developed' suffer from a number of characteristic weaknesses. Exports are relatively few in number and are concentrated in primary commodities, or manufactured goods produced by highly 'mature' industrial technologies. Such exports encounter low income-elasticity of demand in world markets, with aggregate demand falling behind the rate of increase of global wealth or, in some cases, falling absolutely. Moreover, such products can be produced by relatively low-skilled labour forces that, in turn, receive low wages and 'enjoy' poor living conditions. The societies that rely upon these low value-added exports tend to have poorly developed economic, financial, social and educational infrastructures. Externally, they are ill-equipped to exert significant levels of influence, particularly when acting alone. They are, moreover, generally unable to develop substantial levels of military capability and deploy them effectively at any distance from home. Advances in productive technology either bypass such societies or, if available for domestic incorporation, often result in increased local unemployment.[35]

Given contrasting domestic economic and industrial structures, the interconnectedness of the contemporary international political economy exhibits marked asymmetries and imbalances, which underpin, and are reflected in, serious dependencies. The persistence of the disparities between the rich and the poorer countries, the characteristic patterns of which will be explored further in Chapter 5, reflects these structural constraints to a substantial degree. The Advanced Industrial Countries continue to enjoy the many fruits of technological innovation; the poorer Less Developed Countries are unable to obtain, afford, or exploit effectively, the latest technologies and remain condemned, in consequence, to low value-added areas of production. The structural effect of this imbalance in access and capacity has, in the influential analysis of Raul Prebisch, produced a long-term, secular decline in the terms of trade 'enjoyed' by the Less Developed Countries,[36] or, in the view of a critic like Arghiri Emmanuel, a chronic pattern of *unequal exchange.*[37]

Substantial criticisms have been advanced against the statistical basis of Prebisch's terms of trade thesis.[38] Emmanuel's unequal exchange is also open to criticism for its repudiation of market forces and denial of the role, in the generation of the prices of goods and services, of the relative scarcity of factors of production, the real costs of production and, in particular, the embodiment of advanced skills and competencies in high value-added products. However, the over-concentration of Less Developed Countries in a relatively small number of primary, or highly standardised, products[39] is widely acknowledged as a major source of their weakness and vulnerability within the international trade system, of the persistence of low standards of living amongst their populations and of a range of general obstacles to wide-ranging and sustainable development. The persistence of such over-concentration thus condemns a society both to an unfavourable position within the world economy and to the continuation of a disadvantageous 'Sraffian' distribution between capital and labour within the domestic economy, in which cheap and basic technologies both require and justify the low-skilled, low wage, work-forces that sustain the impression of substantial surpluses within the labour pool.[40]

The Structuralist perspective upon the international political economy and contemporary interdependence remains essentially voluntaristic and reformist, in contrast to the deterministic and rejectionist tendencies of many of the derivatives of Marxism. Prebisch, in the role of General Secretary of the United Nations Conference on Trade and Development, played an influential role in the formulation of the programme for a New International Economic Order,[41] that became highly fashionable towards the end of the 1970s. The Structuralist critique also illuminated the Brandt Commission's proposals for negotiated change in the international economic order.[42] In its voluntaristic and reformist character, the Structuralist approach merges, at its borders, with the work of 'compensatory liberals'[43] who do not believe that a liberal order automatically generates optimal outcomes for all participants and often requires a substantial amount of help and guidance from those empowered to exercise such a benign form of influence.

Disappointment was to befall hopes of a negotiated reform of the international economic order. However, many Structuralist propositions were to gain indirect support from the experience of some of the Newly Industrialising Countries (NICs) that made such an impact on the world economic stage during the 1980s. With a clear emphasis on governmentally supported economic diversification and technological advance,[44] a number of the NICs made spectacular economic progress and substantially altered the global division of labour. The established pattern of imbalanced interdependence was, in consequence, subject to a substantial change with the penetration, by at least some of the NICs, of the world markets for the more advanced industrial products.

An approach to international interdependence that emphasises the voluntaristic nature of human activity, and the potential role of governments, places the sources of the beliefs of human agents at the centre of analytical concern. Economic Realist and Structuralist approaches to international affairs differ significantly, in this respect, from both the belief of classical liberalism in the self-revelation of a rational universe and the classical Marxist doctrine of the economic determination of the ideas that underpin, and are representative of, the social, political and legal superstructure of society.Economic Realism recognises the fundamentally problematical character of the relationship between human 'subjectivity' and 'objective' patterns of human behaviour.

Institutionalist perspectives

The effective management of an interdependent, or globalised, world economy is also not held to be either automatic or impossible. The central problem, for Economic Realists, is to construct the appropriate structures and institutions, within which the actions of individual actors on the international economic stage can be effectively co-ordinated. Such structures and institutions could be hegemonical in character, with one, or a small number of the strongest states effectively writing and enforcing rules of conduct for all other members of the international political economy.[45] The establishment of enduring *regimes* , whether by hegemonic influence or through voluntary negotiation, offers another path to such institutional management, that has been much debated by students of the international political economy.[46] Such regimes can be formed either by formal regulatory institutions or less formal sets of 'rules', sustained by a suitable pattern of intersubjectivity amongst pertinent actors. Either type of regime, if effective, can offer a solution to the problems of effective co-ordination within a politically fragmented international political economy.

Hegemonical and regime approaches to management in the international political economy shade across the analytical gap between liberal political economy and Economic Realist approaches. Many of those who have been most prominent in the study of international regimes have, in particular, formed a virtual sub-school of 'regime liberals'. Politics, of a wide and less adversarial character than that envisaged by Realists, is thus central to a distinctive view of the relationship between politics and economics in the contemporary international political economy. An *institutionalist* disposition is evident in a number of perspectives upon the development and condition of the international system. A central proposition here is that the development of a wide range of institutions within the international political economy has both facilitated, and reflected, the steady growth of international interdependence and globalisation.

The precise sources of the contemporary web of institutions, both formal and informal, within the international political economy remains controversial. Those who emphasise the co-operative imperatives generated by conditions within the international political economy contrast sharply with those who identify the central role of beliefs, commitments and political leadership in the establishment of arrangements for the management of the system.[47]

Such issues thus relate to that of the causal connection between the institutional structure of the international political economy and the development of interdependence and globalisation. The perspective provided by 'Structuration Theory' offers, as will be shown later, a methodology that partially bridges the rationalist/reflective divide, by identifying the intersubjective basis of the behavioural patterns that characterise the international political economy and its institutional features. The realm of international relations is thus one of constant structuration and re-structuration by sentient human beings, all seeking to realise their expectations in a world of collectively constructed 'realities' and constraints.

The product of such processes is the profusion of international institutions and collaborative associations.[48] At the level of formal, interstate arrangements, the institutionalisation of the international political economy has a number of tangible expressions. The Group of Seven (G7) constitutes a regular meeting of the leaders of the world's seven leading industrial economies to review global economic developments and pursue, often with limited success, co-ordinated solutions to common economic problems. The Organisation for Economic Cooperation and Development rests upon a more permanent basis and provides support for high-level collective deliberations with its systematic reviews of economic developments and policy prescriptions. The international financial system is supported and surveyed by the Geneva-based Bank for International Settlements and the International Monetary Fund in New York. The lion's share of multilateral economic aid is directed through, and monitored by, the International Bank for Reconstruction and Development (the World Bank). Difficulties encountered by the recipients of 'official' aid are considered by the regular meetings of the Paris Club of representatives of donor countries. The specialist agencies of the United Nations provide additional institutional contributions to the contemporary international political economy.

One of the results of the Uruguay Round of negotiations within the General Agreement on Tariffs and Trade (GATT), during the late 1980s and early 1990s, was the decision to establish a new World Trade Organisation to consolidate, and further institutionalise, the work of the GATT. The ultimate effectiveness of this new organisation, in a world of intensifying economic problems and trade disputes, however, remains open to considerable doubt and, thereby, to questions about the independent influence of international institutions upon the shaping of the international political economy.

Below the level of formal interstate institutions lie a range of non-state 'international' arrangements. The London Club, consisting of representatives of commercial lending institutions, review and restructure the debt of the largest commercial debtors amongst the Less Developed Countries. The Organisation of Petroleum Exporting Countries (OPEC) provided a dramatic demonstration of the potential impact of explicit cartels of commodity-producing countries during the 1970s. On the other side, the 'Seven Sisters', of the world's leading oil companies, have often been accused of operating an informal cartel to regulate the supply and price of petroleum-based products on world markets. Other major industries have been subject to similar accusations, over the years, with co-ordination at varying levels of formal institutionalisation and with differing levels of clarity and effect.

Controversy about all such institutions within the international political economy continues to turn around two axes of debate. The first is whether such institutionalisation is a source or a symptom of growing globalisation, as was indicated earlier in this discussion. The second concerns the division between those who see such institutionalisation as a relatively neutral phenomenon, concerned merely with necessary co-ordination and, where necessary, control, and those who identify it with a global capitalist 'conspiracy'. Such a possibility underlies a number of critical interpretations of the modern international political economy, that see evidence in many institutions, not of benign hegemony and constructive regimes, but of an exploitative and ultimately destructive pattern of global domination.[49]

The institutionalisation of the international political economy is clearly a significant feature of the contemporary system and, whatever the direction of causality, an area of close connection between the economic and political spheres. Whether it establishes the case for growing international interdependence and globalisation, and their benign consequences, is, however, a question which will be considered again later in this discussion.

Methodological considerations

Many of the issues concerning the relationship between the 'subjective' and the 'objective' will be considered further subsequently in this discussion. It is important to note at this stage, however, that the voluntaristic approach of Economic Realism, and many Structuralist approaches, permits a perspective that can attribute considerable influence over the future shape of economic developments, and hence upon patterns of international interdependence, to the role of new ideas and commitments amongst active individuals, communities and their governments. The political economy is thus *constructed,* and may be *reconstructed,* in the same way as may other central human social and political institutions.[50] Positive reconstruction of the political economy, and the consequential patterns of international interdependence, is not, however, easy, merely because it is a possibility. The complex patterns of intersubjectivity, that sustain, and are sustained by, prevailing 'realities', thus generate considerable inertia in human affairs and confront change with substantial obstacles.[51]

The substantial inertia generated by established, constructed 'realities' highlights, in turn, the potential role of dominant ideologies. It thus becomes possible to chart, in a non-deterministic manner, the emergence and influence of basic systems of values, and beliefs, that are both partial in their view of human possibilities, and desirabilities, and clearly beneficial to specific interests, classes or ruling groups. A 'Gramscian' flavour, of a possibilistic type, is thus compatible with richer forms of Economic Realist and Structuralist analyses of the international political economy, contemporary 'interdependence' and globalisation. However, the emphasis within Economic Realist analysis will be upon the specific patterns of resources and processes that generate such ideological primacy: *when* and *where* it is actually found to arise within the international political economy.

Conclusion

The complex interactions between the political and economic dimensions of contemporary life are demonstrated by the character of international interdependence and globalisation. Charting these interactions is a controversial as well as a complex matter. The major competing interpretations of the contemporary political and economic world offer markedly contrasting views of the relationship between economics and politics, and of interdependence and globalisation.

Liberal political economy prescribes a substantial degree of separation between economics and politics. For pure liberals, the political system may 'hold the ring' for free enterprise, but should never impose itself further upon economic activity. While compensatory liberals and regime liberals envisage some role for collective action in the economy, pure liberals are happy with a minimal role for political authorities.

The liberal perspective also identifies, within the contemporary plethora of international economic interconnections, a generally benign condition of international interdependence and growing globalisation. Free trade is held to be generally beneficial and the resulting patterns of production and exchange merely a reflection of prevalent patterns of comparative advantage. Trade and specialisation contribute to new patterns of interdependence amongst societies that actually bind them together with increasing force. Societies will neither wish nor be able to go to war with those with whom they conduct rewarding, and increasingly essential, trade. A mutually advantageous system will thus, with time, engender a new system of harmonious social and political relations.

The Marxist perspective traditionally deemed the political to be determined by the nature of, and developments within, the economic infrastructure of society. Modern derivatives identify a more complex relationship between the economic and the political, but continue to attribute considerable significance to the former. All modern variants of Marxism adopt a distinctive, and generally hostile, attitude towards patterns of interconnectedness, and hence interdependence, within a capitalist world system. Exploitation and instability are integral to the capitalist system for all Marxists. Some contemporary neo-Marxists and near-Marxists also attribute the positive underdevelopment of many of the Less Developed Countries to their past and present relations with the capitalist metropoles. The disruption and transformation of contemporary interdependencies, and the reversal of current globalisation tendencies, are thus essential to the view of an acceptable future offered by many contemporary 'Marxists'.

Economic Realists emphasise the primacy of 'political' influences and interests in the shaping of the foundations of the prevailing economic order and many of its central developments. They remain agnostic about the implications of prevailing patterns of international economic interconnectedness, equivocal about established interdependencies, and sceptical about the pace and prospects of globalisation.[52] Indeed, Economic Realists share the view of many forms of Marxism that international economic associations can generate frictions and potential conflict, not merely harmony and general prosperity.

With an essentially voluntaristic and situational perspective, Economic Realism is open to the variety of possibilities presented by contemporary 'realities'. The relative power and influence of states and other actors on the world economic stage remains a function of their control of appropriate resources. The distribution and control of such resources changes with time and circumstance, as does the will to deploy them to maximum effect. The direct control of peoples, territory and the preponderance of armed force, by states has to be set against the mobility flexibility of many transnational actors and, in particular, the wealth and informational strengths of the Transnational Corporations. In direct confrontations over immediate issues, or in the shaping of the future development of the international political economy, the balance between such disparate forces cannot be predicted with any precision. Moreover, Economic Realists acknowledge the many ways in which the economic relations amongst states may be manipulated to promote political and security objectives.

Economic dependencies can provide the basis of sanctions designed to coerce states, or their leaders, into compliance with the desires or demands of other states, singly or severally. The non-violent appearance of such economic sanctions has commended them to those who have endeavoured to construct systems of international Collective Security or to promote more elevated norms of conduct internationally. The non-violent purity of such sanctions has, however, been disputed, as in the case of post-Gulf War sanctions against Saddam Hussein's Iraq. Their effectiveness was also doubted after the apparent failure of the League of Nations' economic sanctions to curb Italian aggression against

Ethiopia in 1935 and 1936. The pressure exerted upon the apartheid regime in South Africa by widespread economic sanctions does, however, seem to have been substantial, whatever their precise contribution to the eventual dismantling of that political order.

Political purposes may also be promoted by the acquisition of additional economic resources. The impulses of the mercantilist era have not been entirely expunged from the modern world. Indeed, the new 'world disorder' of the post-Cold War era may reveal many issues on which, and areas within which, resource disputes become the central sources of conflicts. Hydro-politics in the Middle East and parts of the former Soviet Union have a potency akin to that of land corridors to the coast in the former Yugoslavia.

Methodologically, structuralist conceptions of the international political economy share the voluntaristic and situational perspectives of Economic Realism. They also emphasise the role of the state in directing the economic fates of societies. Whether through a determined domestic development programme, or through the exercise of influence and power to secure beneficial changes in the functioning of the international economic system, the role of states may be pivotal to economic advance. However, the dense and complex pattern of prevailing international economic interconnections is such as to condemn those Less Developed Countries that prove incapable of effective national action to sustained dependencies of a disadvantageous character.

An institutional perspective then associates the proliferation of associations amongst states, and other prominent non-state actors, with the advance of interdependence and globalisation. However, the pattern of causality in this relationship, and the character of the associations thus formed, remains controversial.

The review of major analytical perspectives, undertaken in this chapter, hints at, but has not explored in detail, a central, though often neglected, aspect of international interdependence, globalisation and the general relationship between the economic and the political. The neglected element is that of the source and role of the basic values and ideas that direct human action and underpin human institutions. Such issues will, however, receive considerable attention within the subsequent discussion and be used to throw a sharper and more critical light upon a number of aspects of international interdependence and globalisation.

Notes and references

1. For general reviews of these three major approaches see: Robert Gilpin, *The Political Economy of International Relations* (Princeton, NJ: Princeton University Press, 1987) esp., pp. 25-54; D.H. Blake, R.S. Walters (Englewood Cliffs, NJ: Prentice-Hall, 1976) and R.J. Barry Jones (ed.), *The Worlds of Political Economy: Alternative Approaches to the Study of Contemporary Political Economy* (London: Pinter Publishers, 1988), esp. Chs. 1, 6, 7 and 8. One of the earliest studies to demarcate these three approaches with clarity was Robert Gilpin, *US Power*

and the Multinational Corporation: The Political Economy of Direct Investment (New York: Basic Books, 1975; and London: Macmillan, 1975), esp. Ch. 9.

2. For a documentary review of classical liberalism, see E.K. Bramsted and K.J. Melhuish (eds.), *Western Liberalism: A History in Documents from Locke to Croce* (Oxford: Clarendon Press, 1978).
3. For a fuller account see R.J. Barry Jones, 'Liberal political economy', in R.J. Barry Jones (ed.), *The Worlds of Political Economy* (London: Pinter Publishers, 1988), pp. 27-56.
4. See the seminal discussion by Mancur Olson, *The Logic of Collective Action: Public Goods and the Theory of Groups* (Cambridge: Cambridge University Press, 1965); and the discussions of this perspective in: N. Frohlich and J.A. Oppenheimer, *Modern Political Economy* (Englewood-Cliffs: Prentice-Hall, 1978), esp. Ch. 2; N. Frohlich, J. A. Oppenheimer, and Oran R. Young, *Political Leadership and Collective Goods* (Princeton, NJ: Princeton University Press, 1971).
5. For a classical expression of this view see Norman Angell, *The Great Illusion* (New York; Putnam, 1913).
6. R.D. McKinlay and R. Little, *Global Problems and World Order* (London: Frances Pinter Ltd., 1986), esp. pp. 27-9, 36-41, 45-8 and 103-14.
7. A peacefulness that was peculiar to Europe, but that was, for Europe, a singular contrast with earlier eras.
8. For a clear account of Marxist political economy see M.C. Howard and J.E. King, *The Political Economy of Marx* (Harlow: Longman, 1975).
9. R. Hilferding, *Finance Capital: the Latest Phase of Capitalism* (Vienna; Vorwarts, 1923).
10. V.I. Lenin, *Imperialism: The Highest Stage of Capitalism* (Little Lenin Library, first published in Petrograd, 1916).
11. For an account that stresses these additional benefits from overseas investments see Michael Barratt Brown, *The Economics of Imperialism* (Harmondsworth: Penguin Books, 1975).
12. For a succinct discussion see Chris Brown, 'Marxist approaches to international political economy', in R.J. Barry Jones, *The Worlds of Political Economy*, pp. 120-41, esp. p. 129.
13. A point emphasised by Chris Brown, in 'Marxist approaches to international political economy', in R.J. Barry Jones (ed.), *The Worlds of Political Economy*, pp. 120-41, esp. p. 125.
14. See, Ian Steadman *et al.*, *The Value Controversy* (London: Verso, 1981).
15. For a brief discussion of which see Andrew Gamble, 'Marxist political economy', in R.J. Barry Jones (ed.), *The Worlds of Political Economy*, pp. 56-73, esp. pp. 68-71.
16. See especially Immanuel Wallerstein, *The Capitalist World-Economy* (Cambridge: Cambridge University Press, 1979).
17. Especially Robert W. Cox, *Production, Power and World Order: Social Forces in the Making of History* (New York: Columbia University Press, 1978).
18. See, particularly, S. Gill, *Gramsci, Historical Materialism and International Relations* (Cambridge: Cambridge University Press, 1993).
19. Jack Woodis, *Introduction to Neo-Colonialism* (London: Lawrence and Wishart, 1967)
20. For a classic exposition of Dependency Theory see Andre Gunder Frank, *On Capitalist Underdevelopment* (Bombay: Oxford University Press, 1975).
21. See, in particular, Immanuel Wallerstein, *The Capitalist World-Economy* (Cambridge: Cambridge University Press, 1979); and Immanuel Wallerstein, *The Modern World System – 2 volumes* (New York: Academic Press,

1980), Volume 1: *Capitalist Agriculture and the origins of the European World-Economy in the Sixteenth Century;* Volume 2: *Mercantilism and the Consolidation of the European World-Economy, 1600-1750.*
22. For two, succinct accounts of this position see: Robert W. Cox, 'Social forces, states and world orders: beyond international relations theory', reprinted in R.O. Keohane *Neo-Realism and its Critics* (New York: Columbia University Press, 1986) (from an original article in *Millennium: Journal of international Studies*, Vol. 10, No. 1 (Summer 1981), pp. 126-55); and Robert W. Cox, 'Multilateralism and world order', *Review of International Studies*, Vol. 18, No. 2 (April 1992), pp. 161-80.
23. See, in particular, Frank, *On Capitalist Underdevelopment*, esp. pp. 9-18; and Malcolm Caldwell, *The Wealth of Some Nations* (London: Zed Press, 1977), esp. pp. 54-68; and see also, Samir Amin, *Accumulation on a World Scale*, 2 vols., trans. B. Pearce (New York: Monthly Press and Hassocks: Harvester Press, 1974).
24. Bill Warren, *Imperialism: Pioneer of Capitalism* (London: Verso New Left Books, 1980).
25. See Chris Edwards, *The Fragmented World: Competing Perspectives on Trade, Money and Crisis* (London: Methuen, 1985), esp. Ch. 4; and R.J. Barry Jones, 'Economic Realism, Neo-Ricardian Structuralism and the political economy of contemporary neo-mercantilism', in R.J. Barry Jones, *The Worlds of Political Economy*, Ch 8.
26. See the brief discussion of this by Andrew Gamble, 'Marxist political economy', in R.J. Barry Jones (ed.), *The Worlds of Political Economy*, Ch. 3, esp. pp. 68-71.
27. For an outline of Gramscian perspectives see S. Gill and D. Law, *The Global Political Economy: Perspectives, Problems and Policies* (Hemel Hempstead: Harvester/Wheatsheaf, 1988) esp. pp. 77-80.
28. On which see Keohane, *Neorealism and its Critics.*
29. Hans J. Morgenthau, *Politics Among Nations* (New York: Knopf, 1948, and 1954, 1960, 1967).
30 Kenneth Waltz, *Theory of International Politics* (Reading, Mass: Addison-Wesley, 1979).
31. For a discussion of which see John A. Hall, *Powers and Liberties: The Causes and Consequences of the Rise of the West* (Oxford: Basil Blackwell, 1985), esp. Chs. 1 and 5.
32. On which see Richard K. Ashley, 'The poverty of neo-Realism', *International Organisation*, Vol. 38, No. 2, (Spring, 1984), pp. 225-61, reprinted in R.O. Keohane (ed.), *Neo-Realism and its Critics* (New York: Columbia University Press, 1986).
33. For an extensive discussion of the manipulation of economic relations see David A. Baldwin, *Economic Statecraft* (Princeton, NJ: Princeton University Press, 1985).
34. For a further discussion of these links, see R.J. Barry Jones, 'Economic Realism', in R.J. Barry Jones (ed.), *The Worlds of Political Economy.*
35. For a further outline of this general interpretation of North-South structural differentiation see Chris Edwards, *The Fragmented World: Competing Perspectives on Trade, Money and Crisis* (London: Methuen, 1985), Chs. 3 and 4.
36. See, in particular, Raul Prebisch, *Towards a New Trade Policy for Development* (New York: UN Publications, 1964).
37. Arghiri Emmanuel, *Unequal Exchange: A Study of the Imperialism of Trade* (trans. Brian Pearce; London: New Left Books, 1972).
38. See, in particular, John P. Powelson, 'The LDCs and the terms of trade',

Economic Impact, Vol. 22 (1978), pp. 33-7.

39. On which see Michael Michaely, *Concentration in International Trade*, (Amsterdam: North Holland Publishing Co., 1962).
40. For a fuller discussion of post-Sraffian economics, and its view of the conditions within Less Developed Countries, see Chris Edwards, *The Fragmented World*, esp. Ch. 4.
41. On which, see J.N. Bhagwati (ed.), *The New International Economic Order: The North-South Debate* (Cambridge, Mass.: The MIT Press, 1977); and E. Laszlo *et al.*, *The Obstacles to the New International Economic Order* (New York and Oxford: Pergamon Press, for UNITAR/CEESTEM, 1980).
42. The Brandt Report: W. Brandt, *North-South: A Programme for Survival* (London: Pan Books, 1980).
43. R.D. McKinlay and R. Little, *Global Problems and World Order* (London: Frances Pinter Ltd., 1986), esp. pp. 27-9, 36-41 and 44-8.
44. For a thorough discussion of the experiences of some of these advancing economies see Robert Wade, *Governing the Market: Economic Theory and the Role of Government in East Asian Industrialisation* (Princeton, NJ: Princeton University Press, 1990).
45. For the now standard exposition of this approach see Robert Gilpin, *The Political Economy of International Relations* (Princeton NJ: Princeton University Press, 1987), esp. pp. 75-80; and for a judicious review of this argument see Andrew Walter, *World Power and World Money: The Role of Hegemony and International Monetary Order* (Hemel Hempstead: Harvester/Wheatsheaf, 1991).
46. See, in particular, Stephen D. Krasner (ed.), *International Regimes* (Ithaca: Cornell University Press, 1983); Robert O. Keohane, *After Hegemony: Cooperation and Discord in the World Political Economy* (Princeton, NJ: Princeton University Press, 1984); and V. Rittberger with P. Mayer (eds.), *Regime Theory and International Relations* (Oxford: Clarendon Press, 1993).
47. A contrast highlighted in R.O. Keohane, 'International institutions: two approaches', *International Studies Quarterly*, Vol. 32 (1988), pp. 379-96; and that is a central theme of many of the contributions to V. Rittberger with P. Mayer (eds.), *Regime Theory and International Relations*.
48. For a view of many of which see A. Leroy Bennett, *International Organizations: Principles and Issues* (Englewood Cliffs, New Jersey: Prentice-Hall (5th edn.), 1991), esp. Chs. 12 and 10; and for an earlier review see J.H. Richards, *International Economic Institutions* (London and New York: Holt, Rinehart and Winston, 1970).
49. See, in particular, Stephen Gill, *American Hegemony and the Trilateral Commission* (Cambridge: Cambridge University Press, 1991).
50. See the discussion of the construction of social 'reality' by Peter L. Berger and Thomas Luckmann, *The Social Construction of Reality* (Harmondsworth: The Penguin Press, 1967) and the discussion of the political construction of 'international reality' by R.J. Barry Jones, 'The political construction of international reality', Paper presented to the meeting of the Seminar on International Political Theory, at the LSE, Friday 7 February 1991.
51. For a general discussion of the force of constructed realities see Anthony Giddens, *The Constitution of Society: Outline of the Theory of Structuration* (Cambridge: Polity Press, 1984).
52. See, for example, Kenneth Waltz, 'The myth of national interdependence', in Charles P. Kindleberger (ed.), *The International Corporation* (Cambridge, Mass. MIT Press, 1970), pp. 205-23.

Section 2

INTERNATIONAL INTERDEPENDENCE AND GLOBALISATION: THE POLITICAL DIMENSIONS

CHAPTER 3

Interdependence and globalisation in a world of states

Discussions of interdependence conventionally take for granted the separate existence of the entities that are supposed to be interdependent upon one another. Thus, considerations of international interdependence, whether economic or political, assume the prior separation of nation-states and national economies. This casual presumption, however, obscures the historical origins of the modern international system, with its characteristic patterns of interdependence, and inhibits a sense of the complex interaction between the differing facets of the contemporary international system.

Some forms of interdependence are inevitable for such social animals as human beings. The prevalent forms of interdependence will, however, be a product of the historically, and technologically conditioned, political, economic and social patterns of each era and location. It is possible that a society experiencing a combination of geographical remoteness, technical limitations, modest expectations and relative social stability might exhibit relatively high levels of internal interdependence amongst its members, but relatively few external interdependencies of substance. A highly aspirant and energetic society, enjoying rapid technical advance, might, in contrast, experience an expanding range of external 'interdependencies', of increasing significance for its continued well-being.

Contemporary patterns of international 'interdependence' are the product of a remarkable process of political and economic transformation that crystallised in the formation of a system of nation-states, and the emergence of industrial capitalism, in the Europe of the sixteenth century onwards. The consequences of this transformational experience have conditioned the modern world and established the framework of contemporary political and economic interdependencies.

Statism, capitalism and the emergence of the modern international system

The central interdependencies of the contemporary world are a function of the two dominant features of the modern era: the nation-state system and industrial capitalism. Historians have long puzzled over the emergence of industrial capitalism within Europe, and particularly Western Europe, in the eighteenth and nineteenth centuries. Recent scholarship has begun to emphasise the central role of the crystallisation of the European states' system, during the sixteenth, seventeenth and eighteenth centuries, in creating suitable conditions for such a transformational experience.

The problem confronting those wishing to explain Europe's centrality to the political and economic shaping of the modern world turns upon the technological superiority of non-European regions before the European take-off.[1] Chinese society had a massive technical superiority in many areas over the medieval Europeans. India enjoyed considerable levels of technical capability, socio-economic organisation and artistic skills. The Middle-East and North Africa were then dominated by an Islamic culture, much devoted to scientific endeavour, technological innovation and aesthetic achievement. In the southern regions of the American continent, too, there were civilisations of considerable strength, domain and sophistication.

A range of circumstances, some accidental, some geographical, but all significant in the historical conditions of Europe, combined to create a dynamic, and ultimately transformational, blend, within a region of intense political and military interactions. The dominion of Rome had been weakened and overthrown, to be replaced by a myriad of jealous tribal groupings. The spiritual heirs to the Roman Empire — the Papacy and the Catholic Church — while succeeding in maintaining a measure of common outlook throughout Europe, were unable to sustain a degree of religious/ideological dominance sufficient to prevent the emergent feudal order incorporating an enduring measure of competitive rivalry.[2] Continuous internal rivalry, coupled with periodic external pressure from an aggressive Islam, prevented the emergence of one, wholly hegemonic centre of political control.[3]

As an arena of persistent rivalry and conflict, the emergent European states provided incentives for those leaders that wished to prevail against their competitors. Whether stimulated by resistance against Islam, or periodic bouts of internecine competition for real estate, military techniques and technologies were subject to waves of substantial innovation. The ruling classes of the emergent European states found that advantage, and even survival, depended upon a willingness to embrace the latest military developments. Moreover, the maintenance of increasingly sophisticated and expensive military establishments required major changes in the political and economic organisation of their societies.[4]

Successive leading states found that the military and economic strains of hegemonical aspirations ultimately eroded their abilities to maintain a dominant position on the European stage. These strains proved crippling partly, if not largely, because of failures to develop effective domestic political and economic structures and institutions.[5] Whatever the fates of particular European states, a general engine of change and innovation remained in constant motion. Moreover, a powerful stimulus to, and capacity for, the expansion of influence and control beyond the European continent had also been created. As the modern European system began to crystallise, it was already beginning to impose its stamp, if not yet its image, upon a growing portion of the wider world.

The dynamic interactions within the emergent European states' system thus constituted a complex and powerful form of interconnectedness: with developments in one part having potentially profound implications for others. Such interconnectedness does not automatically constitute a substantive form of interdependence, as was argued in the introductory section. A number of substantive interdependencies did, however, develop within, and from, the developing European system; some of these were to configure the political and economic shape of the modern international system.

The crystallisation of the modern states' system, itself, constituted one of the central forms of interdependence that accompanied the emergence of modern Europe. The wishes of monarchs, princes and assorted political elites to legitimise and stabilise their territorial control encouraged the gradual development of doctrines of state sovereignty. The 'Janus-faced' character[6] of such notions of sovereignty entailed the linking of absolute domestic jurisdiction with the recognition of comparable rights for the rulers of other territories. The consolidation of such a doctrine required its acceptance by a substantial majority of the rulers of influential European states. Rulers were thus interdependent upon one another for the mutual recognition of rights of domestic jurisdiction and limitations upon the legitimacy of intervention in one another's internal affairs. The growing appreciation of such a measure of mutual interdependence for survival and well-being formed the basis of a mutually supportive set of values, expectations and understandings amongst a preponderance of leaders, such as to generate, cumulatively, a new form of intersubjective 'reality': a form of 'socially constructed reality'[7] whereby practices were progressively incorporated, and hence supported, beliefs about the forms of behaviour that were appropriate and effective under specific circumstances. As such intersubjectively supported patterns and practices became increasingly institutionalised, the European states' system exhibited many of the characteristics of *structuration,* with actors and structures locked into a self-sustaining behavioural cycle.[8]

The emergence of the system of sovereign states in Europe was bloody, hesitant and ultimately incomplete. However, crucial landmarks were passed with the Treaty of Westphalia of 1648 and the Treaty of Vienna of 1815. Westphalia marked the defeat of Habsburg designs for 'universal monarchy', and the proclamation of the rights of individual states and, hence, the continued division of Europe into separate sovereign states.[9] The Treaty of Vienna, in bringing the Napoleonic Wars to a final close, further reinforced the anti-hegemonical principles of the Continental European states' system[10] and provided for a number of practical territorial adjustments to enhance the prospects of an effective balance-of-power against a resurgent France.[11] The settlements of each major period of warfare thus acknowledged, and partly redefined, the element of political interdependence amongst the leading members of the European states' system.[12] Moreover, each settlement defined the basic framework for the subsequent era of economic development and growth.

The institutionalisation of the sovereignty of states, and the use of power balancing mechanisms, formed the basis of what some analysts have dubbed an *international society*:[13] a 'society', albeit, of states (or their ruling groups) devoted to the interests and maintenance of those states (or ruling groups).[14] The *system* brought into being was thus a product of the character, needs and interests of its constituent parts — the member *states* — or, rather, of the dominant interests within those states: the European system of states did not simply spring into life immaculately.

The international system that was created during the emergence of modern Europe, far from shaping the character of its member states uni-directionally, as has often been implied in Realist writings on international relations,[15] was far more a political construction of its constituent states. These states had, initially, been constructed to serve the interests of dynastic ruling groups. The threats posed to their continued suzerainty by ideologically motivated forces, or by hegemonically minded fellow rulers, had prompted the self-interested identification of appropriate 'rules of conduct' within a fundamentally statist political order. The gradual secularisation of the basis of legitimacy for the leaders of states reinforced the need to elaborate a philosophy of the state as a natural, and necessary, form of human political organisation. With the subsequent, albeit gradual, democratisation of political life in the European states, the legitimisation of the state increasingly required its 'nationalisation', as a means of incorporating the 'interests' and support of each state's citizenry. The 'nation-state' was the potent product of this process of consolidation of territorial control, and progressive legitimisation within the territories of Europe's consolidating states.

Politics is as much about fundamental political orders as it is a matter of day-to-day control of office or the making of rules and decisions. The political order prevailing encompasses three basic levels of political life. At the foundational level of a political order are the basic principles that identify the 'legitimate' members of that political order and their proper patterns of interaction. At the institutional, or constitutional, level are treaties, constitutions, organisational structures and any other well-established arrangements, which give expression to the fundamentals of the political order. At the day-to-day level of politics, negotiations are undertaken, elections held, office-holders formulate policies and legislative bodies deliberate upon the proposals and performances of governmental executives. In the political order that crystallised within Europe, states, rather than individuals or other groupings and associations, were enshrined as the legitimate members of the order. A succession of peace treaties, 'concerts', leagues, diplomatic practices and increasingly formalised institutions, gave institutional expression to that statist order. A plethora of diplomatic exchanges, threats, bribes and periodic armed conflicts constituted the 'day-to-day' stuff of an interstate political order.[16] Such behaviour at the level of day-to-day interstate politics provided the regular nourishment for the underlying principles of that basic order.

The dynamism and acquisitiveness of the members of the developing European states' system also encouraged the deployment of military techniques and technologies, forged by the continuing experience of internecine conflict, in an accelerating process of overseas adventure and colonial acquisition. The external expansion of some of the leading European powers produced, for some, a benign symbiosis between enhanced influence within Europe and the spread of trade and acquisitions beyond the Continent. The 'successes' of the early European colonialists owed much to the habits and techniques born of generations of intense conflict within Europe's boundaries: the discipline of individual soldiers and adventurers; the command structures developed by protracted military engagement; a combination of robust ships and ruthless determination. Initial overseas conquests were later to be complemented on a massive scale by European forces endowed with high levels of discipline; effective command structures; regular payment and well-organised logistical support. The final great surge of European colonialism of the later nineteenth century was then sustained by a range of critical technological innovations: the steam engine, and the consequent transformation of long-distance communications; the development of quick-firing, long-range armaments; and substantial advances in medical knowledge.[17]

The contribution of the burgeoning European empires to the general process of capitalist industrialisation has been keenly disputed. The mercantilist impulses that were widespread throughout Europe were particularly favourable towards private economic initiative in the maritime powers of the Netherlands and Great Britain. Prosperous commerce and state power were seen as inextricably linked and wholly supportive of one another, however much war-time costs and taxation have attracted concern and criticism. The growing stimulus to domestic manufacture from military procurements was also significant for the development of early factory-based production. Moreover, the contribution of Britain's overseas colonies and extra-European trade to her efforts during the Napoleonic Wars was considerable.[18] With the final defeat of Napoleonic France in 1815, Britain's colonial preponderance combined with her emergent industrial revolution to drive an unprecedented ascent to 'superpower status' in the Europe of the late nineteenth century. The pivotal interconnection between rising and falling hegemonic powers is a central characteristic of modern European history and, in the eyes of a number of influential analysts, the prime source of major wars.[19]

The spread of industrialisation throughout Europe, and the revival of imperial impulses, then wrought a transformation upon the structure of the world political economy. Europe, and its North American cousin, came to dominate world manufactured output, as Chart 3.1 illustrates.

European colonies had also spread widely by the late nineteenth century, to occupy some eighty-four per cent of the world's surface by 1914,[20] thereby subordinating the economic development of the greater part of the world to the needs of a relatively few industrial societies.

The effects of the global spread of Europe and its colonies were to be two-fold. First, a new global division of labour was created. Artisan manufacture in many parts of the world was overwhelmed by the vast influx of cheap, mass-produced goods from the industries of Europe. In other areas, new regions of primary production were created to meet the burgeoning requirements of the growing populations and industrial systems of Europe's ever expanding economies. A special form of international economic interdependence was thus generated, in which the metropolitan economies became increasingly dependent upon imports of primary products from their overseas colonies, while the colonies became, in their turn, increasingly wedded to imports of manufactured goods and advanced services from their colonial masters. The heritage of this global economic transformation will be addressed further in the later discussions of the economic dimensions of contemporary international interdependence.

Interdependencies being were also being forged, and reinforced, by the progress of industrialisation and the growth of international trade during the eighteenth and nineteenth centuries. The technical consequences of industrialisation added ever more products to the list of imports that became important to one or another industrialised country. Previous net exporters of basic foodstuffs and raw materials, like Great Britain, gradually became substantial importers of staple foods, commodities and ores. Moreover, as competitive advantage in manufacturing sectors switched from one country to another, new dependencies were created in the wake of lost industrial pre-eminence.

Attributed by economists to varying patterns of comparative advantage, and differing endowments of pertinent factors of production, such shifting patterns of specialisation and dependence reflect a range of causes that are interrelated in a complex manner. Strategically motivated governmental direction has frequently played a central role in the emergence of new centres of economic competitiveness and, hence, preponderance in the international supply of sensitive products. Major innovations in military technologies and equipment are one, rather obvious, area of such progress. Sustained efforts to promote highly competitive industries in a range of sectors have, however, had both serious military, as well as simply economic, implications.[21] Government-supported industrialisation in the Germany of the late nineteenth century achieved more than the emergence of modern Germany as a major industrial and military state.[22] It also resulted in a British dependence upon German chemical imports by 1914 that denied the British army sufficient quantities of dyes for uniforms, and propellants for artillery, by the start of the First World War.[23]

The second, but no less salient, consequence of the global expansion of the European states was the projection of a model of the European

Chart 3.1 Relative shares of world maintenance output, 1750-1900 (% shares)

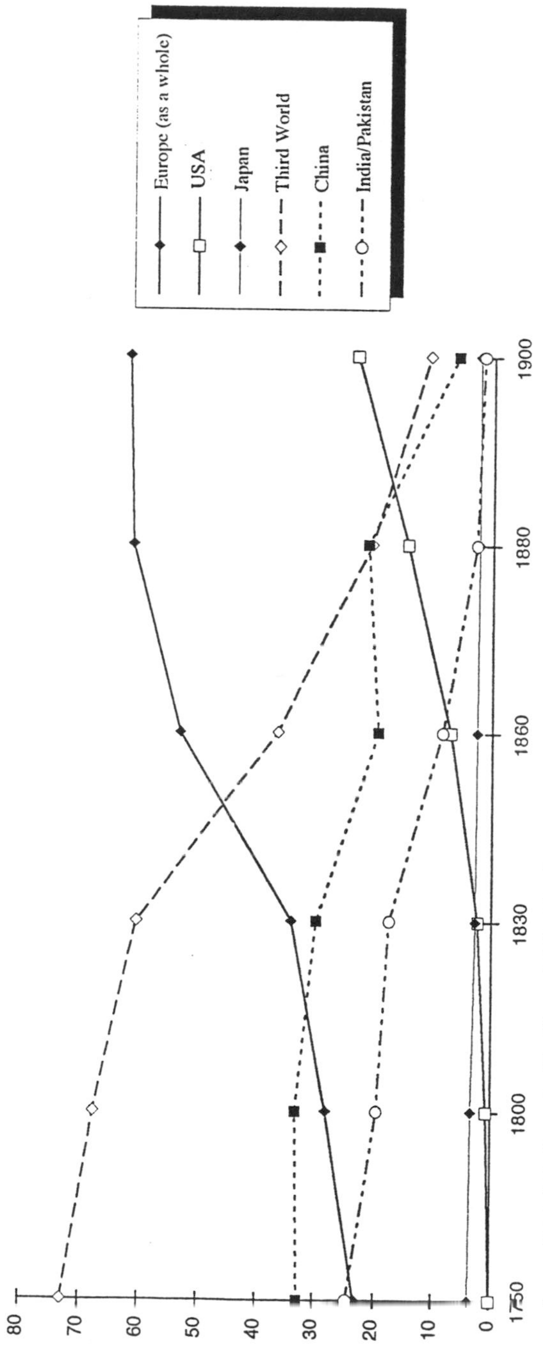

Source: Table 6, P. Kennedy. *The Rise and Fall of the Great Powers*, p. 190

nation-state as an ideal for the rest of the world. This process ensured that those who resisted European encroachments proved to be successful in doing so partly because of their adoption of many of the trappings of such European states. Moreover, when the tides of imperialism eventually began to ebb, it was to the European model that the former colonial territories looked for a blueprint for their futures.

The related emergence of a vigorous, and highly competitive, state system and a dynamic, and expansionary, industrial capitalism within modern Europe thus led, by the start of the twentieth century, to a world largely remade in its service, and aspiring to remake itself in its mould. The general structure of the modern world system was thus constructed and, with it, the politico-strategic problems, and impasses, of a world of states were enshrined.

Politico-military interdependence in a system of conflicting states

One of the more interesting forms of interdependence generated by the complex fusion of interstate competition and the dynamic, but inherently uneven, growth of wealth and economic power in the modern states' system has been that between rich patron states and poorer clients during times of political and military turbulence. Such a relationship is by no means recent in the history of the modern international system. At the height of the Renaissance, Italian princes and city states employed mercenary forces and paid encouragements to 'allied' states. Wallenstein's service to his Habsburg masters during the Thirty Years' War had a distinctly commercial dimension. The spectacular growth of British wealth and economic power during the nineteenth century, however, raised international clientilism to unprecedented levels. The adherence of successive allies was subsidised in the protracted struggle to contain and then defeat Napoleon's France. During the long Victorian 'summer', Britain was able to rest relatively content with a modest army; keeping European troubles at bay through the judicious deployment of largesse to suitable beneficiaries, while securing global and imperial interests through naval preponderance.

The use of massive economic largesse to sustain political and military relationships between patron and client did not disappear with the waning of British strength and wealth, for it was to be adopted with relish by the newly emergent superpower — the United States of America — in the post-World War era. From the time of the initial distribution of Marshall Aid to former friends and foes in Western Europe and Japan, a major criterion of US international aid has been the strategic sensitivity of the recipient state. US aid has flowed freely and in quantity wherever major US bases have been located, or where 'friendly' governments have been faced by an apparent threat from the Soviet bloc. The leading recipients of US aid during the period 1982 to 1991 were thus Israel, $29.9 billion; Egypt, $23.2 billion; Turkey, $6.9 billion; Pakistan, $5.4 billion; El Salvador, $4.0 billion; Greece, $3.7 billion; the Philippines, $3.5

billion; Honduras, $1.9 billion; Spain, $1.9 billion; India, $1.7 billion; Bangladesh, $1.7 billion; Sudan, $1.5 billion; and Portugal, $1.5 billion.[24]

A world of intense bipolar confrontation is also a world of 'follow my leader'. The widespread distribution of US aid towards sympathetic, or allied, states, stimulated comparable actions by the Soviet Union. Fraternal states everywhere were the primary beneficiaries of post-war Soviet assistance, for as long as its straining economy was able to sustain the multiple burdens of military and economic competition from the West. Post-war bipolarity intensified the sense of interdependence between patron and client in such relationships, given the zero-sum atmosphere of the political and military confrontation. It was, however, a real form of interdependence only for so long as, and to the extent that, perceptions remained stable and the interests of elite groups within the participating states remained complementary. Once perceptions, personnel and interests began to change, the nature of the interdependencies within the Cold War alliances underwent a rapid, and profound, re-evaluation.

Strategic interdependence and the security dilemma

Specific political, military and economic interdependencies between patron and client states are not the only consequence of the statist order. The more fundamental, and enduring, legacy of this heritage is that of the political fragmentation of the global 'order' and the endemic insecurity that is its consequence.

The imperatives generated by a system of sovereign states have been the subject of a voluminous literature. It is the primary focus of the Realist School of international relations' theory[25] and those who have deliberated upon the *security dilemma* facing states facing a world that lacks an effective, central political authority.[26] Such concerns for political and military security, within an 'anarchical' international system, are paralleled in the deliberations of those who have reflected upon the problems facing the levels of co-ordination for the operation of a liberal international trading system and other forms of international co-operation.[27]

The central problem facing all forms of co-operation and co-ordination in a states' system is that of interdependent decision-making in the absence of an overarching authority capable of formulating, and enforcing, common rules for the members of the system. The prisoners' dilemma, depicted in Figure 3.1, illustrates such a problematical situation of interdependent decision-making for two actors with two options and identical, and transparent, preference schedules.

Such a prisoners' dilemma replicates the problems of decision-makers faced with a situation in which the outcome will be a function of what both they and the other actor(s) decide. The case illustrated in Figure 3.1 illustrates the problems under one set of assumptions about the preference schedules of the actors involved.

In Figure 3.1 both actors have identical preference schedules. The rows of the matrix represent the options available to State A and the columns represent the options for State B. Each of the outlined boxes then corresponds to one of the four possible sets of joint decisions by Actor A and Actor B. Thus, the top left-hand box represents the situation in which both actors choose to co-operate with one another. The top right-hand box, in contrast, represents the situation in which State A decides to continue co-operating, while State B decides to defect from co-operation. In the bottom left-hand corner A defects while B co-operates, and in the bottom right-hand corner both A and B defect from co-operation simultaneously. The pay-offs, or patterns of benefit or loss, for both actors are contained within the box that corresponds to the choices of action that both have made. In each case, the number in the top right-hand corner of the box represents the pay-off for State B, while the number in the bottom left-hand corner is the pay-off for State A. Thus the pay-offs when State A decides to defect and State B continues to co-operate are: +40 for State A and -40 for State B.

		STATE B	
		Co-operate	Defect
STATE A	Co-operate	+10 (B) +10 (A)	+40 (B) -40 (A)
	Defect	-40 (B) +40 (A)	-20 (B) -20 (A)

Figure 3.1 The prisoners' dilemma

Decision-making is difficult if each actor's decision has to be made before that of the other is known. The aggregate benefit for both states can be maximised if both decide to continue co-operating. Unfortunately, the decision-makers in State A may reason as follows. If they continue with a co-operative strategy and State B realises that this is what they are likely to do, then the decision-makers of State B may calculate that they can secure substantial gains by switching to defection (increasing their gains from +10 to +40). This is a significant gain and may therefore prove attractive. The decision-makers of State A may appreciate the temptations involved and fear that the decision-makers of State B cannot be trusted to resist them. The only way in which State A's decision-makers can protect themselves from the danger of suffering a serious loss (a pay-off of -40) is to undertake a pre-emptive switch of strategy, themselves, to defection.

The problem is that both states' decision-makers have identical preferences and must be assumed to be equally prescient and 'rational' (within the dictates of such a *game theory* framework). If it is tempting for one state to switch from co-operation to defection, it is equally tempting for the other. If it is prudential for one state to protect itself by a pre-emptive move away from a vulnerable co-operative strategy, it is equally prudential for the other. The consequence is that both states opt for the strategy of defection and the 'game' comes to rest in the bottom right-hand box of the 'game' matrix, with both states experiencing losses (-20 in each case). This, therefore, is a paradoxical outcome, since both states, whether through greed or anxiety, have managed to move from a mutually beneficial situation, in which both secured positive outcomes (+10 in each), to one that has created a loss for both.

The impulses, both acquisitive and precautionary, for each state to switch from co-operation to defection are thus powerful and can be contained, in any isolated 'game' of such choices, only by the existence of considerable mutual trust and confidence between the decision-makers of the two states. In continuing sequences of 'prisoners' dilemma' games, consistent co-operation can be confidence-building measures, including the learning effect of adopting 'tit-for-tat' strategies of response to the other's choices,[28] embedding the 'game' within a wider framework of co-operation between the actors and generally creating conditions that effectively alter the cost-benefit patterns that face the participants.[29]

The problem of the prisoners' dilemma faces all states as they consider co-operative relations with other states. International interaction has, in this way, often been conceived of as an n-person prisoners' dilemma (the individual state playing against the large number of other states simultaneously). The conditions and measures that might militate against mutually damaging, defection strategies, have, furthermore, been the subject of a growing literature on co-ordination and management within the international system.

The *security dilemma*[30] thus generated by a fragmented states' system subjects decision-makers to considerable difficulties and dilemmas. Should states trust others and opt for low levels of defensive capabilities, or should they maintain high levels of vigilance, suspicion and military capability? The problem with a high-vigilance, high-armaments strategy is that it is akin to the defection strategy in the prisoners' dilemma and is tempting to all states that lack high levels of trust in their fellows. Worse, the adoption of a high-vigilance, high-armaments level strategy is likely to transmit disturbing signals to other states. Other states may well interpret such a situation as justification of their worst fears and believe that it warrants, indeed compels, the adoption of a similar strategy.

The consequence of states adopting strategies of high-vigilance, and a high level of armaments, is thus that they can stimulate cycles of mutually reinforcing suspicion, arms acquisition and hostility: a classical arms race process.[31] This possibility demonstrates the inherent security interdependence of states in a fragmented international system: if they seek the enhancement of security unilaterally, they may merely precipitate reactions that qualify, and even undermine, that security.

Arms races may end in the outbreak of war or sustain an evolving, and ever more deadly, form of deterrence, as during the era of the nuclear arms race between the USA and the USSR. Whatever the outcome, the ultimate well-being of all participants in an arms race remains dependent upon the behaviour of the other side(s). If the other(s) refrains from armed actions, then peace and well-being can be preserved for all. If the opponent(s) resorts to force, then damage will be suffered by the victim of that action, irrespective of what it had hoped and expected initially. Strategic interaction in a politically fragmented world can thus constitute a potentially deadly form of interdependence.

Anxiety about the durability of deterrence under the psychologically pressing, and economically burdensome, conditions of arms races has long prompted recourse to alternative means of managing the strategic interdependence amongst sovereign states. The relevant interdependencies, here, can be defined in one of two ways. The first approach is to limit them to the states that are participants in some current confrontation and to undertake bilateral, or multilateral, negotiations to secure agreements on arms limitation, or even substantial measures of disarmament. Either outcome acknowledges the direct interdependencies involved in the central relationships and crystallises those interdependencies in explicit agreements and formal measures of mutual inspection, scheduled armaments' destruction and similar procedures.[32]

The alternative approach to the problems of security is to attempt to deal with them at the collective level, thereby constructing an alternative form of a favourable 'balance of power'. The traditional concern of international relations theorists with 'balances of power' arises from the central questions of state security. Highly varied in the range of its possible meanings, a state can pursue some form of 'balance of power' through multilateral or unilateral efforts. Policies and processes can sometimes coincide to establish a favourable 'balance' between *status quo* states and those that pose a threat. If states seek such a balance through the strength of alliance with others, then they commit themselves to a central dependence upon those with whom they ally. Where a state seeks to deter a potential aggressor unilaterally, then its central dependence is upon the restraint of the threatening state. In the modern case of a nuclear 'balance of terror', participating states are locked together in mutual dependence upon one another's restraint for the preservation of peace and, quite possibly, physical survival.

Increased confidence can thus be pursued through the formation of alliances with other, sympathetic states, but the confidence generated by such measures of collective defence may be illusory. The formation of alliances may well assume a competitive form, with alliances prompting counter-alliances. Competitive alliance formation and enlargement processes parallel the arms race process between individual states, merely adding the complexities and uncertainties of multiple centres of decision-making.[33] The interdependencies of international security are thus complicated by the formation of alliances or other international coalitions. Any enhancement of security thus remains, to a significant extent, a function of the response of the other side(s) to the creation, or enlargement, of any alliance. Whether such additional complexity adds to the escalatory pressures within the relationship or reinforces its deterrence effects is a function of the specific empirical conditions within which the alliances have been formed. A favourable outcome will, as suggested earlier, also remain dependent upon restraint from the adversary.

The members of an effective alliance (or coalition) are also in a clear relationship of mutual interdependence for at least some part of their security, perceived or actual. The persistent danger in any alliance, or coalition, is the possibility of 'free-riding' by one, or more, members on the efforts and sacrifices of the other alliance members; a special case of defection in a 'prisoners' dilemma' game amongst supposed friends. Such free-riding might assume one of two forms. A state might fail to fulfil its obligations when the alliance is called into operation by a challenge to the security of one or more of its members. Such defection 'in the face of the enemy' is a possibility that has often reduced the confidence that states are prepared to place in the alliances that they have joined.[34]

More common are instances of free-riding states sheltering behind the shield provided by alliances of conveniently located states, or situations in which participating states are able to gain disproportionately from membership of an alliance. Seminal discussions of the problems of free-riding, and the provision of collective goods, have identified mechanisms by which potential free-riders can be brought into line and persuaded to make some contribution to the provision of a desired collective good, such as an effective politico-military alliance. Mancur Olson's initial list of such mechanisms emphasised the force of common ideological commitments in the alliances of the post-war world.[35] Firm, and possibly compelling, action by alliance leader(s) has also proved significant to the preservation of many alliances throughout history,[36] from the Peloponnesian War[37] to the Cold War. Disproportionate burden sharing is, however, all too common where the participants in an alliance are of significantly differing size, wealth, military capability or commitment to the alliance.[38] The alliances that result from the deployment of such cohesion-maintenance devices amongst a disparate collection of states are likely to embrace a range of striking, and noticeably asymmetrical, interdependencies.

A wider system of universal Collective Security may be preferred to the more limited, and inherently antagonistic, measures of collective defence. Such Collective Security expands the principle of 'one for all and all for one' to the global level. In the event of aggression, all the other members of the Collective Security system are supposed to take appropriate action to protect the victim of the aggression and, if necessary, adopt coercive measures against the aggressor. The threat of overwhelming opposition would, it was hoped, constitute a massive preponderance of 'power', sufficient to deter would-be aggressors. Should such collective deterrence fail, however, the victim would be preserved and the aggressor convincingly punished by the combined efforts of the rest of the international 'community'.[39]

The effectiveness of Collective Security systems, in both theory and practice, has been widely discussed by students of international relations[40] and international history.[41] The problem, however, is essentially that of an attempt to provide a collective good for the international system, under the demanding conditions of voluntary contributions, the semi-visibility of those contributions, ideological diversity and even division, a large 'collectivity', some divisibility of the 'good' itself, and massive disparities of wealth and strength amongst the potential contributors. The necessary levels of mutual commitment and confidence have been difficult to create under such circumstances. Practical expressions of Collective Security operations have thus been limited to operations of three types. Peace-keeping operations, of 'relatively' modest cost, and which can be sustained by contributions from states of a range of size and strength, have been launched in the aftermath of a number of international and civil disputes.[42] There have also been a number of attempts to reverse military aggression, or unacceptable political behaviour, through the imposition of economic sanctions, under the League of Nations and the United Nations. There have, however, only been two serious efforts to reverse aggression, and restore peace under internationally acceptable conditions, through the determined use of force by a wide-ranging coalition of sates. Both have taken place under the clear leadership of the United States of America: the Korean War and the recent Gulf War to liberate Kuwait from Iraqi occupation.

The idea of the interdependence of all states in a world security system, while attractive in principle, has thus been of limited effectiveness. The relevant interdependencies have been modest, somewhat specific and highly asymmetrical in the case of those efforts that have been made to resist, or reverse, major challenges to the *status quo*. States that wished to oppose the threat were effectively dependent upon the strength, wealth and commitment of the United States of America. The USA's dependence on its fellow states has, in contrast, been for legitimising statements and limited measures of practical support from the relatively small number of its current allies. Such a situation departs substantially from that envisaged by the intellectual founding fathers of Collective Security and carries clear dangers of self-interested dictation by dominant, if not hegemonical, powers. Such dangers have, however, been integral to all the arrangements thus far contrived by, and for, the system of states. Indeed, effective action in international affairs, freed from the enervating potentialities for free-riding, may always require the decisive influence of the stronger states, while the system of states is, itself, maintained.

In the United Nations' more modest, peace-keeping actions, the central dependencies have, again, been rather limited in scope and range. The United Nations Organisation, and those directly involved in the violent confrontations, have been largely dependent upon the goodwill of the relatively small number of states that have proved willing to supply the troops, and logistical services, necessary for sustained peace-keeping presences.

Rationalist perspectives

Functionalism, interdependence and globalisation

The gap between the hopes and limited realities of Collective Security highlights the wider difficulty of rationalist[43] expectations about the potentialities for international collaboration, peace and harmony. A general disposition to equate that which reason suggests ought to be the case in international affairs, with what is likely to be achieved, has a long lineage in human thought. The notions of benign interdependence that were so dear to late nineteenth-century liberals, embraced such expectations. These were, however, to be frontally challenged by the cataclysmic events of the early twentieth century, as was indicated in Chapter 2.

Functionalist doctrines[44] of peace, co-operation, organisation and even formal integration at the international level are a more recent development of rationalistic notions of the relationship between apparent imperatives, whether moral or material, and consequential developments in international behaviour and institutions. International organisations have proliferated, with accelerating pace, beyond the Collective Security institutions of the League of Nations and the United Nations. Whereas nineteenth-century interdependence theories envisaged the automatic translation of increased levels of economic interdependence into enhanced peace and security, internationally, the focus of modern Functionalist theory is upon the construction of institutions through which international difficulties can be resolved and effective co-ordination orchestrated. In this vein, Functionalist analysis has been applied both to studies of the origins, and potentialities, of global-level international organisations and to the experiences of integration within such regional associations as the European Community.

Cumulative imperatives are central to Functionalist interpretations of the growth of international organisations or the progressive integration of regional associations. As practical difficulties of interaction and co-ordination are encountered in one area, or another, pressures build for the establishment of suitable fora within which they can be considered and solutions developed. Successful collaborative responses to existing difficulties contribute to further collaboration in the future in two ways. First, the experience of successful collaboration is, itself, encouraging: it provides a vision of, and a model for, future efforts. Second, the fruits of effective international collaboration and co-ordination often provide stimulation for new, or intensified, forms of international interactions which, themselves, generate new difficulties which require resolution through further international collaboration. The Functionalist engine thus drives the continuous development of international association and organisation through the cumulative effects of past collaboration and co-ordination. Interdependencies in the real world thus exert clear and cumulative imperatives upon the development of human institutions. The processes through which such pressures exert their influence will, in Functionalist theory, be equally operative at the levels of regional integration, international organisation or the institutional manifestations of globalisation.

The automaticity implied by the earlier Functionalist models of international organisations and international integration troubled some of those whose familiarity with the actual histories of international organisation and regional integration led them to envisage a rather more complex, and variable, process. The continuing, and often critical, role of states, state institutions, 'spill-over' effects, and political decision-makers in the development of international organisations or regional integration is thus central to the approach of *neo-Functionalists*.[45] The role of conscious political activity is thus restored to a central role in the construction of new institutions in the international arena. Such a mid-range theoretical perspective upon international and regional association thus better captures many of the empirical features of the actual processes that have led to the creation of international organisations and regional associations, but loses much of the causal confidence of Functionalist theory.

International societies, international regimes and hegemons

The possibilities of explanation, and the range of salient features of international organisation, are not, however, exhausted by the close cousins of Functionalism and neo-Functionalism. Two additional perspectives accept the persistence of a politically fragmented states' order and seek to identify, and emphasise, those features of international interaction that offer keys to the successful management of interdependence within such a system.

The *international society* concept, propounded by the so-called 'English School' of international relations' theory,[46] identifies a societal component within international relations that provides for the partial transcendence of the 'anarchical' and brutal features of a system of sovereign states, and that reflects, and preserves, a pattern of intrinsic interdependence. Not a full-blown society of the kind encountered in well-knit, local communities — *Gemeinschaft* — but rather a looser, emergent social form — *Gesellschaft* —[47] international society which is bound by the development of a shared set of understandings and expectations, generated by a long history of international interaction and the gradual acknowledgement of the essential interdependence of life in a system of states. The nominal basis of international society thus lies in reflective or cognitive approaches to international relations. However, this foundation is neither as clear or as secure as might initially appear, given the contested empirical reality of such an 'international society'.

The existence of such an international society remains controversial.[48] Analyses of international society also have an in-built tendency to meander between reflective and rationalist perspectives on human activity. The important point in this discussion, however, is that such a concept constitutes a device for establishing a durable basis for restraint and orderliness within a system that lacks effective, central authority. Rationalist analysis thus identifies a possible path towards the resolution of the apparent contradiction between the perceived need for collaborative behaviour in many areas of international affairs and the clear dangers inherent in a politically fragmented system. This *Grotian* vision[49] of international relations allows that states may be the enduring, and even desirable, component of the international order, but the worst dangers of that condition might be evaded through the ameliorative influence of the component of international society. Realism prevails, but a Realism less red in tooth and claw than that depicted by some of the founding fathers of modern Realist theory.

Comparable results to those of international society theory can also be derived via a different, though closely related, branch of theory in international relations, which also straddles the rationalist/reflective methodological divide.[50] The means of constraining disorder within the international system, and its economic component in particular, have been identified in the creation of international *regimes*, often under the guidance, if not coercive pressure, of dominant, or *hegemonic*, powers, as was suggested briefly in Chapter 2. The core concept here is that, in the absence of suitable structures and organisation, states will emphasise their own immediate interests at the expense of the interests of other states and, indeed, at the expense of new international arrangements that would ultimately serve everyone's interests. The temptation to free-ride may, as was suggested in the earlier discussion of Collective Security, prove irresistible. The impulse to protect themselves against the effects of others' free-riding will merely reinforce the self-regarding behaviour of states. The consequence of such free-riding and self-protective impulses will be to undermine efforts to create, or sustain, mutually advantageous forms of international co-operation in many spheres of international interaction.[51] Suitable international arrangements might overcome such impulses and sustain co-ordinated behaviour by states. Such arrangements might warrant the term *regimes*, if the term can remain sufficiently precise in the face of the breadth of its potential referent.[52]

The use of the concept of international regime has become extensive in contemporary studies of international relations. Indeed, its breadth of application has reinforced many doubts about its analytical efficacy. In his introduction to the seminal survey of regime analysis, Stephen Krasner defines the concept thus:

> International regimes are defined as principles, norms, rules, and decision-making procedures around which actor expectations converge in a given issue-area.[53]

The existence of discrete issue-areas within international relations is, itself, a problematical matter. The definition of regimes, thence, is so wide as to encompass happily a wide diversity of empirical conditions; from highly formalised, treaty-based organisations, such as the International Monetary Fund and linked monetary institutions, to situations wholly lacking formal recognition or regulation, but with widely acknowledged 'principles'.

Given the range of possible international 'regimes', the paths to their formation may be highly varied. Three obvious avenues present themselves: spontaneous emergence; negotiated establishment; and imposition.[54] A critical variable in determining the feasible paths to regime creation is likely to be the costs entailed by participation in, and support for, any potential regime. Where low costs are involved in a minimal 'regime', then spontaneous emergence is a clear possibility. Where costs to states are significant, but potential benefits considerable, then a negotiated path to regime creation may well be pursued. Where possible costs are considerable, and the temptations to free-ride obvious, then it may be necessary to impose any regimes that may be created or underwrite them through the disproportionate contributions of one, or a small number, of *hegemonic* states.

The development and maintenance of valuable regimes in areas of costly international interaction are thus held to rest upon the efforts of the states that are dominant economically, and possibly militarily. *Hegemonic Stability* thus arises and serves the needs of the entire membership of the international system, as in the heyday of British economic dominance in the late nineteenth century and the dominance of the United States of America throughout the non-Soviet world for the two to three decades following the Second World War.[55]

Hegemonic Stability thus offers a partial resolution to the problems created by interdependencies within a politically fragmented world. Stable conditions can be sustained for those exchanges that states, and their populations, wish, or need, to undertake with one another. Moreover, as will be emphasised later in this discussion, the stability endowed by such hegemonic leadership may encourage the further development of interdependence: existing interdependencies may be intensified; and new interdependencies may be born as states, and their populations gain the confidence to identify and respond to new possibilities of production and trade.

Three questions, however, arise about the role of hegemonic powers in the international political economy. The first concerns the influence actually exercised by the supposed hegemon, given the ease within which it can be exaggerated by enthusiastic analysts. Detailed studies of Great Britain's role in the nineteenth century certainly suggest that her role in the international financial system of that time was less that of a straightforward hegemon than has sometimes been claimed.[56]

Should a measure of hegemony exist, however, there is still the question as to whether all members of the international system benefit equally. The clear danger is that the prime beneficiaries of any regime, or set of international regimes, established under the influence of a hegemon will be the hegemon itself. Great Britain, and the group of 'core' industrial economies, was able to transmit the greater share of the costs of adjusting to trade imbalances to weaker economies through the operation of the Gold Standard during the later nineteenth century. The United States of America benefited considerably from the liberalisation of trade during the era of her economic dominance after the Second World War. In the international political realm, the operation of the United Nations was dominated by the USA, and her Western allies, during the initial decades of that institution's life.[57]

In the extreme, the condition of international hegemony might reflect, and contribute to, the exploitative dominance of the international system by a small number of states and/or their economic and political leadership groups. Such a critical perspective upon international hegemony is offered by the neo-Gramscian analysis that has become popular in recent years. This approach identifies an insidious form of intellectual and ideological hegemony that has been generated by dominant capitalist interests, and sympathetic state actors, and that subordinates the peoples of much of the world, mentally as well as materially.[58] As with most theoretical perspectives upon human activity, this neo-Gramscian approach captures *something* of the nature of the contemporary international political economy; as a *meta-theory*,[59] however, it remains inherently untestable in any simple, and straightforward, manner and retains its force primarily as a critical perspective.

The third central question about hegemony, and its effects, is that of the durability of the conditions generated by hegemony, if and when the material basis of that condition begins to dissolve. Two linked possibilities provide the specific regimes, and the general stability, generated by the previous hegemon, with some prospects of survival.

Many specific regimes may be sustained, as Robert Keohane has been at pains to argue,[60] as a result of experience of those regimes, themselves. In game-theoretical terms, the cost-benefit schedules faced by individual states when considering behaviour that might sabotage an established regime will differ, in significant ways, from that facing a state considering participation in the creation of a new regime. The diplomatic costs of destroying a valued regime will be far heavier than those of merely failing to join a new venture. Moreover, the understandings and expectations of political decision-makers, business leaders and citizens may all have been changed significantly by past participation in the regime. Finally, material changes to production patterns and trade flows might have followed from participation in the regime, which would now be costly to disrupt through withdrawal from the regime, or its destruction. Self-interested behaviour may still prevail in an essentially Hobbesian world, but calculations of self-interest may have been substantially modified by changing institutional conditions and experiences.

The cumulative effects of hegemonic leadership upon the international political economy may also provide a basis for sustained general stability. It is possible that expectations, practices and patterns of trade will have been progressively altered by a world in which stability and co-ordination were underwritten by the hegemon. One possible result of such a situation might be the gradual emergence of a world, in Robert Keohane and Joseph Nye's terms, of *complex interdependence*,[61] if such a phenomenon is held to be a real-world condition, rather than a heuristic model.[62] The emergence of such a world, with multiple channels of association amongst societies and their peoples, an absence of a simple hierarchy amongst the issues of political and economic decision-making and the diminished utility of force in the relations amongst states,[63] would have been generated by a period of stability and confidence in world affairs and would, in turn, demonstrate a deepening and widening of prevailing international interdependencies. Globalisation, in its benign sense, could well be the product of the further deepening of any such empirical condition of complex interdependence.

The vision of the world presented by the set of ideas that embraces notions of regimes, structure, hegemony and complex interdependence has a complex, and not entirely clear, relationship with that of international society.[64] Both dispositions accept the centrality of states in the contemporary international order. Both also embrace notions of norms, and other constraints, that moderate and modulate state behaviour. Grotian presumptions are, however, absent from the theories of regimes, hegemony and complex interdependence, as are explicit references to the idea of international society. A neorealist strain,[65] that flows from Hobbesian and Machiavellian roots, directs such thinking. The progressive adoption of this intellectual tendency to the complex characteristics of the modern world has, however, brought it ever closer to some of the central referents of the theory of International Society. Moreover, the persistence of functionalist and neo-functionalist tendencies in the work of some members of this broad school of international relations' theorists, confirms the optimistic rationalism of both them and their distant cousins in the 'English School'. Functionalist echoes are also strong in many visions of contemporary globalisation, whether benign or malign in form and effect.

Conclusion

Contemporary international interdependence, and contemporary tendencies towards globalisation, has its roots and reality in the system of states and industrial capitalism that emerged in early modern Europe. A complex system of military and economic interaction drove the process of 'modernisation' within the emergent European states that was to prove transformational, first for itself and then for the rest of the world. With the 'triumph' of the West, the extra-European world was progressively drawn into the Euro-American dominated economic system. With the maturation of the new world system of states, former colonies found formal independence on the model of the European nation-state. Interdependencies have been created, transformed and endowed with their politico-economic context by this historical process.

The consequences of the enshrinement of the nation-states are many. The world is fragmented into states that jealously guard their sovereignty. A central problem has thus been created for the peace of the world and the security of states and their populations. The conventional means through which enhanced security has been pursued have had to take the existence of separate states as their starting-point and accept the limitations that this central reality places upon the confidence that can be placed in collaborative approaches to enhanced security. Indeed, it is all too easy to precipitate unintended, and undesirable, consequences through misjudged attempts to improve security, as the eruption of destabilising arms races has demonstrated all too often in the past. The prospects for effective collective solutions to the problem of security have, thus far, been equally compromised by the nature, and consequences, of the system of sovereign states. States may remain ultimately interdependent upon one another for their real security, but their separation condemns them to a fear-laden form of such interdependence. Conflict, rather than harmony, is thus integral to the character and developments of many forms of international interdependence.

Interdependencies may also underlie, and be promoted by, institutional changes in international relations. Many theories that seek to account for the prominent institutional innovations of the post-war international order attribute considerable significance to the influence of such interdependencies as have arisen. Moreover, theories of regime formation and hegemonic influence highlight the significance that such phenomena can have for the emergence of new, and possibly higher, levels of interdependence within the international political economy. Much of the perceived momentum towards globalisation also reflects such factors and influences. However, many of the institutional developments characterising such 'progress' reflect the tensions and potential conflicts inherent within an arena of growing, and often deepening, international associations and transactions.

Interdependencies in the real world are, however, rarely symmetrical and balanced in their significance for all parties. In the extreme, it is possible that hegemony has followed a fundamentally exploitative agenda and generated a set of interdependencies that are overwhelmingly to the advantage of a few states, or of their dominant economic interest groups. Visions of future world well-being will be profoundly influenced by judgements made about the character, and general effect, of such hegemony as has prevailed in the post-war world.

While the bulk of discussions of international interdependence take the centrality of the sovereign state as a given, such an assumption is not common to all approaches to the phenomenon. A range of perspectives upon contemporary world affairs challenge the moral and empirical priority of the 'nation'-state. Some discussions put people before states. Many studies of the evolving global ecosystem, and general globalisation, are concerned with processes and developments that transcend the frontiers of states and potentially overarch the considerations and concerns of their decision-makers. It is to such non-statist approaches to interdependence that the next chapter is devoted.

Notes and references

1. For a review of these regions of the early medieval world see John A. Hall, *Powers and Liberties: The Causes and Consequences of the Rise of the West* (Oxford: Basil Blackwell, 1985), Chs. 2, 3 and 4.
2. Ibid., Ch. 5.
3. See, in particular, Paul Kennedy, *The Rise and Fall of the Great Powers: Economic Change and Military Conflict from 1500 to 2000* (London: Unwin Hyman, 1988), esp. Ch. 2.
4. See Geoffrey Parker, *The Military Revolution: Military Innovation and the Rise of the West, 1500-1800,* (Cambridge; Cambridge University Press, 1988), esp. Ch. 2; Frank Tallett, *War and Society in Early Modern Europe, 1495-1715* (London: Routledge, 1992); and Kennedy, *The Rise and Fall of the Great Powers,* esp. Ch. 3.
5. Kennedy, *The Rise and Fall of the Great Powers*, esp. Ch. 2; and see also Tallett, *War and Society in Early Modern Europe.*
6. See the discussion in Yale H. Ferguson and Richard W. Mansbach, *The State, Conceptual Chaos, and the Future of International Relations Theory* (Denver and London: University of Denver/Lynne Rienner Publishers, 1989), esp. pp. 75-6.
7. See Peter L. Berger and Thomas Luckmann, *The Social Construction of Reality* (Harmondsworth: The Penguin Press, 1967).
8. On 'structuration' see Anthony Giddens, *The Constitution of Society: Outline of the Theory of Structuration* (Cambridge: Polity Press, 1984); and Ira Cohen, *Structuration Theory: Anthony Giddens and the Constitution of Social Life* (London: Macmillan, 1989); and on its application to international relations, see Andrew Wendt, 'The Agent-Structure problem in international relations theory', *International Organization*, Vol. 42, No. 3 (Summer 1987), pp. 335-70.
9. On which see K.J. Holsti, *Peace and War: Armed Conflicts and International Order 1648-1989* (Cambridge: Cambridge University Press, 1991), esp. pp. 37-46.
10. But not extra-European 'hegemony', the capacity for which passed to Great Britain with the massive reduction of the maritime and overseas capabilities of France, and her erstwhile European allies, brought about by the outcome of the Napoleonic Wars.

11. On which see Kennedy, *The Rise and Fall of the Great Powers,* esp. pp. 178-80; and Holsti, *Peace and War,* pp. 129-37.
12. See, in particular, the discussion in K.J. Holsti, *Peace and War: Armed Conflicts an International Order 1648-1989,* (Cambridge: Cambridge University Press, 1991).
13. On which see Hedley Bull, *The Anarchical Society: A Study of Order in World Politics* (London: Macmillan, 1977); C.A.W. Manning, *The Nature of International Society* (London: G. Bell and Sons Ltd., 1962); M. Wight, *'The theory of international society'* in M. Wight (ed. G. Wight and B. Porter), *International Theory: The Three Traditions* (London: Leicester University Press/RIIA, 1991), Ch. 3; H. Bull and A. Watson (eds.), *The Expansion of International Society* (Oxford: Clarendon Press, 1984); and Adam Watson, *The Evolution of International Society: a Comparative Historical Analysis* (London: Routledge, 1992).
14. For a further critique of 'international society' theories see Roy E. Jones, 'The English School of international relations: a case for closure', *Review of International Studies,* Vol. 7, No. 1 (January 1981), pp. 1-13; and R.J. Barry Jones, 'The English School and the political construction of international society', in B.A. Roberson (ed.), *The English School Revisited,* (forthcoming).
15. A point made forcefully, if rather densely, by Richard Ashley in 'The poverty of neo-Realism', *International Organization,* Vol. 38, No. 2, pp. 225-61, reprinted in an edited form in R.O. Keohane (ed.), *Neo-Realism and its Critics* (New York: Columbia University Press, 1986), Ch. 9.
16. For a further discussion of this conception of politics and political orders, see Jones, 'The European School and the political construction of international society', in B.A Roberson (ed.), *The English School Revisited* (forthcoming).
17. See Michael Howard, 'The military factor in European expansion', in Bull and Watson (eds.), *The Expansion of International Society,* Ch. 2, esp. pp. 34-40.
18. Kennedy, *The Rise and Fall of the Great Powers,* esp. pp. 167-9.
19. See, in particular, Robert Gilpin, *War and Change in World Politics* (Cambridge: Cambridge University Press, 1981); Charles Doran, *Systems in Crisis: New Imperatives of High Politics at Century's End,* (Cambridge: Cambridge University Press, 1991); and Paul Kennedy, *The Rise and Fall of the Great Powers: Economic Change and Military Conflict from 1500 to 2000* (London: Unwin Hyman, 1988).
20. Kennedy, *The Rise and Fall of the Great Powers,* p. 192.
21. For a more extensive discussion, see R.J. Barry Jones, *Conflict and Control in the World Economy: Contemporary Economic Realism and Neo-Mercantilism* (Brighton: Wheatsheaf/Harvester, 1986), esp. Part IV.
22. For a general discussion of the economic significance of military rivalry see Gautam Sen, *The Military Origins of Industrialisation and International Trade Rivalry* (London: Frances Pinter Ltd., 1984).
23. Corelli Barnett, *The Collapse of British Power* (London: Eyre Methuen, 1972), pp. 85-8.
24. Figures quoted in the report 'Kind words, closed wallets', *The Economist,* 27 March 1993, pp. 58-61.
25. See, in particular, Hans J. Morgenthau, *Politics Among Nations: The Struggle for Power and Peace* (New York: Alfred Knopf, 1948, various editions); Reinhold Niebuhr, *Moral Man and Immoral Society: A Study in Ethics and Politics* (New York: C. Scribner's, 1952). For a specific discussion of Realism and interdependence see Richard Little, 'Power and interdependence: a Realist critique', in R.J. Barry Jones and Peter Willetts (eds.), *Interdependence on Trial: Studies in the Theory and Reality of Contemporary Interdependence* (London: Frances Pinter Ltd., 1984), pp. 111-29.

26. See, particularly, Barry Buzan, *People, States and Fear* (Brighton: Wheatsheaf/Harvester, 1983).
27. See, in particular, R.O. Keohane and J.S. Nye, Jr., *Power and Interdependence: World Politics in Transition* (Boston: Little, Brown, 1977); S.D. Krasner (ed.), *International Regimes* (Ithaca: Cornell University Press, 1983); and Robert Keohane, *After Hegemony: Cooperation and Discord in the World Political Economy* (Princeton, NJ: Princeton University Press, 1984).
28. See, especially, Robert Axelrod, *The Evolution of Cooperation* (New York: Basic Books, 1984), Part 2.
29. For further discussions of game theory and its implications for such situations, see Michael Nicholson, *Formal Theories in International Relations* (Cambridge: Cambridge University Press, 1989), esp. Ch. 3.
30. See, in particular, Buzan, *People, States and Fear.*
31. On which see Michael Nicolson, *Formal Theories in International Relations,* Ch. 8.
32. For a seminal discussion of arms control negotiations, see Hedley Bull, *The Control of the Arms Race: Disarmament and Arms Control in the Nuclear Age* (London: Weidenfeld and Nicholson/ISS, 1961).
33. On alliances and other coalitions in international relations see J. Friedman, C. Bladen and S. Rosen (eds.), *Alliance in International Politics* (Boston: Allyn and Bacon, 1970); and Nicolson, *Formal Theories in International Relations,* Ch. 7; and on coalitions see William H. Riker, *The Theory of Political Coalitions* (New Haven: Yale University Press, 1962).
34. See, for illuminating discussions of the problems of maintaining confidence in the Anglo-French alliance before the outbreak of the Second World War, Arnold Wolfers, *Britain and France between Two Wars* (New York: Harcourt Brace and Co., 1940, reprinted New York: W.W. Norton and Co., 1966); and R.J. Barry Jones, *'Challenge and response in international politics: an analysis of the development of British policy towards Germany during 1935 and early 1936'* (Unpublished D.Phil thesis, University of Sussex, England, 1975).
35. See Mancur Olson, *The Logic of Collective Action: Public Goods and the Theory of Groups* (Cambridge: Cambridge University Press, 1965).
36. On the theoretical significance of which see N. Frohlich, J.A. Oppenheimer and O.R. Young, *Political Leadership and Collective Goods* (Englewood Cliffs, NJ: Prentice-Hall, 1971).
37. Thucydides, *The Peloponnesian War* (trans. Rex Warner; Harmondsworth: Penguin Books, 1954).
38. On which see, Mancur Olson, Jr. and Richard Zeckhauser, 'An economic theory of alliances', *The Review of Economics and Statistics,* Vol. 48, No. 3 (August 1966), pp. 266-79.
39. For the classical statement of the theory of Collective Security see Inis Claude, *Swords into Ploughshares* (New York: Random House (3rd edn.), 1964).
40. See, for example, Otto Pick and J. Critchley, *Collective Security* (London: Macmillan, 1974; and Claude, above.
41. See, for example, F.P. Walters, *A History of the League of Nations* (single volume edn. Oxford: Oxford University Press, 1953); and Evan Luard, *A History of the United Nations; Volume 1: The Years of Western Domination, 1945-1955* (London: Macmillan, 1982) and *Volume 2: The Age of Decolonization, 1955-1965* (London: Macmillan, 1989).
42. On which see Alan James, *Peacekeeping in International Politics* (London: Macmillan/IISS, 1990)
43. On rationalism in philosophy and less formal thought see J. Cottingham, *Rationalism* (London: Paladin, 1984).

44. On which see in particular, A.J.R. Groom and P. Taylor (eds.), *Functionalism: Theory and Practice in International Relations* (London: University of London Press, 1975), esp. Part I.
45. On which, see C. Pentland, 'Functionalism and theories of international political integration', in Groom and Taylor (eds.), *Functionalism,* pp. 9-24, and esp. pp. 16-20; N. Heathcote, 'Neo-functional theories of regional integration,' in Groom and Taylor (eds.), *Functionalism,* pp. 38-52.
46. On the existence of such an 'English School' see Roy E. Jones, 'The English School of international relations: a case for closure', *Review of International Studies,* Vol. 7, No. 1 (January 1981), pp. 1-13; Sheila Grader, 'The English School of international relations: evidence and evaluation', *Review of International Studies,* Vol. 14, No. 1, (January 1988), pp. 29-44; and Peter Wilson, 'The English School of international relations: a reply to Sheila Grader', *Review of International Studies,* Vol. 15, No. 1 (January 1989), pp. 49-58.
47. On which distinction see: C.A.W. Manning, *The Nature of International Society* (London: G. Bell and Sons Ltd., 1962), esp. p. 176; and Evan Luard, *International Society* (London: Macmillan, 1990), esp. p. 2.
48. See the critical comments of Roy E. Jones in 'The English School of international relations' and R.J. Barry Jones, 'The English School and the political construction of international society', in B.A. Roberson (ed.), *The English School Revisited* (forthcoming).
49. On which, see Martin Wight (ed. G. Wight and B. Porter), *International Theory: The Three Traditions* (Leicester and London: Leicester University Press/RIIA, 1991), esp. Ch. 1; and Hedley Bull, *The Anarchical Society: A Study of Order in World Politics* (London: Macmillan, 1977), esp. pp. 28-32 and 35-6.
50. Robert O. Keohane, 'International institutions: two approaches', *International Studies Quarterly,* Vol. 32 (1988).
51. See, especially Robert O. Keohane, 'The demand for international regimes', in S.D. Krasner (ed.), *International Regimes,* pp. 141-71; and Robert O. Keohane, *After Hegemony,* 1984.
52. See Susan Strange's critical comments on the concept, and attendant analysis: Susan Strange, *'Cave! hic dragones:* a critique of regime analysis', in S.D. Krasner (ed.), *International Regimes,* pp. 337-54.
53. Stephen D. Krasner, 'Structural causes and regime consequences: regimes as intervening variables', p.1, in S.D. Krasner (ed.), *International Regimes,* pp. 1-21.
54. See Oran R. Young, 'Regime dynamic: the rise and fall of international regimes', in S.D. Krasner (ed.), *International Regimes,* pp. 93-113; and see also a number of chapters in Rittberger and Mayer, *Regime Theory and International Relations* (Oxford: Clarendon Press, 1993).
55. On Hegemonic Stability theory see Charles P. Kindleberger, *The World in Depression, 1929-1939* (Berkeley: University of California Press, 1973); and Charles P. Kindleberger, 'Hierarchy versus inertial cooperation', *International Organization, Vol.* 40 (Autumn 1986). But on the limitations of the role of the hegemon, see Timothy J. McKeown, 'Tariffs and Hegemonic Stability theory', *International Organization, Vol.* 37 (Spring 1982), pp. 73-91; and on its continuing analytical difficulties see David A. Lake, 'Leadership, hegemony and the international economy: naked emperor or tattered monarch with potential', *International Studies Quarterly,* Vol. 37, No. 4 (1993), pp. 459-89.
56. See Andrew Walter, *World Power and World Money: The Role of Hegemony and International Monetary Order* (Hemel Hempstead: Harvester/Wheatsheaf, 1991).

57. See Luard, *History of the United Nations, Vol. 1.*
58. For a full account of this perspective, see S. Gill and D. Law, *The Global Political Economy: Perspectives, Problems and Policies* (Hemel Hempstead: Harvester/Wheatsheaf, 1988), esp. Chs. 5, 6 and 7.
59. On the idea of *meta-theory* see F.G. Castles, *Politics and Social Insight* (London: Routledge and Kegan Paul, 1971).
60. Keohane, *After Hegemony.*
61. Keohane and Nye, *Power and Interdependence.*
62. Keohane and Nye, themselves, later suggest that complex interdependence was intended to be no more than a heuristic model. See R.O. Keohane and J.S. Nye Jr., '*Power and Interdependence* revisited', *International Organization,* Vol. 41, No. 4 (Autumn 1987), pp. 725-53.
63. Keohane and Nye, *Power and Interdependence op. cit.* pp. 24-5.)
64. See, for instance, Andrew Hurrell, 'International society and the study of regimes: a reflective approach', in Rittberger and Mayer (eds.), *Regime Theory and International Relations,* pp. 49-72; and B. Buzan, 'From international system to international society: structural realism and regime theory meet the English school', *International Organization,* Vol. 47, No. 3 (Summer 1993), pp. 327-52.
65. Keohane, *Neo-Realism and its Critics.*

CHAPTER 4

Interdependence, globalisation and challenges to the international order

Introduction

Many discussions of contemporary interdependence, and globalisation, challenge the fundamentals of the prevailing order of separate, and jealously sovereign, states. This challenge is sometimes explicit; more commonly it emerges as an implication of arguments that focus upon problems that transcend state frontiers, challenge the competence of state authorities, or encourage the conclusion that sovereign states are a significant part of the problem of many of the difficulties currently facing humanity and its natural environment.

The subject matter of this chapter will thus be those perspectives and arguments that, when confronting various aspects of interdependence, and globalisation, seek to transcend the character and limitations of a system of sovereign states. The foundations for such an endeavour may be moral or practical, but frequently a combination of the two.

Global interdependence and the moral transcendence of the states' system

The triumph of the modern states' system has not been without its critics. Such critical reactions have generally followed one of two paths. The first rejects the fragmentation of the world order into separate, and potentially conflictful, states; advocating, in its place, a unified global system. The second approach proceeds further into a thoroughgoing critique of the authoritative state, as such; promoting an alternative vision of human self-regulation.

The unity of man, world society and a world state

A rejection of the fragmented international political order may reflect views about the moral and practical interdependence of the peoples of the world. The concept of the essential unity of humanity is both long-standing and frequently evoked. Many of the world's major religions proclaim the essential commonalty of all human beings and, in particular, their equal prospects for redemption. The religious foundations of such cosmopolitan[1] impulses have been progressively complemented by a range of secular propositions about the *essential* identity of all the members of the human 'family', in which all are interconnected in respect of their moral entitlements and ethical fulfilment. Such universalistic views have been directed equally towards identifiable groups and individual human beings.

The ethical elaboration of such universalistic perspectives underlies a range of contemporary sentiments and formal pronouncements. The notion that the suffering of peoples in 'far-away-places', whether from famine, war or disease, should be a matter of general concern reflects a moral universalism and constitutes an assertion that interconnections exist amongst people even in the absence of direct interaction. More specifically, the proposition that the barbarous actions of one group of people against another group should be a matter of concern, and possible practical response, by those not directly involved in those situations is an assertion of a moral cosmopolitanism that is contentious and by no means universally accepted.[2] Wider notions of world society, however, reflect a clear cosmopolitan outlook and expectation.[3]

The widespread adherence to moral cosmopolitanism, if only at the formal level, is enshrined by the United Nations' Universal Declaration on Human Rights.[4] Despite its clear practical qualification by Article 2.7 of the Charter of the United Nations, which asserts the domestic sovereignty of member states, this Declaration enunciates a set of 'rights' to which all inhabitants of the world are entitled, irrespective of time, place or prevailing political situation. The Declaration thus forms the apex of cosmopolitan ethics in world affairs, but remains under challenge from those who assert the primacy of the individual states, and 'their interests'; and by cultures that do not entertain notions of 'human rights' identical to, or even compatible with, those enunciated in the Universal Declaration.[5]

The rejection of a system of separate states also reflects concerns about practical problems, the solution of which is inhibited, and even blocked, by such a fragmented political order. The division of the world into separate states has often been identified as a major source of war, and all its attendant ills. The best path to prolonged peace has often been identified with the emergence of a central political authority to govern the affairs of the world as a whole.[6] Even without any further changes in the personalities of human beings, or the politico-economic ordering of their lives, such a development might be sufficient for the construction of a peaceful world.

Many recent concerns have reinforced such well-established views about the desirability of moving from a world of many states to a unified system of global political power and authority. Growing anxieties about environmental threats, and the danger of the exhaustion of a range of vital resources, have further stimulated scepticism about the contribution of states to effective global management.

Numerous examples highlight the considerable difficulties encountered by collective attempts to create, and implement, clear and effective rules for the management of the global 'commons'. The United Nations Law of the Sea Conference generated a treaty that remained unratified for far too long and was then ratified by too few of the more important states to be of much practical effect. The International Whaling Commission stands threatened by the defection of Norway and Japan;[7] while the more recent Rio Conference on environmental protection generated far more rhetoric than substance.[8]

The response to such frustrations of attempts to establish effective collective management of the global environment has followed two, often linked, courses. The first is the rhetorical assertion of ecological interdependence. This, in turn, can encourage a similar rejection of the states' system to that motivated by perennial aspirations for perpetual peace. At the heart of such notions of ecological interdependence, however, is a sense of Common Fate in the affairs of humanity: a Common Fate that generates imperatives for closer co-operation amongst peoples, if not their reorganisation into a new, global polity.

Common Fate

Notions of Common Fate, however, embrace a range of significantly different phenomena, with different implications for collaboration, and political organisation, amongst peoples. Four analytically distinct forms of Common Fate can be identified: *transmitted effects; shared consequences of unilateral actions; shared consequences of joint actions;* and *common exposure.*

The notion of interdependence is often, misleadingly, applied to situations in which one agent suffers the consequences of actions taken by another. Where an industrial enterprise discharges toxic waste into a river, it may experience few, if any adverse consequences. Those downstream of the polluter may well, in contrast, suffer severe damage to the quality of their water supplies and general environment. While they are clearly exposed to the consequences of upstream pollution, they are not necessarily in a relationship of real interdependence with the polluter. Rather, those facing the consequences of upstream pollution are unilaterally vulnerable to the polluter; and such *unilateral vulnerability* does not constitute a genuine form of interdependence.

Pure unilateral vulnerability may actually be a more unusual condition within our complex environment than has often been supposed. The nuclear pollution unleashed by the explosion of the Chernobyl nuclear reactor in the former Soviet Union illustrated a case in which the meteorological conditions prevailing at the time of the accident determined the subsequent areas that were affected by the pollution: the consequences might have been confined to the polluting country; might have fallen predominantly upon neighbouring countries; or might, as proved to be the case, have been spread widely around the immediate locality and territories to the west. Chernobyl thus became an instance of *shared consequences of unilateral actions,* in which both the polluter and its neighbours were vulnerable to the consequences of the actions of the polluter. The element of real interdependence in such situations is minimal, as there is little that the victims of the actions of the polluter can do to prevent such pollution in the short term, other than exercising strong pressure upon the potential polluter to mend its ways before perpetrating a mutual disaster.

There is a set of conditions, however, in which both the perpetrators and the victims of pollution, or other forms of ecological damage, are basically the same actors. The agents of pollution within the Mediterranean, and its primary victims, are the same group of littoral Mediterranean states. However, even here, there is no necessary symmetry between pollution and suffering. With water-born pollutants, damage that is generated by the industries of one country could be inflicted disproportionately upon the coastal regions of a neighbour. Certainly, the depredation of Mediterranean fishing stocks by the fleets of a small number of the richer maritime nations has had severe consequences for the prospects of the fleets of the region's smaller states. However, such situations of *shared consequences of joint actions* , such as that of Mediterranean pollution and resource exhaustion, do require the participation of, and effective action by, a considerable majority of the pertinent states. It is here that genuine interdependence begins to appear within the broad weal of Common Fate in contemporary human affairs.

Common Fate may also arise in situations in which all the actors are exposed to a common threat, arising from sources other than themselves and their own actions. Science fiction has long envisaged the threat of invasion from outer space and such a development would constitute a form of such *common exposure.* Again, common exposure does not constitute a genuine form of interdependence for those faced by the common threat, for the common threat does not arise from the actions of those affected. Moreover, it may be that the common threat does not call for collective action in response. It is possible that nothing practicable could be done in the face of certain kinds of threats or that the action that was available could be taken by one member of, or a small group within, the larger body of exposed states.

Common Fate may, therefore, involve forms of interdependence, but it is unsound to assume that all situations of Common Fate entail interdependence in any meaningful sense of the term. Such situations may not be produced by the actions of a number of mutually involved states and may not warrant responses by a plurality of states. Where Common Fate is neither a product of joint action (or inaction) nor amenable to co-ordinated responses it is doubtful that a genuine case of interdependence, or mutual dependence, exists.

The moral and practical issues within which genuine forms of interdependence arise, have, as has been suggested, stimulated two kinds of response. Those that hold, explicitly or implicitly, to the necessity of authoritative and, if necessary, powerful, government will tend to seek solutions to the problems of political fragmentation, and the dilemmas of collective action in vital spheres of global management, in a move towards world government and, hence, some form of world state. Whether on confederal, federal, or unitary lines, such a state would resemble the states of the modern states' system. Whether such a state would be viable and cohesive in the absence of the compulsions and constraints of the competitive states' system, considered in Chapter 3, is, however, a question that has rarely been addressed.

Given the major obstacles to the formation of a world state, regional integration has seemed attractive to many as a promising half-way house. If a profusion of separate states finds it difficult to deal effectively with a range of pressing global problems, then might not a smaller number of regional 'states' be more suitable. The domain of such states would be far greater than any contemporary states, and would therefore be able to internalise substantial elements of many of the difficulties that are currently 'international' or global. Moreover, negotiations to deal with joint problems might be simpler amongst a significantly smaller number of principals. Common problems, various patterns of interconnectedness and some forms of real interdependence might thus encourage sets of states to integrate into new regional states that would be better able to conduct effective negotiations with a small number of similar regional 'states'.

The supposed imperatives driving regional integration are, however, still not sufficient to overcome all practical obstacles, as the recent history of the European Community demonstrates. Moreover, there are persisting doubts about the desirability of such regional, 'super' states, both in practice and in principle. Thus the origins, character and impact of the modern states have been such as to alienate many political theorists, and critics, and persuade them of the intrinsic undesirability of a state writ large on the world stage. From ultra-liberals, through to revolutionary anarchists, the actions of the state are viewed in hostile and threatening terms.

A world without states

The character of the modern state has been condemned as destructive of true liberty and fraternity internally, and as a major source of conflict externally. With roots in an individualistic Christian rejection of the intervention of human authorities between the individual and his/her God, anti-statism developed through such critical experiences as the English Civil War and the rise of the Napoleonic dictatorship in post-Revolutionary France. By the mid-nineteenth century, anti-statist impulses had crystallised into a powerful, and highly articulated, theory of anarchism: of human self-management without the state.[9]

The anarchist critique depicts the state as the product, and a primary source, of violence. A critical view is taken of the processes of state formation throughout history that is wholly concordant with the description of the emergence of the European state system in the previous chapter. The story of violent competition between states, requiring domestic control for external effectiveness and using external pressures as an excuse for internal discipline, accords with the anarchist characterisation of the integral violence of the established state.

The inherently violent state has a number of implications for individual and collective life. The needs, and ideologies, of the state prevail within, and are dominant over, society. Structures of belief and doctrine are developed to institutionalise the position, and preservation, of the state. The presentation of the state as necessary and natural encourages its passive acceptance by the population. People are no longer able to conceive of the ability of human beings to regulate their affairs in a participatory manner. The members of all state-dominated societies are thus, in anarchist theory, alienated from their true characters and potentialities, by the false consciousness induced by the deceitful philosophy of statism.

Supine acceptance of the state by a population that has been indoctrinated with an insidious philosophy of statism, allows the established state to present and preserve a pacific image domestically. Should people seek to challenge the state and overthrow its physical and psychological shackles, however, the state will instantly reveal its fundamentally violent character. Nothing, indeed, will provoke a more violent reaction for the state, and its myriad acolytes, than a direct challenge to its legitimacy, authority and integrity. The excuses for its violent response may invoke threats to life and property, but in the suppression of anti-statist forces the state will rarely constrain itself by undue concern for either.

Rejection of the philosophy of statism, and the psychology of the *status quo* thus implied, has been the constant refrain of anarchist thinkers and writers. It is a sentiment that has also found strong echoes throughout many of the radical dispositions that have illuminated the nineteenth and twentieth centuries, from the more libertarian prescriptions of Karl Marx[10] through to the polemics of such modern 'critical' theorists as Michel Foucault.[11]

Not only will the state preserve itself by any means necessary, domestically, but it also promotes a moral dualism with regard to the external environment. Thus, the kinds of moral constraints and concerns with which the state seeks to justify its existence internally, are explicitly denied in its external behaviour. The doctrine of *raison d'état* justifies otherwise immoral behaviour when applied to foreigners or other states, and when the needs of the state are seen to be at stake.

Beyond a shared anti-statism, and a general hostility to the private ownership of property beyond immediate personal or professional needs, anarchist thinking has varied considerably. Collectivist dispositions have surfaced in the gentle 'federalism' of Pierre Proudhon[12] and the revolutionary anarcho-communism of the Ukrainian Nestor Makhno and his followers.[13] The ultra-individualistic tendency in anarchist thought has found its extreme expression in the writings of Max Stirner.[14] The more collectivist and communalist variants of anarchist thought have asserted the fundamental interdependence of all the peoples of the world and envisaged a highly cosmopolitan global community of self-governing, and mutually accommodating, individuals and groups. The ultra-individualist, or egotistical, tendency has had little to say about the organisation of human affairs on the global scale, save to sustain its critique of all state-like institutions, whether at the local or the global level. In this, egotistical anarchism has been broadly at one with the ultra-liberalism which has experienced a recent revival of popularity, particularly within the United States of America, and which envisages the dissolution of the chronic problems of world affairs within a world of fully rational, self-interested individuals, emancipated from the constraints of overbearing government and all forms of collectivist philosophy.[15]

Many critical analyses of the current state of international affairs, that invoke a range of supposed forms of interdependence, thus pose frontal challenges to the prevailing international order: the states' system that has held sway since the crystallisation of the modern European states' system. The persistence of separate, sovereign states is, as has been seen, challenged by those who assert the need for world government, or some close analogue, to meet one or other of a variety of pressing problems the solution of which, it is claimed, is inhibited by political fragmentation. The state is not so much the problem here, rather the plurality of such institutions in the contemporary world.

Not all critics of prevailing conditions are, as has been suggested, equally sanguine about the prospects of a world state. Strong anti-statist traditions exist in anarchist political theory and ultra-liberalism. States, themselves, are here held to be intrinsically malignant institutions, not merely their multiplicity. To replace a set of states by one, omniscient state would merely be to replace one source of ill with another. Indeed, the monopoly of power and force that such a single, world state would enjoy might actually generate the very worst of conditions: of perpetual, and unchallenged, tyranny and human alienation. A choice between the conflictful, and often violent, character of established states and the unchecked tyranny of a possible world state, would not be easy for either anarchists or ultra-liberals.

Many of the critical dispositions towards the existing international (or interstate) order are of more than mere academic importance. Echoes of these perspectives permeate many of the more popular, albeit diverse, arguments that abound about the nature of contemporary international interdependence and its implications for international action and order. Beyond such critical perspectives, references to interdependence and globalisation, and their supposed implications, are also recruited for all manner of political and economic causes. Indeed, as the diverse uses of interdependence rhetoric by Britain's Prime Minister, Margaret

Thatcher, in the early 1980s and the radical Brandt Commission on North-South relations (the relations, broadly, between the Advanced Industrial Capitalist Countries and the Less Developed Countries) in the late 1970s[16] demonstrated, international interdependence can be interpreted in a manner supportive of just about any political or economic agenda.

Interdependence and globalisation: rhetoric and reason

The abiding difficulty with the notions of international interdependence and globalisation is their evocative character. So emotive are these terms that their invocation has become one of the standard rhetorical devices of those who wish to provide their political arguments with substantial reinforcement. Rarely, however, has political discourse included any attempt to define, or refine, the concepts of interdependence or globalisation: the listener is assumed to have an automatic, and unquestioning, comprehension of all that is entailed by such ritual incantation.

Neo-liberalism, interdependence and globalisation in the international economy

The rhetorical content of many references to interdependence is central to competing efforts to construct alternative political and economic 'realities'. References to the constraints and imperatives of established interdependencies in the realms of international trade, finance and resources was central to many of the arguments of the neo-liberals of the 1980s, particularly Britain's then Prime Minister, Margaret Thatcher, and her followers. The proposition, here, was that the prevailing patterns of trade, the global division of labour and the progressive integration of the international financial system, confronted all 'national' economies with 'realities' that could not sensibly be ignored. The imperative, in this view, was to 'liberalise' national economies to the greatest possible level, minimise state interference in industry and encourage the maximum competitiveness, and flexibility, in financial services. Such a policy framework promised its own guarantees of success, while alternative approaches to economic and industrial policy were condemned as inappropriate, misconceived and doomed to failure.

Such arguments about the implications of contemporary international economic interdependence and globalisation were central to the construction of a 'radical', neo-liberal political and economic agenda. The state activism, and general 'collectivism', of post-war politics in many of the industrialised countries was to be reversed. Faith was to be invested in individual enterprise, and self-reliance, and the vigour and virtues of competitive capitalism.

The degree to which the prevailing 'realities' of the international economy were, and remained, a consequence of the persisting policies, and past decisions, of the governments of the most influential Advanced Industrial Countries[17] was consistently ignored in such advocacy. As a constructed 'reality', the international political economy could carry few of the automatic implications for 'national' action that neo-liberals claimed. Moreover, significant institutional changes were wrought in many of the Advanced Industrial Countries (AICs) in the name of neo-liberal principles and the behaviour of many individual citizens was similarly influenced, or at least rationalised and legitimised. Within limits that were to become increasingly apparent with the passage of time, the neo-liberal agenda thus constituted a self-constructing, and hence self-justifying, politico-economic doctrine.

The Brandt Commission and North-South interdependence

Politically coloured interpretations of contemporary international economic interdependence have not been unique to neo-liberals, however. Much of the discussion of 'North-South' relations during the later 1970s was based upon equally convenient concepts of the nature of international interdependence and its supposed imperatives. The Brandt Report[18] on the nature, and reform, of North-South economic relations based its proposals, not on moral sentiments, but upon the supposed imperatives of the prevailing pattern of North-South interdependencies. The proposition was that the rich North was sufficiently dependent upon the economies of the South for self-interest to warrant the concession of those negotiated changes to the functioning, and management, of the international economic order that would improve the position of the Southern economies and, hence, ensure a stable future for the international political economy.

Despite its intentional neglect of moral arguments, the Brandt Commission's report nevertheless proposed the active construction of a new international economic order. Statements about the supposed nature, and implications, of contemporary international economic interdependence were central to such advocacy. However, as will be seen from the discussion in later chapters, the picture of North-South 'interdependence' painted in the Brandt Commission's report was, at best, highly simplistic and, at worst, seriously misleading.

Southern radicalism and Northern 'dependence'

The picture of North-South interdependence presented by the Brandt Commission dovetailed with, and reinforced, a view of Northern economic dependence upon the South that was already in wide currency and that had roots in far more radical critiques of the nature of the politico-economic order. A variety of Marxist and quasi-Marxist analyses asserted the critical significance of the economies of the Less Developed

Countries for the prosperity and continued well-being of the Advanced Capitalist Countries.

As was seen in Chapter 2, classical Marxist-Leninist analysis had identified the supposedly critical role of the acquisition and control of colonies for the survival of capitalism in the capitalist economies during the later nineteenth and early twentieth centuries.[19] The subsequent diversification of 'Marxist' perspectives generated a variety of interpretations of the central significance of the Less Developed Countries for the advanced capitalist economies. For some, the developing exploitation of the Southern economies had provided the colonial countries with a vital stimulus to their own industrial development.[20] Dependency Theorists share such a view of the origins of Western capitalism, but also claim the continuing centrality for the Northern economies of the exploitation of the South and the crippling consequences of such exploitation upon the developmental prospects of the latter.[21] Structuralist analysis, as was seen in Chapter 3, adopted weaker versions of many of the propositions of the radical/Marxist model of North-South relations.

The general picture of Northern economic dependence upon the South, presented by many radical analysts, encompasses a number of elements. First, the South is held to be the predominant source of primary commodities, whether raw materials or foodstuffs, upon which the North is said to be dependent for its very survival. Second, investments in, and sales to, the South are a critical source of the profitability, and viability, of Northern capitalist institutions.[22] Finally, the continuous exploitation of the South, by the capitalist North, is identified as the major source of obstacles to the sustainable development of the Less Developed Countries. The radical vision is thus that of a global capitalist economy, characterised by a form of structured interdependence between exploiter and exploited.

There are many difficulties with the radical perspective upon North-South economic relations. The empirical and conceptual shortcomings of its analysis of North-South interdependence will be considered further at a later stage. Radical views have also encountered serious set-backs in their apprehension of contemporary developments. The apparent success in development of many of the Newly Industrialised Countries (NICs) has posed serious questions about the fundamental obstacles to development that are supposed to derive from the structure of North-South economic relations. The success of the NICs has, moreover, contrasted markedly with the sad fates of those economies that have experimented, during the post-war era, with the more extreme forms of socialist organisation and development. Such analytical difficulties add their weight to the more fundamental objections raised against highly deterministic models of human action and economic developments.[23]

The Green critique and the preservation of an 'interdependent' world

Critical and radical perspectives upon international economic interdependence are not, however, confined to those derived explicitly from Marxist origins. Few approaches to the world economy are more radical in their potential implications, or more dependent upon general notions of interdependence and globalisation, than the political and economic agenda of the environmentalist, or 'Green', movement. Indeed, with the widespread fall from favour of Marxist and conventional socialist doctrines, environmentalist politics have attracted the loyalties of many who would previously have adhered to more traditional forms of political and economic radicalism.

The 'Green movement' is of considerable breadth in its range of views and intensity of commitment. Many 'Greens' go little further than modest proposals for more environmentally sensitive modifications to the existing pattern of economic and industrial patterns and policies. There is, however, a powerful 'Deep Green' agenda which is fundamentally critical of the economic, industrial and political institutions and arrangements of the contemporary system, and particularly within its more affluent regions.[24]

The environmentalist critique, in its more extreme forms, rests upon the identification of a compelling form of Common Fate for humanity: of shared consequences of joint actions; of complex patterns of economic interconnectedness shading into real interdependencies and true ecological globalisation. It perceives a fundamental threat to the survival of the very planet, if current economic and industrial policies and practices are maintained. The combination of resource exhaustion with escalating levels of pollution will, it is argued, ultimately destroy the very foundations of life on earth, let alone the prosperity of the established economic system. A wholesale switch to non-polluting and resource-preserving forms of production is therefore an ever more urgent necessity. A major move towards more modest levels of personal consumption will be necessary, and life in smaller, and more dispersed communities a desirability. Most of the major established economic and political institutions would, however, be threatened, if not overturned, by such a radical transformation of the patterns of economic life. Their resistance can therefore be expected and, in the 'Green' view, their wholesale replacement ultimately required.

The rhetoric of the more extreme environmentalists echoes the preachings of those nineteenth-century anarchists and communitarians who saw the political and economic virtues of the small, relatively self-sufficient, rural communities as the model for an acceptable and sustainable form of future human organisation. Common to both modern environmentalists and earlier anarchists is a suspicion of substantial levels of material possessions and an outright hostility towards large-scale government and all its doings. The natural harmony of those who acknowledge their intrinsic interdependence, moral as well as practical, is viewed as the ultimate guarantor of human harmony and global survival.

The 'Green' agenda, in its extreme, thus exemplifies a conception of human world-wide interdependence, and globalisation, that warrants a thoroughgoing critique of the prevailing political and economic order. It contends that the current pattern of exploitation of the world's natural environment is unsustainable and echoes other arguments that the prevailing patterns of production and consumption are inequitable and exploitative, both of human beings and the natural world. Moral and practical interdependencies are thus central to the Green critique and sustain a fundamental attack upon the contemporary statist and capitalist order.

Interdependence and a New World Order

Many references to international interdependence are central to wider political and economic agendas that challenge the basic principles of the prevailing order. Some analyses of interdependence serve to highlight the shortcomings of a world divided into formally sovereign states and focus on the obstacles to the solution of general problems that are created by such a system. The emergence of a world state then appears as one, obvious path to the dissolution of the problems of international political fragmentation. It is feasible, moreover, that a world state, unchallenged by potentially threatening competitors, might have less need for substantial levels of institutionalised force than the states of the traditional international system.

Not all those concerned about the variety of interdependencies, and their many implications, are equally sanguine about the prospects of a world state. Many critics believe that the alienated, and alienating, character of all states would merely be compounded by the emergence of a monopolistic world state. The prospects for any effective challenge to a tyrannical state would be diminished by such a development and the opportunities for individual exit from its political, economic and social system, eliminated. The implications of extant interdependencies, for the assorted radicals who entertain such views of states, and of a world state in particular, thus reinforce the perceived need for people to regain control over their lives, establish participatory forms of self-government and adopt more modest patterns of consumption and less damaging forms of production. Many variants of anarchist political thought have long reflected such views. The Green movement has posed a similar challenge to the basic principles of the prevailing capitalist/consumptionist economic order and the statist world political order.

Arguments about the moral interdependence of humanity are a matter of the principles and preferences of the individual analyst or advocate. The empirical 'reality' of practical interdependence and globalisation is, however, another matter, particularly in the economic realms. Indeed, when confronting a world of extreme complexity, the purposes of analysts continue to colour the criteria of selection from, and simplification of, the range of phenomena that are to be examined. The complexities of the interdependencies and globalisation in the international economy, their identification and analysis, and the role of personal and theoretical preferences, will be the subject of the next section of this discussion.

Notes and references

1. For a fuller elaboration of the *cosmopolitan* impulse, see Chris Brown, *International Relations Theory: New Normative Approaches* (Hemel Hempstead: Harvester/Wheatsheaf, 1992).
2. For instance, the views expressed by the former British Defence Minister, Alan Clarke, in defending British sales of weapons to Saddam Hussein's repressive regime in Iraq.
3. See, in particular, John Burton, *World Society* (Cambridge: Cambridge University Press, 1972); John Burton, *Systems, States, Diplomacy and Rules* (Cambridge: Cambridge University Press, 1968); and, for a general discussion of world society approaches, see W.C. Olson and A.J.R. Groom, *International Relations then and now: Origins and Trends in Interpretation* (London: Harper Collins, 1991), Ch. 9.
4. On the UN and human rights, see Tom J. Farer and Felice Gaer, 'The UN and human rights: at the end of the beginning', in A. Roberts and B. Kingsbury, (eds.), *United Nations, Divided World: The UN's Roles in International Relations* (Oxford: Clarendon Press (2nd edn.), 1993), pp. 240-96.
5. As has been contended by some Islamic 'fundamentalists' and/or representatives of the governing regimes of some Arab countries.
6. Garthorne Hardy, *The International Anarchy, 1904-1914* (London: George Allen and Unwin, 1926); Bertrand Russell, *Has Man A Future?* (Harmondsworth: Penguin Books, 1961); K. Waltz, *Man, the State and War: A Theoretical Analysis* (New York: Columbia University Press, 1954), esp. Ch. 6.
7. See 'Harpooned', *The Economist*, 27 June 1992, p. 90.
8. See 'Reading for RIO', *The Economist*, 30 May 1992; and 'Outlook, cloudy', *The Economist*, 12 February 1994, p. 62.
9. For surveys of anarchist political theory see G. Woodcock, *Anarchism: A History of Libertarian Ideas and Movements* (Harmondsworth: Penguin Books, 1963); and April Carter, *The Political Theory of Anarchism* (London: Routledge and Kegan Paul, 1971).
10. See, for example, Karl Marx, *The Communist Manifesto* and *The Civil War in France*.
11. For an example of arguments in this vein, see Michel Foucault, 'Nietzsche, genealogy, history', in Michael T. Gibbons (ed.), *Interpreting Politics*, (Oxford: Basil Blackwell, 1987), pp. 221-40.
12. Pierre Proudhon, *The Philosophy of Misery*, (trans. Benjamin Tucker; Boston: 1988).
13. See Woodcock, *Anarchism*, Ch. 13, esp. pp. 376-7 and 392-9.
14. Max Stirner, *The Ego and His Own* (trans. T. Byington; London: 1907).
15. See, for an outstanding example, Robert Nozick, *Anarchy, State and Utopia* (New York: Basic Books, 1974)

Independent Commission on International Development Issues (ICIDI) (London: Pan Books, 1980).

17. On the sources of the contemporary conditions of the international financial system see Susan Strange, *Casino Capitalism* (Oxford: Basil Blackwell, 1986).
18. The Brandt Report.
19. See, in particular, V.I. Lenin, *Imperialism: The Highest Stage of Capitalism* (Petrograd, 1916); and M. Barratt-Brown, *The Economics of Imperialism* (Harmondsworth: Penguin Books, 1974).
20. See, especially, Bill Warren, *Imperialism: Pioneer of Capitalism* (London: Verso/New Left Books, 1980).
21. See, in particular, Andre Gunder Frank, *On Capitalist Underdevelopment* (Bombay: Oxford University Press, 1975).
22. Ref. Samir Amin, *Accumulation on a World Scale*, 2 vols. (trans. B. Pearce; New York: Monthly Review Press, and Hassocks: Harvester Press, 1974).
23. On which, see the discussions in R.J. Barry Jones, 'Political Economy: contending perspectives on a changing world', and Chris Brown, 'Marxist approaches to international political economy', in R.J. Barry Jones (ed.), *The Worlds of Political Economy: Alternative Approaches to the Study of Contemporary Political Economy* (London: Pinter Publishers, 1988), pp. 1-26 and pp. 122-41.
24. For a thorough analysis of which see Andy Dobson, *Green Political Thought: An Introduction*, (London: Unwin Hyman, 1990).

Section 3

INTERNATIONAL INTERDEPENDENCE AND GLOBALISATION: THE ECONOMIC ISSUES

CHAPTER 5

Patterns of economic interdependence

Introduction

The problem with the ideas of international interdependence and globalisation is that they embrace a range of overlapping terms and proximate ideas. Basic distinctions thus have to be established before enquiry and investigation can proceed further.

The earlier discussion has suggested a number of possible distinctions between closely related terms and, indeed, between alternative conceptions of 'interdependence' and 'globalisation' themselves. Popular discussions of the contemporary international situation commonly employ such terms as integration, interdependence and even globalisation, as if they were synonyms or at least very close cousins. These concepts have to be differentiated, however, if serious imprecision is to be avoided.

Integration

Integration is an increasingly important concept in the study of the contemporary international system. It also has a complex relationship with the phenomena of international interdependence and globalisation. In common usage, the Oxford Shorter English Dictionary defines integration as:

> the making up of a whole by adding together or combining the separate parts or elements; a making whole or entire.

Such a definition is consonant with the way in which the term integration has been employed in the context of the integration of European states within the European Community.

The formal association between states in treaties establishing new economic and political entities is the clearest, and least problematical, use of the term integration in international affairs. Somewhat more problematical is the use of the term 'integration' within the context of the contemporary international monetary and financial system. Here again, however, the notion of integration might be suggested by the plethora of institutions, both intergovernmental and 'private', that exist to 'manage' various aspects of the monetary and financial transactions amongst states, and across their frontiers, and the formal instruments, such as the Bretton Woods Agreement, that have been concluded for international monetary regulation.

As the number of treaties and organisations that exist to regulate developments within a particular realm or region of international affairs diminishes, or the influence of those that do exist weakens, then the notion of integration becomes decreasingly appropriate.

The notion of integration that emerges from this discussion, then, embraces differing possibilities. Formal international integration will be a measure of the extent and effectiveness of treaties, and other legal instruments, that exist to regulate the relevant range of activities amongst the otherwise distinct political and economic communities that are held to have 'integrated'. Informal integration may exist where the attitudes and expectations of critical participants accord over the principles and practices that bind their communities together in important respects. The existence of an effective international 'regime', not based upon any formal treaty or agreements, would evidence such informal integration.

Integration may also take place in the unofficial domain. Private enterprises may well establish close patterns of association of varying degrees of formality. Strategic partnerships amongst manufacturing corporations parallel treaties amongst states. Elsewhere, less formal, but widely acknowledged, arrangements might develop for the co-ordination of activities. Ultimately, the pattern of association might constitute little more than mutual accommodation to one another's behaviour within a tacit cartel of producers, distributors or purchasers of specific goods or services.

Integration amongst political and economic communities, whether formal or informal, may be closely connected with the other characteristics of these communities, and prevailing patterns of international interaction, but remains analytically, and in some respects practically, distinct from them. Convergence amongst 'national' economies is thus not synonymous with integration, as defined above.[1] Neither are patterns of interconnectedness or true interdependencies.

Convergence

It is entirely possible that closer economic and political association amongst economies will promote convergence across a wide range of basic economic indicators. However, it is also possible that closer economic association within a more 'integrated' economic area will subject the industries of many regions to intensifying competition and, hence, generate new patterns of production, an altered geographical division of labour and greater *divergence* on many economic measures.

The complex relationship between integration and convergence is well illustrated by the European Community. The pursuit of monetary integration within the Community, as enshrined in the Maastricht Treaty of 1992, required participating national economies to satisfy a number of criteria of convergence *before* the final adoption of a common currency on 1 January 1997, if feasible, or 1 January 1999, if a reasonable minority of potential participants had then satisfied the criteria.[2]

Such provisions implicitly acknowledged the requirement for a high measure of convergence amongst national economies before formal integration could be advanced successfully. In this, the Maastricht provisions reflected the wider debate about 'optimal currency areas'. The issue here is whether a common currency is acceptable for an economic area only if its various geographical regions are all equally exposed to the same economic pressures and/or its population enjoys high internal mobility.[3]

The concerns that underlay the Maastricht criteria for monetary union and the debates on 'optimal currency areas', reflect the view that any significant measure of integration requires the rapid promotion of convergence if it is to prove durable. Thus it was conceded from the outset that the implementation of the single market, under the Single European Act, would require the promulgation and implementation of extensive measures to ensure the rapid convergence of economic conditions and the harmonisation of 'national' economic regimes.

Such examples of the active, and often intensive, *promotion* of convergence, to *create* the necessary conditions for successful economic, and political, integration suggest that the traditional Functionalist model of integrative pressures is inadequate. Indeed, it will be a recurrent theme in this discussion that theories of Functionalist imperatives, whether in the guise of naïve interdependence theory or globalisation doctrines, present a seriously simplistic picture of a far more complex reality. Many developments in the international economy may well generate a need for enhanced co-ordination, regulation, or other forms of formal association. However, many of these developments are, themselves, the products of prior political decisions and developments and the resulting needs do not automatically guarantee the satisfaction of such requirements.

Interconnectedness

One of the greatest sources of difficulties in many discussions of the contemporary international situation is the confusion of patterns of interconnectedness with true interdependence. This confusion has been compounded by the adoption of interconnectedness as the definition of interdependence and the development of associated numerical measures as the indicators of empirical interdependence.

The work of Richard Rosecrance, and his associates, exemplifies the conflation of interconnectedness with interdependence.[4] Such a definitional device was highly convenient for studies that sought to measure international 'interdependence' through readily available aggregate data on economic variables in the countries to be surveyed; the argument being that any close associations in changes in the values of such variables would provide clear indicators of underlying patterns of interdependence. Moreover, wholesale prices, consumer prices, interest rates and wage rates in a number of the more 'advanced' economies could all be compared with relative ease. Sophisticated statistical tests could then be applied to the data to establish patterns of co-variance across national frontiers. High levels of such co-variance were then taken to signal high levels of interdependence amongst the countries involved.

Tests of statistical correlation, using Pearson's 'r' test, were applied to the data on the four economic variables of wholesale prices, consumer prices, interest rates and wages. In the case of interest rates, a further test of 'convergence' was also applied. This measure of 'convergence' constituted a calculation in which the absolute value of the sum of the differences in interest rates between each pair of countries was divided by the number of dyads (pairs of countries) surveyed.[5]

The statistical work undertaken by Richard Rosecrance and his associates produced results which were of positive value. Particularly interesting was the finding that patterns of interconnectedness, as evidenced by levels of co-variance amongst the variables analysed, had fluctuated during the twentieth century. The study, completed in the mid-1970s, suggested that such interconnectedness had intensified during the period 1950-8, but had then diminished from 1958 onwards.[6]

A similar attraction was exerted by data concerning a range of transactions and flows of communications amongst the members of any potential community or arena of integration. Karl Deutsch undertook some seminal, early work in this area, establishing the massive preponderance of intranational flows over international flows, at least by such measures.[7]

Findings about the co-variance amongst national economies of a number of central economic indicators is clearly interesting and significant. Similar calculations, based on more recent data, are presented in the early part of Chapter 6 of this study. More debatable, however, is whether such data demonstrate real interdependencies amongst the countries involved and, hence, whether a definition of international economic interdependence based upon such variables is sound.

Mutual influence

A notion that is very closely related to many of those that have been considered thus far is that of mutual influence, which can take place in either the economic or the political spheres. Much of the sensitivity and mutual responsiveness addressed by the work of Richard Rosecrance and his associates concerns patterns of mutual influence within economic arenas exhibiting relatively high levels of interconnectedness. The substantive importance of such forms of mutual influence is, however, dependent upon circumstance and interpretation, as has been emphasised at various points in this discussion.

In the political and military arena, unintentional mutual influence may also be exerted with potentially profound consequences. Much of the dynamic of 'power politics' turns around the perceived, and actual, relativities of military strength and general capability of the central actors in the global system or its regional sub-systems. Considerable analytical efforts have been directed towards identifying the precise relationships between changes in the 'power' and potential of states and the incidence of tension or armed conflict within the international system. There has been a widespread view that the dangers of major wars increase as the capabilities of major challengers come closer to those of current, dominant states. Controversy continues, however, as to the stage of the 'power cycle' at which major conflicts are likely to erupt,[8] controversy which is compounded by the difficulties of explaining away the absence of major conflagrations at some times of transition in hegemonical patterns.

Theoretical and methodological difficulties notwithstanding, it is clear that a significant level of mutual effect continues to exist within the worlds of international economic interconnectedness and international political rivalry.

Globalisation

The concept of 'globalisation' has become popular recently and overlaps significantly with the notions of convergence and interdependence as was shown in Chapter 1. The idea of 'globalisation' has, however, been taken up by analysts with diverse interests and perspectives. To some with neo, or perhaps post, Marxist leanings, 'globalisation' marks the hegemony of transnational capitalism in general, and the institutional primacy of the Transnational Corporation, in particular.[9] To others, 'globalisation' marks the general progress of the internationalisation of finance, production and economic transactions, to a level that now threatens the traditional functioning of the nation-state, the capacities of governments for effective action and, ultimately, the potency of the democratic polity.[10]

To yet another group of observers of the contemporary scene, the significance of 'globalisation' is seen to lie in the standardisation of production technologies and capabilities, world-wide, and the increasing exposure of all states to a common set of practical problems and competitive economic pressures.

Convergence and interconnectedness, if not true interdependence, are clearly involved in such notions of 'globalisation'. As a terminological shorthand for the development of some common experiences and problems within a world of intensifying interconnections it is an unobjectionable concept. The problem, however, comes with the assumptions of automaticity that are often associated with the supposed progress of 'globalisation'. Mere interconnectedness, as will be argued elsewhere, does not carry simple, uncontested, or irreversible, implications for other important conditions. Such assumptions are, moreover, mechanistic, and even deterministic, in a way that is rejected in this study and that discords with the points made above about the role of political commitments in the creation of the prior conditions that are necessary for many forms of durable economic association amongst formerly discrete economic communities.

Mutual dependence

The central difficulty with a definition of interdependence in terms of patterns of interconnectedness, or of equating it with general notions of globalisation, is that it is indiscriminate with regard to the sources, ultimate significance and even reversibility of the conditions under examination. The world market for used postage stamps is no less interconnected internationally than is the market for oil. Few societies, however, are exposed to serious dangers by virtue of philatelic interconnectedness. Many, in contrast, have been wracked by the costly effects of the dependencies that accompany, and largely characterise, the internationally interconnected world oil market.

Measures of interconnectedness may thus do little more than demonstrate linkages, of various sorts, between otherwise discrete societies. However, as David Baldwin argued in his seminal discussion of the issue,[11] interdependence suggests the existence of relations of real substance amongst the involved societies. Such issues, in turn, embrace dependencies involving real costs, actual or potential, for those that experience such dependence. In Chapter 1 dependence was defined thus:

> *Dependence* exists for any actor when a satisfactory outcome on any matter of significance for that actor requires an appropriate condition or development elsewhere.

True interdependence could then be defined in comparable terms:

> *Interdependence* exists for a set of two or more actors when each is dependent upon at least one other member of that set for satisfactory outcomes on any issue(s) of concern.

This, it is contended throughout this study, is the only coherent, and etymologically sound, approach to the definition of international interdependence. It applies critical tests of significance, defined in terms of potential or actual costs, to any pattern of linkage or association amongst states. In the world oil market, price changes transmit themselves rapidly around the globe, to producers and consumers alike. There is also a complex, and highly varied, pattern of dependencies, with some states dependent upon the importation of oil, while others are critically dependent upon the receipt of oil revenues. It is thus possible to speak of the world oil market as exhibiting *both* a high level of general interconnectedness *and* linked, but far more complex, patterns of dependence and interdependence.

The global oil market illustrates the close association between interconnectedness and interdependence in the empirical world. The analytical distinction between the two concepts remains critical, however, if discriminating analysis of the differential impact of prevailing economic and political patterns upon different societies is to be possible. The capacities for coercion within, or the extraction of disproportionate advantage from, any relationship will rarely be signalled by mere measures of interconnectedness. Real dependencies are the conditions that often expose societies to the threat of coercion and to the toleration of unequal exchanges with other societies.

Dependence or interdependence?

The definitional relationship between the concepts of dependence and interdependence is relatively easy to establish. Far more problematical, however, is the question of when, and under what conditions, the overall relationship between any two societies is to be characterised as the dependence of the one upon the other, rather than one of genuine ***inter***-dependence. The attempt to address this complex question takes the discussion into the ultimately linked issues of the relative vulnerabilities of societies and the broader politico-economic system within which they operate.

There are two general paths by which a condition of one-way dependency might be identified and differentiated from that of mutual interdependence. The first, and in some ways easiest, approach is to deduce its necessary existence from some prior theory. Dependency Theory, as discussed in Chapter 2, defines the condition of many Less Developed Countries as that of structural dependency. The historical experience of subjugation to formal or informal empire endowed such economies with distorted domestic social, economic and political structures, and seriously imbalanced external trade patterns. Domestic distortions remained the source of profound obstacles to 'authentic' and sustainable development. Imbalanced trade patterns, with over-concentration on a few exports and a requirement for an extensive range of imports, left such economies seriously vulnerable to adverse developments in the international economy. Many empirical indicators can provide 'evidence' for the existence of such structured Dependencia. Many of these indicators are, indeed, similar or identical to those employed in less theoretically ambitious approaches. Within Dependency Theory, and its close cousins, however, the identity and significance of these indicators is established in advance by the theory itself: a potential source of evidential circularity.

The second approach to the identification of dependency is that of establishing individual, and aggregate, patterns of substantial asymmetry in the economic, and associated, relations between any state and its international partners. Many indicators of such asymmetries are available, and are similar to those referenced by Dependency Theory. In the theoretically agnostic, aggregative approach to dependence, however, three interrelated questions continue to arise. The first is that of how much asymmetry there has to be in any bilateral relation before it qualifies as a relationship of dependence rather than mutual interdependence. The second is that of differentiating qualitatively between conditions of dependence that are to be deemed significant as opposed to relatively trivial. The third, then, is whether, and how, patterns of specific dependencies aggregate to create something much more serious for the 'dependent' state, or society, than any one dependence, or lesser set of dependencies, would suggest.

In the absence of prior theory, judgements about the significance of specific imbalances and asymmetries within the external relations of any states will remain difficult and inherently controversial. However dramatic the evidence of such inequalities may appear at first sight, their significance for the economies, societies and political systems of the affected states cannot be taken for granted. Their implications for the development prospects of Less Developed Countries thus affected can certainly not be presumed, as the recent experience of many of the Newly Industrialised Countries suggests.

A caveat is, however, necessary before considering potential indicators of state dependencies in the contemporary world. A range of factors will, clearly influence the degree to which dependencies are experienced as *sensitivities* as opposed to enduring *vulnerabilities,* as defined in Chapter 1. Two societies might be equally exposed to adverse developments in the international exchange values of their national currencies. However, if one is highly dependent upon food imports and the value of currency falls sharply, it might experience far greater difficulty in feeding its population adequately, than might the society that is relatively self-sufficient in foodstuffs.

It is not merely a matter of the relationship between specific dependencies and the broader pattern of domestic production and external relations of any society. Different states also have differing levels of capacity for orderly and effective response to adverse developments and adjustment requirements. Where the institutions of a state are effective, its legitimacy and authority widely acknowledged, and its population capable of vigorous and cohesive collective response, then adverse developments may be met with relative ease. Where such conditions are absent, a state and its population may experience considerable damage and dislocation from demanding developments in one, or more, of its relationships of dependence. Such difficulties, when manifest, may provide evidence of structural weakness in the domestic, and international, circumstances of any society. Whether they demonstrate the truth of Dependency Theory is, however, a rather more complex and controversial matter.

Sensitivities and international interdependence

As was suggested in Chapter 1, the use of the term 'sensitivity' in discussions of international interdependence suffers from a potential ambiguity. Sensitivity is often used, as in Keohane and Nye's *Power and Interdependence,* to denote an 'objective' quality of the dependence of any one society upon any other(s).[12] Such 'objective' sensitivity is thus a measure of the exposure of the sensitive economy to costs imposed by external developments before there has been the time and opportunity to introduce polices that might reduce, or even eliminate, such costs. A less demanding conception would relate merely to the respective responsiveness of societies to one another, as suggested by the approach of Richard Rosecrance, and his associates, to 'interdependence'.

Sensitivity in common usage, however, often includes some sense of the subjective. A society would thus be sensitive to any externally generated development if its leaders, or population, were particularly attuned to, or apprehensive about, such a development. The relationship between such subjective sensitivity and the 'objective' realities bearing in upon any society is highly complex. Some subjective sensitivities may well reflect serious 'objective' dependencies. Others, however, may derive primarily from peculiar conceptions of the world, and of their society, that leaders and their populations have developed in the past. Imagined 'realities' or desirabilities may thus form as powerful a basis for the subjective sensitivities of societies as 'objective' realities.

This neat distinction between clear, 'objective' sensitivities and those that are merely a function of local imagination is, however, far too simple. The two dimensions of 'sensitivity' come together in the general framework of policies, practices and aspirations that have been adopted in any society over time. The deep-seated view of the world, and their proper place within it, of the leaders and populations of any country might so constrain their capacity for adjustment to any 'objective' sensitivity that such sensitivity begins to assume many of the qualities of profound vulnerability. The mental set of many in modern Greece towards the situation and status of the Macedonian region of the former Yugoslavia exhibits many of the qualities of such a condition.

Connections, vulnerabilities and dependencies

A number of other considerations thus support the desirability of treating the 'objective' sensitivity and true vulnerability of societies as two poles of a continuum, marked by the varying time and costs of adjustment to external changes, rather than simple alternatives, as was suggested in Chapter 1. Empirically, location on this continuum will be a matter of judgement, informed by a range of evidence about the scale of any dependence, its link with other dependencies, and its intrinsic significance to the dependent society. 'Objective' sensitivity is often, but not always, indicated by the kinds of measures of co-variance considered by Richard Rosecrance, and his associates.[13] Levels of true vulnerability are, however, a more difficult matter. Accurate judgements of such vulnerability are possible only for those possessing highly specialised knowledge of the situation prevailing within any industry, sector of the economy or component of the security structure of a state. More general evaluations thus have to rest upon the cumulate judgements of a range of sectoral specialists and 'common sense' judgements based upon aggregate data.

Modern states encounter potential difficulties in most areas of their external economic relations. Whether all such difficulties reflect true dependencies is, however, a more complex and controversial matter. The current exposure of many Advanced Industrial Countries to speculative international flows of finance and, hence, volatile exchange rates, is as much a product of their own past policy decisions as it is a function of true, and inevitable, international dependencies.[14] The widespread dissolution of exchange controls, without the introduction of other measures to penalise primarily speculative international financial movements, exemplifies this largely self-inflicted difficulty.

Distinctions thus have to be drawn between those economic conditions that reflect the external connectedness of any state and those that demonstrate true dependencies. The current need of many Less Developed Countries for substantial supplies of financial assistance from the international 'community' thus marks a real dependence, which contrasts markedly with the financial 'integration' amongst the Advanced Industrial Countries, which brings undoubted advantages to a minority of their populations at the expense, sometimes high, of their fellow citizens.

Where dependencies are real and unavoidable, at least in the medium term, they may characterise many dimensions of a state's external economic relations. The most obvious, and most frequently discussed, area of dependence is that upon imports of commodities and manufactured goods. Concentration upon this one dimension of dependence underlay the popular view, of the late 1970s, of 'Northern' dependence upon the 'South'.[15] The international flows of goods and commodities, however, have to be broken down into their components, to reveal the far more complex picture actually presented by the contemporary international trade system. Differing patterns of import dependence can thus be identified in the distinct areas of: raw materials; primary foodstuffs; luxury foodstuffs; standardised manufactured, and semi-manufactured, goods; and advanced industrial products.

International trade is not confined to the 'products' identified in the preceding paragraph, however. Important patterns of 'trade', and non-traded international transfers, also take place in the area of services and 'know-how'. This broad sector of international transactions is far from trivial, for it ranges from education in nuclear physics (and hence the capacity to manufacture nuclear weapons), through to training in business and marketing 'know-how' for industrialists in the states of the former Soviet Empire. The entire gamut of financial services also occupies a position somewhere between trade in 'real' products and pure services.

A number of general dimensions of dependence can be identified in the contemporary world, with a major distinction being drawn between import dependencies and export dependencies. The Advanced Industrial Countries are the traditional subjects of dependence analysis. They experience a number of significant dependencies. Some AICs are clearly dependent upon external sources of a number of basic commodities, foodstuffs, manufactured products and advanced services. The international financial viability of many AICs is also heavily dependent upon the health of exports in areas of established specialisation and, for an important minority, earnings from financial, and allied, services. Past patterns of international investment and lending have also left a number of AICs significantly dependent upon remittances of profits from overseas assets and interest from overseas loans.

Less widely understood, however, is the wide range of dependencies experienced by the Less Developed Countries, as will be illustrated more fully below. Many LDCs exhibit substantial levels of dependence upon imports across a considerable range of products and services. Their earnings of foreign currency, and hence their abilities to pay for necessary imports, are often heavily dependent upon the production and export of a narrow range of goods and commodities. Persisting, and inevitable, balance-of-payments deficits also compound the technical deficiencies of many LDCs and combine to create a need for continued external financial support.

States are not, however, the only actors with significant dependencies beyond their home territories. Many individual business enterprises have developed increasingly complex patterns of transnational dependence that are now essential to their short and medium-term functioning. 'International' dependencies have always characterised those Transnational Corporations (TNCs) that engaged in extraction and processing of raw materials. However, transnational dependence has become particularly marked in the cases of those TNCs that have promoted transnationally integrated systems of production. Here, patterns of dependence have been created within individual firms that cross state frontiers. The politico-economic conditions under which TNCs feel confident to establish such transnationally integrated patterns of production, as well as their politico-economic implications, will be a major subject for discussion later in this study.

Dependencies upon external supplies and supports may also arise for individuals and groups. Dependency Theory emphasises the particular dependence of local elites within dependent economies upon the metropolitan economies for their wealth, luxury goods, advanced services, and, if necessary, political and even military support. This particular form of transnational group dependence illustrates a wider phenomenon of elite interdependence that has often characterised the political and economic relations amongst elites historically and that bears important implications for their relations with the populations of their home states.

Conclusions

The purpose of this chapter has been to review some of the conceptual and definitional issues raised by the ideas of interdependence, and such proximate notions as integration and globalisation. In common parlance, many of the terms in which general patterns of relations and developments in the international arena are described are seriously vague and undifferentiated. Distinct terms are treated as if they were synonyms, while discrete concepts are deployed in an imprecise manner.

Central issues are encountered when judging the character and force of many forms of interconnection, interdependence and globalisation. Time plays a critical, though infrequently acknowledged, role. The tempo of developments in any relationship, or pattern of relationships, in the international political economy can materially affect their impact. Rapid developments frequently have far more dramatic effects than changes of similar magnitude that are more leisurely in their crystallisation. Sets of relationships are also extremely difficult to judge in isolation.

Much of the talk about complex interdependence, and/or globalisation, also reflects views about the consequences of the increased density of international and transnational interactions and transactions. Here again, however, difficult questions concerning the relationship between quantity and quality in human affairs are to be encountered. What density of interactions is required before a qualitatively new condition can legitimately be identified within the general set of relationships. Most of the answers to such fundamental questions turn, as will be argued at length subsequently, upon established theoretical formulations and dispositions.

General views about the current condition of international interdependence and globalisation are further complicated by the multifaceted character of international interactions. The problem is that patterns in one area of international interaction do not, necessarily, parallel those in other areas. Susan Strange has identified four major 'structures' within the general international political economy: the production structure; the financial structure; the knowledge structure; and the 'security' structure.[16] While clearly related, these structures do not necessarily exhibit identical structural characteristics at any one time. The complexities of contemporary patterns of international economic interaction, at the level of immediate empirical experience, are an issue that will be addressed further in this examination of interdependence and globalisation.

A number of basic issues thus raise the possibility that contemporary talk about increasing interdependence or advancing globalisation may be exaggerated. Few of the empirical foundations of such interdependence and globalisation are new in international relations. Many have existed for centuries within regional contexts. The modern era may merely have witnessed the world-wide spread of such interactions and transactions and, in some cases, their intensification. These developments do not, however, pre-empt a range of critical and demanding questions about the ultimate significance of the range of contemporary international relationships, however numerous and apparently intense, nor doubts about their durability and even reversibility.

Notes and references

1. For an interesting discussion of the problems of using simple convergence measures as indicators of integration, see D. Dosser, D. Gowland and K. Hartley, *The Collaboration of Nations: A Study of European Economic Policy* (Oxford: Martin Robertson, 1982), pp. 26-8.
2. These criteria initially included, for each potential participant, a recent inflation rate of no more than 1.5% above or below that of the three best performers; an annual government deficit of no more than 3% of GDP; an accumulated National Debt of no more than 60% of GDP; a track record of currency stability within the ERM's + or – 2.25% 'narrow band'; and long-term interest rates no more than 2% above those of the best three performers during the previous year. For a further discussion of Maastricht and Monetary Union see M.J. Artis, 'The Maastricht road to Monetary Union', *Journal of Common Market Studies*, Vol. XXX, No. 3, (September 1992), pp. 299-309.
3. See Martin Feldstein, 'The case against the EMU', *The Economist*, 13 June 1992, pp. 23-6.
4. See especially Richard Rosecrance *et al.*, 'Whither interdependence', *International Organization*, Vol. 31 (1977), pp. 425-71; Richard Rosecrance and W. Gutowitz, 'Measuring interdependence: a rejoinder', *International Organization*, Vol. 35, (1981), pp. 533-60.
5. Rosecrance *et al.*, 'Whither interdependence', above.
6. Ibid., p. 442.
7. Karl Deutsch, *Nationalism and Social Communication* (Cambridge, Mass.: MIT Press, 1953).
8. For some of the major arguments see R. Gilpin, *War and Change in World Politics* (Cambridge and New York: Cambridge University Press, 1981); F.A. Beer, *Peace Against War: The Ecology of International Violence* (San Francisco: W.H. Freeman and Co., 1981); C.F. Doran, *Systems in Crisis: New Imperatives of High Politics at Century's End* (Cambridge: Cambridge University Press, 1991).
9. See S. Gill and David Law, *The Global Political Economy* (Hemel Hempstead: Harvester/Wheatsheaf, 1988), esp. Chs. 7 and 11.
10. See David Held, 'Democracy: from city-states to a cosmopolitan order?', *Political Studies*, Vol. XL, Special Edition (1992), pp. 10-19.
11. David Baldwin, 'Interdependence and power: a conceptual analysis', *International Organization*, Vol. 34 (Autumn 1980), pp. 471-506.
12. R.O. Keohane and J.S. Nye, Jr., *Power and Interdependence: World Politics in Transition* (Boston: Little, Brown, 1977), esp. pp. 12-13.

13. Richard Rosecrance *et al.*, 'Whither interdependence', *International Organization*, Vol. 31 (1977), pp. 425-71; Richard Rosecrance and W. Gutowitz, 'Measuring interdependence: a rejoinder', *International Organization*, Vol. 35, (1981), pp. 533-60.
14. See, in particular, Susan Strange, *Casino Capitalism* (Oxford: Basil Blackwell, 1986), esp. Ch. 2.
15. As exemplified in the Brandt Report: W. Brandt (ed.), *North-South: A Programme for Survival* (London: Pan Books, 1980).
16. Susan Strange, *States and Markets: An Introduction to International Political Economy* (London: Pinter Publishers, 1988).

CHAPTER 6

Patterns of interconnectedness, interdependence and globalisation — the empirical picture

Benign theories of international economic interdependence view the growth of interdependence as a beneficial tendency within a developing international political economy. Globalisation theorists identify a steady advance in the level of interconnectedness and interdependence within the modern world economy, differing only in their view of the benign or malign effects of such a development. The purpose of this chapter is to investigate the contemporary patterns of interconnections, interdependencies and globalisation to establish the general state of play in the international political economy and to begin the process of identifying the possible consequences of the prevailing situation.

The empirical evidence concerning international interconnectedness, dependence, interdependence and globalisation is complex and rarely unambiguous in its implications. Moreover, the data upon which indications of dependence and interdependence have to be based are not without difficulties. Much of the pertinent data is accumulated by international agencies from national governments, many of which confront serious practical problems in gathering sound data and which, furthermore, may have many political motives for the presentation of inaccurate information about their societies and economies.

International and comparative data are also beset with a further range of technical difficulties. Many valuations of national GDP and trade are made in terms of local currencies and have, in the past, ignored much non-traded economic activity. Where governments operate official exchange rates, that diverge markedly from the probable international 'market' value of their currencies, then the real value of domestic wealth, and wealth creation, may differ considerably from the levels indicated by official figures. There is thus growing evidence that the value of economic activity within mainland China is substantially greater than official figures on GDP or GDP per capita would suggest.[1]

Such difficulties, notwithstanding, the available data have to be used, albeit cautiously, to develop a picture of contemporary international patterns of wealth creation and trade. Many of the problems of national disparities are overcome, in part, by analytical procedures that do not compare raw data values from different countries. Trends will be apparent even from disparate data, if the sources of that data remain broadly similar in their identity, methods and purposes. Moreover, proportional forms of analysis might be a little less vulnerable to distorting influences than examinations of aggregate volumes, or values, lacking direct 'local' comparisons. Such approaches do not, however, overcome all the analytical pitfalls confronting the analyst of contemporary international and comparative economic data; the analytical traveller can, beyond a point, merely proceed with prudence.

Interconnections in the contemporary international economy

The studies undertaken by Richard Rosecrance and his associates identified international interdependence with the level of interconnectedness existing among nominally separate states.[2] Their findings, as reviewed in the previous chapter, suggested an uneven pattern of growth of global interconnectedness. Certainly, if the international economy was exhibiting the increasing characteristics of globalisation, suggested by some observers, then various indices of interconnectedness should reveal steady growth.

However, the range of empirical evidence on contemporary levels of international economic interconnectedness reveals a mixed picture. This reflects two persisting features of the contemporary international political economy: the differential impact of 'local' influences upon some features of economic and financial activity; and the varying transnational implications of different 'national' and international economic developments. Moreover, the rapid transmission of some effects internationally can have contrary effects: share prices globally may either move in the same direction in response to a general improvement in confidence[3] or in the opposite direction if investment funds flow from one set of countries to another (in a manner similar to that of currency exchange rates, where gold or other tangible assets are not preferred to currencies).

Closely correlated movements in some economic indicators internationally would be indicative of a high level of interconnectedness or even globalisation. Correlation is a statistical measure of association between two or more variables. A figure of +1 indicates perfect association: a development in one variable would be perfectly paralleled by developments in another; an increase in ice-cream consumption in one country would thus be matched by a comparable growth of ice-cream consumption in the other. A figure of -1 indicates a perfectly inverse relationship, with increases in ice-cream consumption in one country being matched by proportional decreases of consumption in the other. A strong negative correlation of this kind might indicate a close interconnection, with flows of funds or physical resources between the two societies furnishing the basis for the statistical relationship. Low correlations, whether positive or negative, are indicative of weak, or virtually non-existent relationships, while a figure of 0 indicates that there is no regular relationship whatsoever between the two variables in question and movements in one cannot be predicted from movements in the other.

An increasing level of financial integration is held to be a critical indicator of global economic interconnectedness. With electronic transmission of funds, a close correlation amongst interest rates in comparable economies would indicate a high level of globalisation and homogenisation of the world economy. The persistence of significant differences amongst the major economies, however, continues to qualify their relative attractiveness to financial inflows and dampens outflows in response to contrary movements in interest rates. Such dampening of sensitivity in the financial system, moreover, provides governments with some flexibility in setting local interest rates to suit the needs of current economic and industrial policies. This, in turn, encourages a measure of divergence amongst the short-term interest rates maintained within the major economies. Within the global 'triad' of Europe, Japan and the United States of America such moderate dampening is demonstrated by correlations amongst interest rate movements, between 1984 and 1993, of only +0.5601 between Japan and the UK, +0.4486 between the UK and the USA and +0.36759 between the USA and Japan.[4] The development of this relationship during this period is illustrated by Chart 6.1. Within Europe, the same period saw an ever wider variation in correlations of interest rate movements, from +0.5055 between France and Germany to the low figures of +0.1913 for Germany and the UK and +0.2123 for the UK and France,[5] with the development of these 'relationships' indicated by Chart 6.2.

More elaborate analysis of the correlations, contemporary or lagged, among real interest rates (where nominal rates are adjusted for the rates of inflation in the respective economies) would reveal more of the complex interconnections among the members of the international economy. This, however, would require a considerable extension, and complication, of an analysis that is primarily concerned with establishing a rough measure of interconnectedness through the patterns of short-term response of national economies to developments in the international financial and economic system.

Movements in the prices of stocks and shares in the world's major stock exchanges are also believed to be increasingly related in a world of growing interconnectedness and globalisation. The problem here, however, is that while all stock exchanges may respond in parallel to changes in the general level of confidence in the international economy, some movements may be in opposite directions as funds withdrawn from one stock market are transferred into others. The overall record on the relationships amongst the stock exchanges of different countries is mixed and the current situation a matter of speculation. *The Economist* identified an inverse relationship between bond yields in the USA and Europe before 1989, but also argued that the dominance of the USA's stock and bond markets is still such as to trigger corresponding responses in other stock markets around the world.[6]

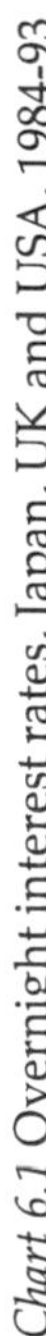

Chart 6.1 Overnight interest rates, Japan, UK and USA, 1984-93

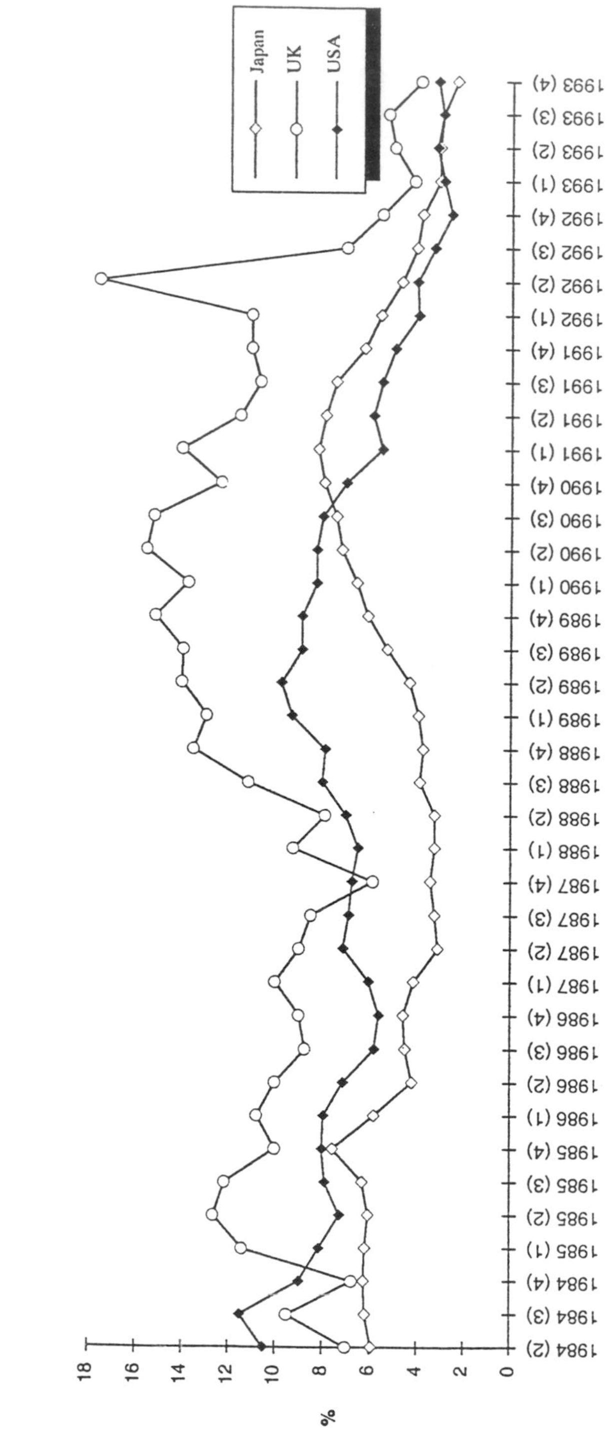

Sources: various calculated from data on overnight interest rates

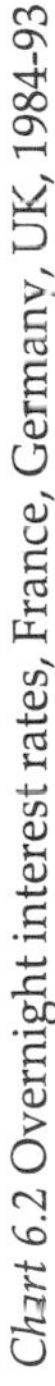

Chart 6.2 Overnight interest rates, France, Germany, UK, 1984-93

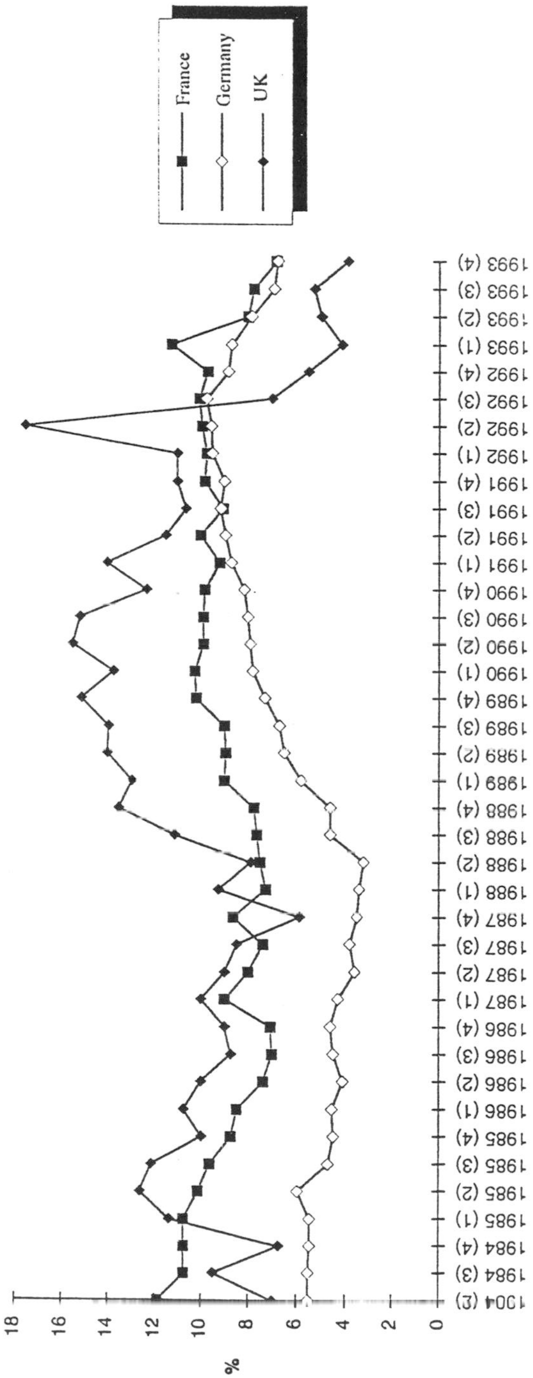

Sources: various; calculated from data on overnight interest rates

Table 6.1 Correlations of stock exchange price index movements, 1986–93

	UK	USA	Canada	Japan	France	Italy	Germany
UK	1						
USA	0.95393165	1					
Canada	0.6496038	0.65810327	1				
Japan	–0.00180101	–0.13426943	0.36054947	1			
France	0.86088547	0.86401724	0.73125263	0.09363621	1		
Italy	–0.36148498	–0.36550748	0.07123204	0.20701613	0.03667026	1	
Germany	0.14360988	0.15072081	0.30430341	0.12157193	0.48132158	0.65458564	1

Sources: various; computed from quarterly data stock exchange price indices

Table 6.1 indicates the considerable range of correlations amongst the movements of price indices in various national stock exchanges during the period 1986-93. The very variation in these correlations suggests differences amongst the level, and nature, of the connections amongst the financial sectors of the countries concerned. As indicators of general financial globalisation, such correlations thus suggest a highly uneven situation. While the correlation between the movements in stock exchange price indices for the UK and the USA was high, those between Japan and the UK and the USA were extremely low. These varying patterns of association are illustrated by Chart 6.3.

Developments in the 'real' economy should also be expected to reveal evidence of growing interconnectedness and globalisation within the world system. Consumer prices should homogenise rapidly in a highly integrated global market-place, as price competition from any one country, or group of countries, forces manufacturers and retailers elsewhere to match those prices or risk the collapse of demand for their products. In practice, however, significant national and regional differences persist within the international economy. The levels of correlation between movements in quarterly consumer prices, across a range of paired economies, vary considerably. Japan is seen to be a pace-setter in the contemporary international market, yet the correlation between its consumer price movements with those of other major market economies ranges from the low value of +0.13 in the case of France to +0.37 in the case of Canada and the United Kingdom (positive but relatively low), as Table 6.2 demonstrates. Within Europe, however, correlations of more than +0.5 between consumer price movements can be found between a number of economies. Such evidence suggests the persistence of national and regional differentiation within the international economy.

The returns to factors of production are also supposed to converge as the international economy becomes increasingly interconnected and globalised. The evidence of correlations amongst increases in wages and earnings in a number of the world's major economies does not, however, suggest a very high level of convergence, as Table 6.3 indicates. Unemployment rates, and their movement, have also proved to be highly variable amongst the world's major economies. The range of correlations between unemployment rates is indicated by Table 6.4. The variation within Europe is further illustrated by Chart 6.4, and that amongst the UK, the USA and Japan by Chart 6.5.

The growth of individual economies should also be increasingly related in a world of growing globalisation. Here, again, the empirical evidence is uneven. As Table 6.5 indicates, correlations amongst the growth rates of the world's major market economies are highly variable. Where significant positive correlations do occur, they take place primarily amongst regional partners: +0.503795 for Germany and France; and +0.475893 for the USA and Canada. Low, or even negative, correlations characterise the relationships between growth rates for most of the remaining leading economies. Chart 6.6 illustrates the discordant fluctuations in the growth rates of the UK, the USA and Japan between 1984 and 1993.

Chart 6.3 Stock exchange price movements in the USA, the UK and Japan, 1986-93

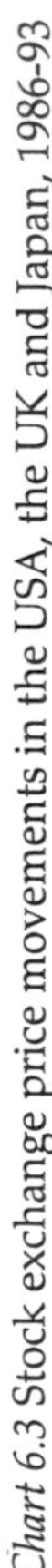

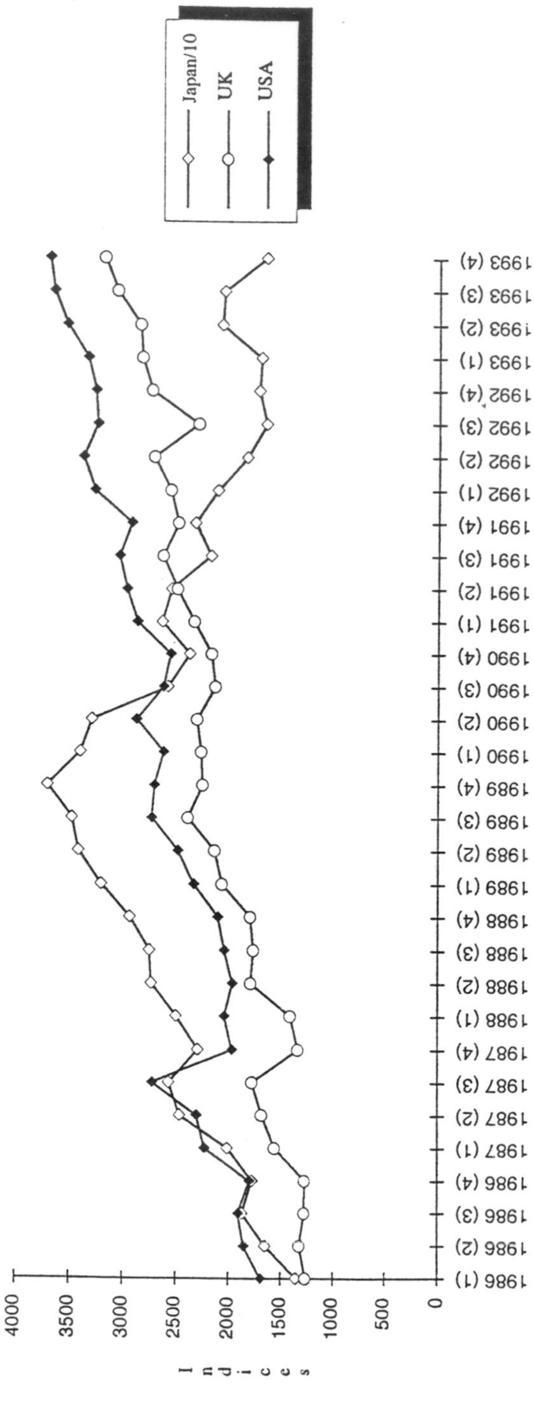

Sources: various; plotted from quarterly data on stock exchange price indices

Table 6.2 Correlations of consumer price increases, 1986-93

	UK	USA	Canada	Japan	France	Italy	Germany
UK	1						
USA	0.4988202	1					
Canada	0.3668093	0.3034145	1				
Japan	0.3689481	0.2559168	0.3737868	1			
France	0.4950587	0.7236087	0.2685899	0.130072	1		
Italy	0.1922253	0.1145463	0.3438162	0.4268109	-0.10217634	1	
Germany	0.1646154	0.2437377	-0.183576	0.22234	0.23099887	0.22091653	1

Sources: various; computed from quarterly data on consumer price increases

Table 6.3 Correlations of wages earnings, 1986-93

	UK	USA	Canada	Japan	France	Italy	Germany
UK	1						
USA	0.26749775	1					
Canada	0.49670125	0.10463545	1				
Japan	0.01138724	0.0010389	0.4283021	1			
France	0.06884079	0.36982492	0.13552768	0.17581228	1		
Italy	0.21831046	0.14200138	-0.07677774	-0.17065179	0.04461421	1	
Germany	-0.24165411	-0.10436236	-0.02842889	0.23931448	0.24865715	0.23796262	1

Sources: various; computed from quarterly data on wages/earnings

Table 6.4 Correlations of unemployment rates, 1986-93

	UK	USA	Japan	France	Italy	Germany
UK	1					
USA	0.70807828	1				
Japan	0.70815767	0.07966915	1			
France	0.63185402	0.29712156	0.66656943	1		
Italy	0.00762416	-0.56845191	0.45399374	0.2025015	1	
Germany	0.47887027	-0.23655009	0.85926024	0.60162767	0.68737956	1

Sources: various; computed from quarterly unemployment data

Chart 6.4 European unemployment rates, 1986-93

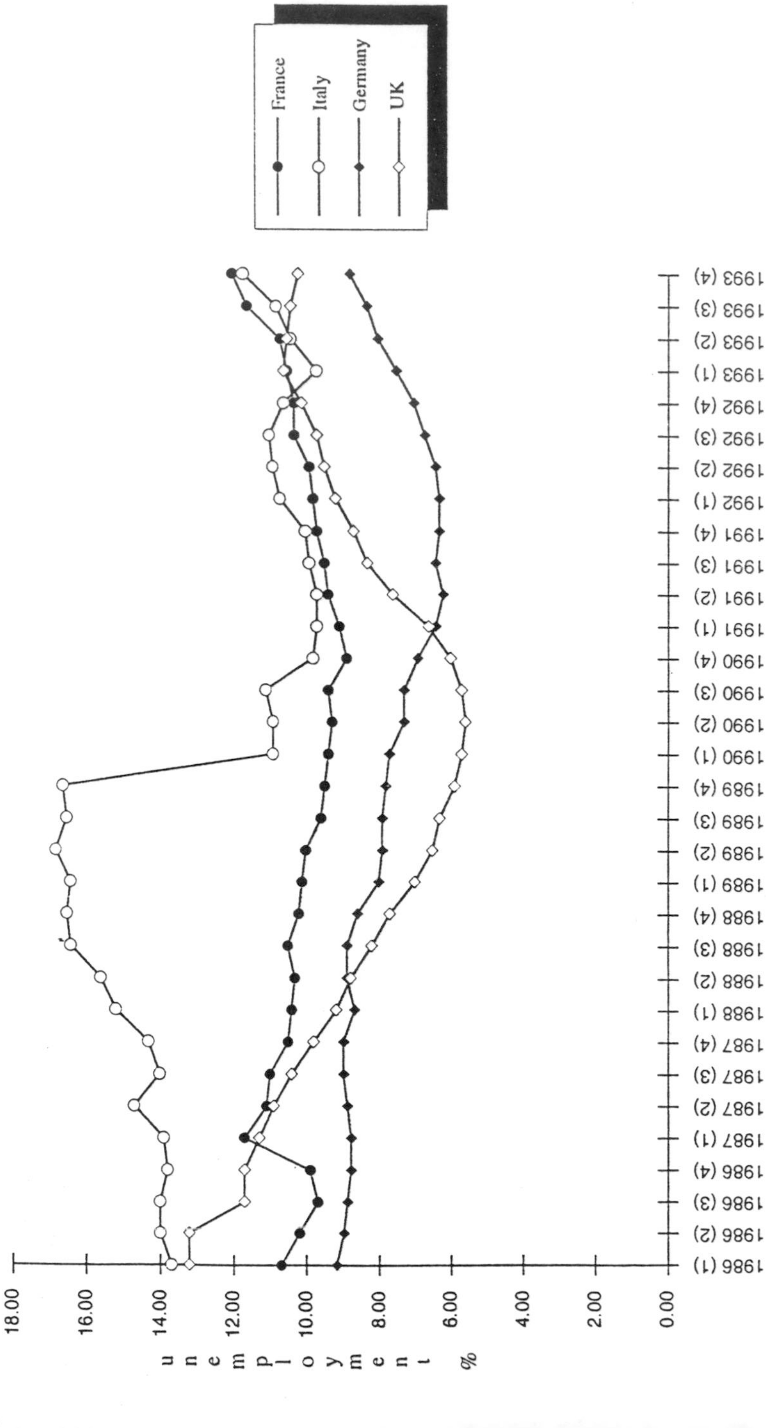

Sources: various; plotted from quarterly data on unemployment rates

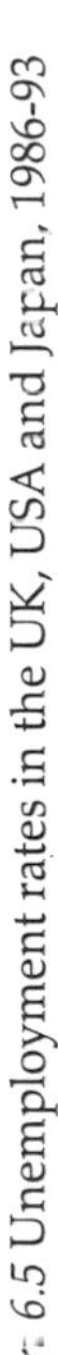

Chart 6.5 Unemployment rates in the UK, USA and Japan, 1986-93

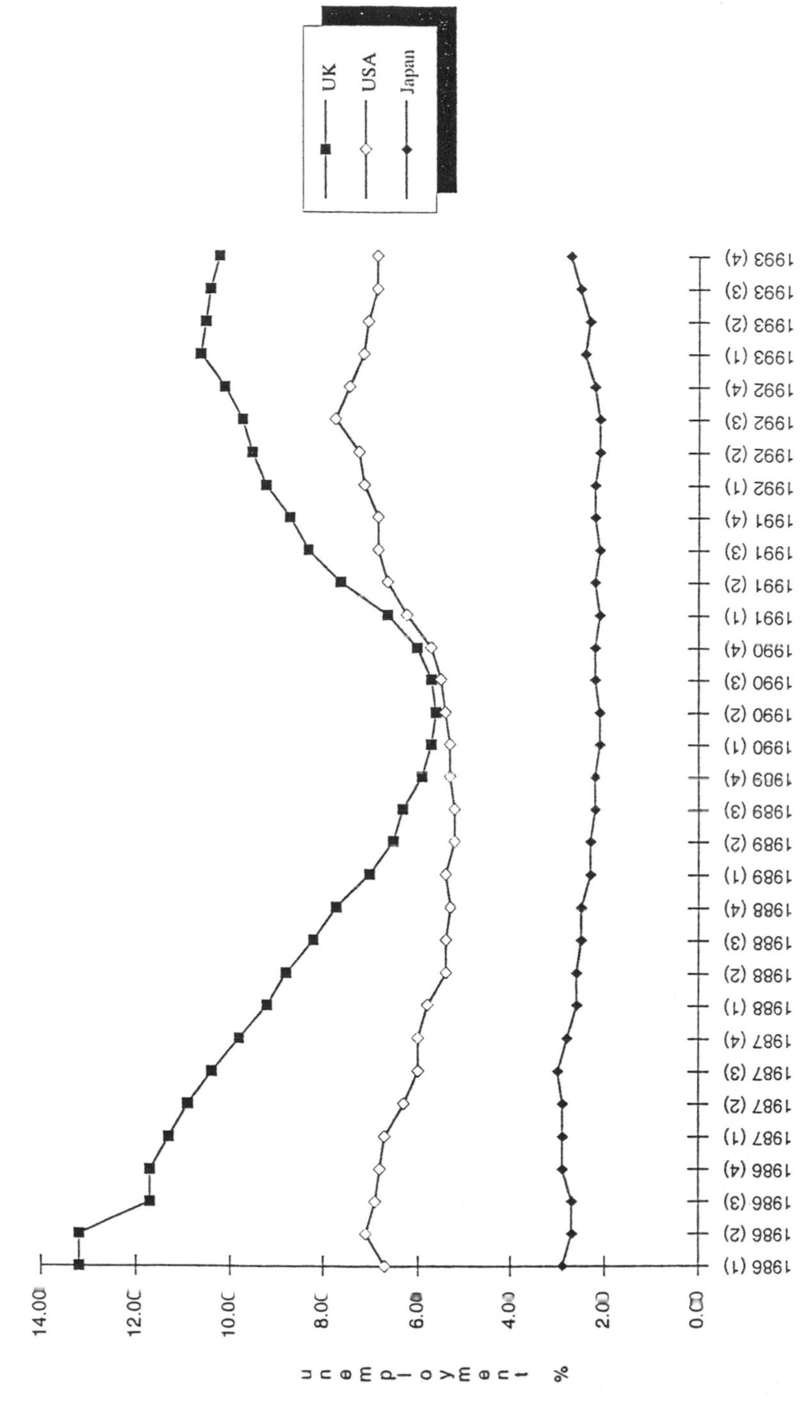

Sources: various; plotted from quarterly data on unemployment rates

Table 6.5 Correlations of growth rates, 1984-93

	UK	USA	Canada	Japan	France	Italy	Germany
UK	1						
USA	0.1353155	1					
Canada	0.18929039	0.47589343	1				
Japan	-0.04661834	0.21138229	0.00442476	1			
France	-0.16693429	0.35757296	0.2223651	0.26848893	1		
Italy	0.01744528	0.0930633	-0.08324883	0.31267842	0.37833756	1	
Germany	-0.24098622	-0.10060497	-0.12109257	0.28640378	0.50379506	0.32311876	1

Sources: various; computed from quarterly data on growth rates

Chart 6.6 Growth rates in the UK, USA and Japan, 1984–93

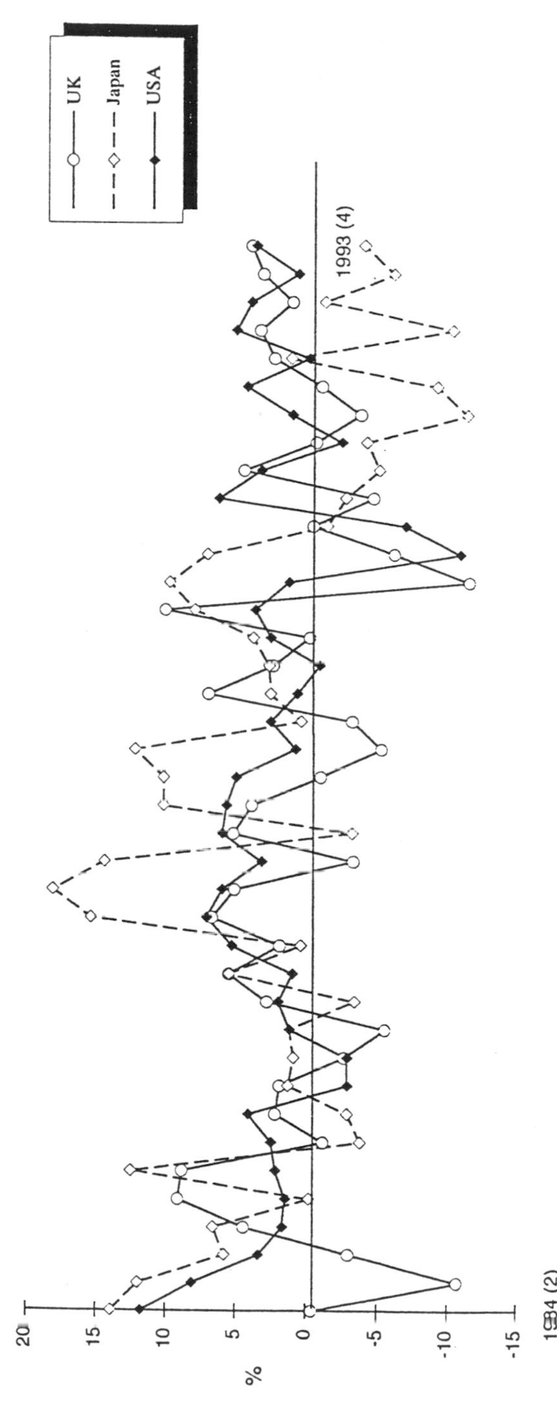

Sources: various; plotted from quarterly data on growth rates

The picture of levels of interconnectedness and globalisation in the contemporary international political economy is thus highly varied. Correlations amongst some indices of interconnectedness are higher than for others. Regional patterns of economic association are also suggested by some of the evidence. Certainly the world has a long way to go before interconnectedness reaches high levels in all important respects, and globalisation, identified in terms of specific flows and associations, is complete.

Trade and dependence

The general significance of trade for human prosperity is a complex matter. While trade clearly provides societies with access to products that would otherwise be unobtainable and permits specialisation in areas of production to which they are best suited, the relationships between trade, economic stability and the general development of economic societies are far less simple and straightforward. Much depends upon the conditions prevailing within any society and the international trade environment within which it has to operate.

Societies have tended to increase the volume of trade that they undertake with the wider world as they grow and prosper. This is not, however, a simple, linear or unidirectional relationship. While simple correlations have to be handled with considerable care, the figures that are available for the world's economies on export growth and GDP growth between 1979 and 1991 produce a correlation of only +0.382.[7] Moreover, the general relationship between the level of exports, as a percentage of Gross Domestic Product, and wealth, expressed in terms of Gross National Product per capita, varies considerably by groups of countries: +0.47849247 for the poorest thirty-four states; +0.24956628 for the lower-middle income countries; -0.03622587 for the upper-middle income countries; and -0.30573439 for the richest twenty-four economies.[8]

Many very poor societies are heavily involved in international trade through their production and export of primary commodities. The United States, in contrast, maintained a remarkably low ratio of trade to Gross Domestic Product (GDP) until recent decades, and still continues to record relatively low scores on this measure of involvement with the international trade system. The ratio of trade to GDP is thus a prime indicator of any society's involvement in the international economy and one index of its possible short-term exposure to externally induced economic shocks. Table 6.6 provides the ratios of exports to GDP for a selection of countries for 1991.

The complexity of the relationship between trade and true dependencies cannot, however, be indicated by aggregate data. The dependencies, be they sensitivities or real vulnerabilities, are far more varied in circumstance and context.

Table 6.6 Exports and prosperity

A. Coefficients of correlation between exports as percentage of GDP and GNP/Capita, 1991

Low-income countries,
coefficient of correlation = 0.47849247

Lower middle-income countries,
coefficient of correlation = 0.24956628

Upper middle-income countries,
coefficient of correlation = -0.03622587

High-income countries,
coefficient of correlation = -0.30573439

B. Exports as percentage of GDP and GNP/capita for selected countries

Country/Group (1989 rankings by GDP/Capita)	**Exports as % of GDP**	**GNP per Capita ($ US)**
Low income, average	*18*	*350*
5. Bangladesh	7	220
13. Nigeria	35	340
16. Mali	14	280
18. Burkina Faso	4	290
20. India	8	330
21. China	20	370
23. Kenya	17	340
24. Pakistan	16	400
27. Ghana	15	400
33. Indonesia	25	610
34. Mauritania	43	510
Average for all middle income countries	*25*	*2,480*
Lower-middle income, average	*15*	*1,590*
44. Egypt	13	610
48. Philippines	19	730
49. Côte d'Ivoire	41	690
55. Congo, People's Rep.	50	1,120
56. Syria	32	1,160
64. Thailand	30	1,570
65. Jamaica	31	1,380
66. Tunisia	32	1,500
67. Turkey	14	1,780
70. Panama	6	2,130
72. Costa Rica	27	1,850
77. Malaysia	73	2,520

Upper-middle income, average	*?*	*3,530*
85. Brazil	8	2,940
89. Gabon	65	3,780
91. Trinidad & Tobago	40	3,670
93. Portugal	25	5,930
94. Korea Rep.	25	6,330
95. Oman	38	6,120
97. Greece	15	6,340
High income economies, average	*16*	*21,050*
101. Ireland	62	11,120
105. Singapore	147	14,210
106. New Zealand	22	12,350
108. United Kingdom	21	16,550
110. Netherlands	46	18,780
112. Belgium	60	18,950
113. Austria	25	20,140
114. France	18	20,380
116. Canada	24	20,440
117. Germany	26	23,650
118. Denmark	32	23,700
119. USA	7	22,240
120. Sweden	27	25,110
121. Finland	21	23,980
123. Japan	9	26,930
124 Switzerland	26	33,610

Source: Tables 3 and 14, *World Development Report 1993,* (New York: World Bank, 1993)

The import dependence of the Advanced Industrial Countries

The late 1970s witnessed the emergence of acute sensitivity within the industrialised world about the levels of import dependence that their economies had developed as a result of their remorseless industrial growth and increasing reliance upon supplies of energy, raw materials and other basic commodities from external sources. This concern was paralleled by a belief, amongst the Less Developed Countries and many of their sympathisers, that the major sources of the Advanced Industrial Countries' necessary imports lay within the Less Developed World. Such a vision of a new 'Northern' dependence upon, and hence vulnerability to, the 'South' underlay the influential prescriptions of the Brandt Commission's 'North-South' study[9] and encouraged the assertiveness of the 'Southern' negotiators in discussions on a New International Economic Order (NIEO) within such fora as the United Nations Conference on Trade and Development (UNCTAD).

The popular picture of Northern economic dependence upon the South was, however, unrealistic. A serious simplification, at best, this model of North-South economic interactions obscured a reality that was both far more complex and actually embraced substantial Southern dependence upon the North. The combination of such complexity, and reverse dependencies, contributed to the overwhelming failure of the South to secure and consolidate the New International Economic Order that had been pursued with such passion and expectation.

The salience of import dependencies is a matter of considerable technical complexity. Extensive knowledge is required about the economic and industrial structure of a given country, and the technical significance of any commodity, component or service, before an accurate judgement can be made about the true nature, or extent, of the vulnerability inherent in any specific pattern of net imports. Some sense of the broad pattern of import dependence for the Advanced Industrial Countries, as a group, can, however, be provided by general statistics of net import levels for a range of basic commodities and goods.

An analysis of import dependence, as a source of strategic weakness, requires the identification of both the net levels of imports and their sources. The nature of dependence is different if the source of a valued import is a friendly and reliable neighbour rather than a geographically distant, potential adversary. The Advanced Industrial Countries (AICs) exhibit high variation in the range and levels of their import dependencies. Indeed, the AICs include national economies that are actually net exporters of a considerable range of energy sources, primary commodities and basic goods.[10]

Table 6.7 illustrates the overall dependence of the AICs on imports of a range of important minerals in 1986. It demonstrates the range in import dependencies, from 100 per cent in the case of a number of the minerals, down to an import requirement of only 15 per cent of total regional usage in the case of mercury within the European Community. The wide variety of sources of such minerals can be illustrated by the origins of the European Community's imports for 1992, with the United States of America, Canada, Australia and South Africa featuring amongst the top three suppliers for eight of the ten minerals considered. Moreover, another Developed Market Economy was the EC's leading supplier for six of the ten minerals. Minerals also constitute a special case in international trade as many, despite their critical role in a number of industrial processes, are actually required in modest quantities and can be stockpiled with ease and at relatively low costs, as the strategic stockpiles held by the United States of America throughout the era of the Cold War demonstrated.

Import dependence for energy is also highly varied amongst the AICs. There is considerable variation amongst the members of the European Community, as Table 6.8 illustrates. Such dependence is also influenced by changes in local patterns of demand and production, as can be seen from the major variation in the balance between the United Kingdom's energy imports and exports between 1980 and 1990. Moreover, a sound analysis of energy import dependence can only be based upon a comparison of levels of energy imports with levels of domestic energy

Table 6.7 Major AIC's raw material import dependence (1986)

Raw Material	Country	Imports (tonnes)	Total (Consumption + Exports + Stocks) (tonnes)	Imports as % of Total	Three largest suppliers to EC, 1982
Tin	EUR 12	43,035	82,079	52	Bolivia (24); Indonesia (18.7); Malaysia (13.1)
	USA	39,704	53,681	74	
	Japan	32,406	36,706	88	
Cobalt	EUR 12	9,083	9,083	100	Zaire (16.5); Zambia (10.7); USA (8.1)
	USA	5,880	5,880	100	
	Japan	2,390	2,390	100	
Molybdenum	EUR 12	48,703	48,703	100	USA (38.3); Canada (21.3); Chile (16.7)
	USA	45,728	45,728	100	
	Japan	12,141	12,141	100	
Niobium	EUR 12	3,694	3,694	100	Canada (19.1); USA (2.4); Others (78.2)
	USA	2,566	2,566	100	
	Japan	1,848	1,848	100	
Tantalum	EUR 12	430	590	73	USA (59.5); Australia (3.2); Others (37.3)
	USA	..	..	..	
	Japan	52	52	100	
Vanadium	EUR12	7,489	7,855	95	China (32.3); Finland (21.4);Australia (10.0)
	USA	..	..	..	
	Japan	1,960	1,960	100	
Tungsten	EUR 12	1,422	11,916	12	Austria (23.7); China (21.2); USA (9.3)
	USA	5,222	8,034	65	
	Japan	1,259	1,770	71	
Mercury	EUR 12	769	5,299	15	Spain (66.1);* USA (12.0)
	USA	696	1,585	44	
	Japan	30	..	..	
Antimony	EUR 12	20,418	29,176	70	Bolivia (28.5); China (7.7); S.Africa (7.6)
	USA	23,044	36,878	62	
	Japan	10,672	10,672	100	
Zirconium	EUR 12	122	125	98	Australia (58.4); S.Africa (40.1)
	USA	36	36	100	
	Japan	86	86	100	

Source: Table 4.4, *Basic Statistics of the Community,* (29th edn., Luxembourg: EUROSTAT, 1992) pp. 176-7; and Table 5.4, G. Faber (ed.), Trade Policy and Development, University of Rotterdam, 1990, p. 131.
Note: * - Spain was not a member of the EC in 1982.

consumption, as illustrated in Table 6.8C. A clear view of the varied sources of energy within the 'dependent' economies, as provided in Table 6.9, may also be indicative of the possibilities of substitution amongst different types and sources of energy supplies. The significance of any energy source may also vary with time, as Table 6.10, on EC energy source exploitation between 1983 and 1991, illustrates. The slight decline in the proportion of energy derived from oil, and the steady rise of nuclear power generation despite the growth of criticism, is interesting in this respect.

National economies do not live by power consumption alone; they also 'march on their stomachs'. Here, and in marked contrast to popular conceptions, the Advanced Industrial Countries are in a relatively comfortable position for they enjoy a marked level of self-sufficiency in staple foodstuffs. The European Community (EC) is particularly productive in the area of basic food, as Table 6.11 demonstrates. Here, figures in excess of 100 indicate foodstuffs in which the EC is a net exporter. Indeed, of the product groupings surveyed, the EC is a net importer of only Oils and Fats.

Such figures should come as no surprise to students of the European Community's Common Agricultural Policy and when it is recalled that the group of Advanced Industrial Countries also includes the major food-exporting economies of the United States of America, Canada, Australia and New Zealand. The great proportion of food products also continue to be consumed within the regions in which they are produced. This underlies the relatively modest level of trade as a proportion of apparent consumption of agricultural products and foodstuffs (including drink and tobacco products) throughout the Advanced Industrial Countries, as demonstrated by Table 6.12. This table also highlights the atypical high level of Japan's dependence on imports of foodstuffs, at some 27 per cent of apparent domestic consumption.

The import dependence of the Advanced Industrial Countries presents a complex and varied picture. There are instances of major import dependence amongst some, at least, of the Advanced Industrial Countries. However, the more extreme dependencies are confined to a small number of the AICs and to a relatively small number of commodities. Japan is an extreme case in its dependence upon imported energy sources, particularly oil. Moreover, where general import dependencies do exist, as in the case of some important minerals, they exist for commodities that are required in modest quantities and that can be readily stockpiled. The AICs, as a group, are relatively low in their level of import dependence for food and agricultural products. Japan manifests a substantially higher level of dependence in this respect and this, in combination with social and cultural factors, goes some way to explain her sensitivity towards any developments that might increase the share of her food needs satisfied through imports.

Table 6.8 EC (12) energy trade and consumption 1980-90

A. Energy trade (million Tonnes equivalent)

					net imports (+); net exports (-)								
Year	EC(12)	Belgium	Denmark	W.Germany	Greece	Spain	France	Ireland	Italy	Luxembourg	Netherlands	Portugal	UK
1980	591.8	41.25	19.05	157	13.55	54.37	149.1	6.535	119.4	3.611	5.302	9.882	12.72
1982	476.4	35.42	15.54	130.1	10.75	48.13	119.1	5.286	112.3	2.948	9.037	9.894	-22.13
1984	461.3	31.6	14.38	129.1	11.24	44.58	114.6	4.797	112.6	2.985	7.187	10.14	-21.9
1986	479.5	34.72	14.34	147	13.38	45.94	112	6.739	113.9	3.054	12.78	10.77	-35.18
1988	511.3	36.37	11.17	143.5	13.68	53.47	110.8	6.26	120.1	3.087	20.27	11.65	-19.04
1990	573.2	39.56	9.08	146.8	15.38	59.85	120	7.077	131.9	3.516	17.52	15.19	7.35

Source: Table 4.17, *Basic Statistics of the Community* (29th edn.; Luxembourg: Eurostat, 1992), pp. 192-3.

B. Energy consumption (million Tonnes equivalent)

Year	EC(12)	Belgium	Denmark	W.Germany	Greece	Spain	France	Ireland	Italy	Luxembourg	Netherlands	Portugal	UK
1980	1,022.10	45.74	18.9	270.3	15.1	66.92	184.5	8.109	134.4	3.628	65.02	9.53	199.9
1982	963.7	41.33	16.94	148.8	15.2	67.01	175.2	8.093	127.2	2.98	56.72	10.38	193.9
1984	990.9	41.88	16.48	257.9	16.18	68.38	188.5	8.334	129.4	3.025	60.19	10.37	192.3
1986	1,042.40	44.77	18.8	265.1	17.04	71.6	197.6	9.056	133.3	3.066	63.5	11.13	207.4
1988	1,076.90	46.14	17.87	269.8	19.4	80	200.9	9.437	143.6	3.144	64.53	12.71	209.3
1990	1,115.30	47.85	17.13	272.8	21.42	85.77	212.6	10.03	151.2	3.537	66.37	15.16	211.6

Source: Table 4.18, *Basic Statistics of the Community* (29th edn.; Luxembourg: Eurostat 1992), pp. 194-5.

C. Imports as percentage of consumption

Year	EC(12)	Belgium	Denmark	W.Germany	Greece	Spain	France	Ireland	Italy	Luxembourg	Netherlands	Portugal	UK
1980	58	90	101	58	90	81	81	81	89	100	8	104	6
1982	49	86	92	87	71	72	68	65	88	99	16	95	-11
1984	47	75	87	50	69	65	61	58	87	99	12	98	-11
1986	46	78	76	55	79	64	57	74	85	100	20	97	-17
1988	47	79	63	53	71	67	55	66	84	98	31	92	-9
1990	51	83	53	54	72	70	56	71	87	99	26	100	3

Source: Tables 6.8A and B above.

Table 6.9 EC (12) energy sources, 1990

	Hard coal	Lignite	Crude oil and oil products (%)	Natural gas	Nuclear elect.	Primary elect.
EUR 12	17.9	3.1	44.8	18.6	14.1	1.2
Belgium	21.5	0.1	38.7	17.4	22.5	-6.3
Denmark	35.9	..	49.1	10.5	..	4.1
W. Germany	19.9	8.2	40.6	17.7	13.3	0.5
Greece	4.5	33.7	59.3	0.5	..	1
Spain	19	3.2	53.6	5.8	16	2.4
France	8.8	0.4	41.4	11.7	37.2	0.3
Ireland	21.6	13.3	46	19	..	0
Italy	9.5	0.2	58.9	25.8	0	3.8
Luxembourg	31.4	..	45.7	11.4	..	8.6
Netherlands	14.1	..	37	46.4	1.4	1.2
Portugal	17.3	..	38.6	22.3	7.8	0.7
UK	30.3	..	38.6	22.3	7.8	0.7

Source: Table 4.20, *Basic Statistics of the Community* (29th edn.; Luxembourg: EUROSTAT, 1992) p. 197
.. = not available.

Table 6.10 Energy sources, EC (12), 1983-90 (percentages)

	Hard coal	Lignite	Crude oil and oil products	Natural gas	Nuclear elect.	Primary elect.
1983	19.4	3.8	49.7	16.9	8	1.78
1984	17.8	3.8	48.9	17.4	10.1	1.6
1985	19	3.8	46.3	17.5	11.7	1.5
1986	18.8	3.4	45.4	17.9	12.7	1.5
1987	18.6	3.1	44.9	18.6	12.8	1.6
1988	17.9	3.1	45.3	17.9	13.6	1.7
1989	17.8	3.2	44.8	18.3	14.3	1.2
1990	17.9	3.1	44.8	18.6	14.1	1.2

Source: Table 4.20, *Basic Statistics of the Community* (29th edn.; Luxembourg: EUROSTAT, 1992) p. 197

Table 6.11 Self-sufficiency of European Community members, percentages

	EUR 12	Belgium	Denmark	W.Germany	Greece	Spain	France	Ireland	Italy	Luxembourg	Holland	Portugal	UK
Product						*Crop Products 1989/90*							
Wheat	136.00	87.00	153.00	109.00	135.00	100.00	271.00	67.00	72.00	:	57.00	63.00	123.00
Rye	122.00	50.00	181.00	123.00	200.00	95.00	123.00	-	78.00	:	52.00	112.00	97.00
Barley	123.00	82.00	133.00	105.00	81.00	110.00	222.00	134.00	68.00	:	27.00	46.00	137.00
Oats	96.00	61.00	83.00	88.00	100.00	102.00	115.00	124.00	80.00	:	49.00	128.00	103.00
Maize	94.00	4.00	-	59.00	104.00	72.00	191.00	-	93.00	:	0.00	49.00	-
Total grain	120.00	56.00	140.00	101.00	113.00	96.00	228.00	101.00	78.00	:	32.00	60.00	116.00
Rice	75.00	-	-	-	115.00	78.00	23.00	-	229.00	:	-	64.00	-
Potatoes	100.00	144.00	97.00	92.00	96.00	93.00	89.00	79.00	93.00	:	154.00	86.00	89.00
Sugar	128.00	222.00	265.00	141.00	109.00	90.00	211.00	187.00	104.00	:	194.00	1.00	54.00
Vegetables	:	130.00	:	38.00	:	105.00		85.00	119.00	:	:	:	:
Fresh fruit	:	69.00	:	22.00	:	110.00		15.00	113.00	:	:	:	:
Citrus fruit	:	0.00	:	0.00	:	199.00		0.00	109.00	:	0.00	:	0.00
Wine	112.00	0.10	0.00	88.00	124.00	136.00	115.00	0.00	135.00	106.00	0.00	136.00	0.30
						Livestock Products — 1989							
Cheese	101.50	49.60	379.50	94.20	86.70	89.20	114.80	493.30	80.20	:	255.30	100.00	66.70
Butter	114.90	105.10	176.90	87.40	38.50	104.40	110.10	780.00	66.90	:	453.20	109.10	62.20
Beef	99.70	150.00	209.30	114.90	25.70	96.10	109.20	716.40	50.50	:	116.80	82.60	86.50
Veal	114.80	152.00	100.00	81.90	61.00	100.00	102.60	:	89.30	:	416.70	85.70	871.40
Pork	102.50	172.20	350.60	84.90	64.70	95.50	84.80	116.80	68.00	:	271.40	91.60	68.20
Poultry	104.40	94.50	213.30	60.30	95.60	95.10	131.60	100.00	97.20	:	194.50	98.40	95.50
Total meat	100.60	140.10	289.10	88.50	65.70	95.70	98.70	275.20	71.70	:	228.70	91.70	82.80
						Oils and Fats — 1989							
Veg. oils and fats	65.00	3.00	73.00	34.00	127.00	75.00	83.00	-	63.00	:	0.00	17.00	31.00
Slaughtering fat	86.00	72.00	114.00	117.00	57.00	83.00	92.00-	240.00	72.00	:	71.00	69.00	55.00
Marine oils and fat	22.00	-	96.00	7.00	-	33.00	40.00	400.00	1.00	:	-	300.00	5.00
Total oils and fats	70.00	34.00	96.00	57.00	117.00	77.00	82.00	59.00	64.00	:	33.00	30.00	35.00

Source: Basic Statistics of the Community (29th edn.; Luxembourg: EUROSTAT, 1992), Table 5.14, pp. 244-5
: = not available

Table 6.12 Imports as a percentage of apparent consumption

	EC			USA/Canada			Japan		
	1984-5	1986-7	1988-9	1984-5	1986-7	1988-9	1984-5	1986-7	1988-9
Agricultural products									
From World	18.79	15.59	15.58	8.38	9.58	9.15	29.19	24.71	27.78
From LDCs	10.52	9.11	8.61	6.61	7.49	7.09	10.52	10.04	10.26
From EC	12.91*	14.23*	14.87*	0.8	0.93	0.78	0.68	0.68	0.79
From USA/Canada	4.44	2.86	2.63	0.16	0.16	0.13	0	0	0
Food, drinks and tobacco									
From World	4.11	3.69	3.84	3.27	3.25	3.07	3.77	3.74	4.98
From LDCs	2.18	1.85	2.02	1.23	1.12	1.1	1.03	1.1	1.24
From EC	10.25*	10.97*	11.57*	1.32	1.35	1.12	0.66	0.67	0.91
From USA/Canada	0.66	0.66	0.6	0.69*	0.72*	0.79*	1.06	1.14	1.75

Source: Table 7.1, *Handbook of International Trade and Development Statistics, 1991* (New York : UNCTAD, 1992), pp. 535 and 537

* for European Community states - imports are only imports from outside the EC — imports from other EC members are excluded.

The import dependence of the Less Developed Countries

Popular illusions notwithstanding, the Less Developed Countries exhibit patterns of import dependence that are both substantial and of considerable significance. This import dependence ranges from basic foodstuffs through to a range of high value-added goods and services in which the Advanced Industrial Countries and a few Newly Industrialised Countries retain an effective oligopoly.

While many LDCs produce and export agricultural commodities, they are not commonly staple foodstuffs. The skewed pattern of agricultural production of many LDCs reflects historical influences, distorting governmental policies and the short-term attractions of international markets for 'luxury' food products. Export production in most LDCs also harks back to the era of imperial control and remains oriented towards the requirements of the metropolitan economies. Governmental policies have, moreover, often compounded the distorting influence of the past by depressing the prices of staple foodstuffs to reduce the living costs of urban dwellers. This has reduced the incomes, and incentives, for domestic farmers and generally discouraged food production for the local market.

The traditional pattern of LDC agricultural specialisation has been compounded, in recent years, by a pursuit of the more lucrative markets for foodstuffs within the AICs. Higher returns can be secured from the export of luxury and unseasonal foodstuffs than from production of staple food for the domestic market. This underlies the apparent paradox of LDCs exporting agricultural commodities and luxury foodstuffs whilst being dependent upon imports of staple foodstuffs, often from Advanced Industrial Countries. The European Community, the USA, Canada, Australia or New Zealand remain major sources of such basic foodstuffs. Table 6.13 outlines the sources of food and agricultural imports by the LDCs.

The combination of a high measure of dependence on imports of basic foods, and agricultural inputs, with a reliance upon external sources of advanced industrial goods and services, condemns many LDCs to a position of serious structural weakness within the contemporary international economy. Too much that is vital for the basic survival of their populations, and too much that is necessary for economic growth and development, has to be supplied from outside. The requirement for foreign exchange, that such dependencies create, adds its weight to the demand for foreign earnings to satisfy the demands for luxuries by the elites of many of LDCs. The combined effect of such import dependencies, and desires, is to place the balance of payments, and currency values, of many LDCs under considerable strain, with a damaging effect on their financial dependencies.

Table 6.13 LDCs' sources of food and agricultural raw material imports, 1970-89

LDC Group	Products	Year	AICs	EC (12)	USA	Canada	Australia/NZ	LDCs
All LDCs	All Foods	1970	61.4	18.6	25.3	4.2	5.5	28.5
		1980	62.7	24.6	24.6	3.1	6.4	27.8
		1989	60.6	23.3	24.4	2.7	6.7	30.3
	Agri Raw Materials	1970	46.1	8.2	20	2.3	5.2	47.7
		1980	47.3	7.3	20.4	2.9	4.9	41.3
		1989	52	8	24.9	3.8	4.1	35.7
Developing America	All Foods	1970	64.9	15.7	33.6	7.8	2.3	27
		1980	72.2	15.5	46.6	7.2	1.5	23.2
		1989	69.5	19.3	42.3	4	2.3	24.2
	Agri Raw Materials	1970	51.6	7.4	31.5	3.8	1.8	40
		1980	57	7.6	38.6	5	1.3	35.8
		1989	57.4	7.1	44.3	3.4	1	35.6
Developing Africa	All Foods	1970	68	36.8	12.9	3.8	3.6	22.8
		1980	74.5	46.4	15.8	2.6	3.2	19.3
		1989	70.5	45.1	17.4	2.1	3.2	24.7
	Agri Raw Materials	1970	51	19.9	9.4	3.5	2.1	33.9
		1980	59.6	21.4	8	5.6	2.1	26.9
		1989	58.5	21.1	13.6	5.3	2	30.5
Developing West Asia	All Foods	1970	51.6	22.9	16.8	2.4	6.2	40.2
		1980	58.3	33.4	10.6	1.3	10	35
		1989	61.2	31.3	15.7	4.5	8.1	34.2
	Agri Raw Materials	1970	49.3	17.4	6.1	0.5	7	33.8
		1980	51.4	14	4.6	2.3	5	36.9
		1989	49.3	17.6	17.6	1.3	4	32.5
Developing S & SE Asia	All Foods	1970	58.3	8	31.2	3.1	7	28.1
		1980	49.2	7.7	25.7	1.6	8.9	34.1
		1989	51.8	9.8	25.7	1.5	9.2	34.9
	Agri Raw Materials	1970	39.1	1.8	21.1	1.3	5.1	58.5
		1980	43.4	2.1	23.8	2.1	4.7	50.8
		1989	53	4.3	25.8	4.4	8.6	40

Source: Table 3.3 C, G, H, I and J, *Handbook of International Trade and Development Statistics, 1991* (New York : UNCTAD, 1992), pp. 96-111

The export dependence of the Advanced Industrial Countries

Much of the debate about the dangers attendant upon any weakening of international free trade turns on notions of the export dependence of the AICs. This notion is rather more elementary than any theoretical arguments about the gains from trade to be enjoyed by societies that are able to specialise in the production of those goods and services in which they have a *comparative advantage*.[11] Rather, the notion of export dependence highlights the extent to which many industries in the AICs have become heavily committed to exports and would suffer seriously from any disruption of this trade. The net effect of such damage to export markets would, it is believed, have serious consequences for the societies involved, as the damaging consequences ripple throughout the industrial and economic system: the *multiplier effect* compounding the damage of export losses.

Moreover, a boost to export opportunities provides one of the most attractive options for policy-makers grappling with the problems of promoting industrial and economic growth within economies that are sluggish, if not in actual recession. If expanded export opportunities can be guaranteed, growth in the national economy can be promoted with diminished dangers of damage to the balance of trade and, hence, to the balance of payments and the value of the national currency. Domestic economic expansion without enhanced export opportunities might result in the attraction of increased volumes of imports. Domestic policies directed towards recovery and growth will be more secure if they can be accompanied by improved export opportunities. This was acknowledged, implicitly, by the widespread support for the conclusion of the Uruguay Round of the General Agreement on Tariffs and Trade (GATT) during the recession-beset early 1990s, which held the promise of providing a substitute for the wider co-ordination of economic and industrial policies internationally.

The paradox is thus that a significant measure of openness to the international economy renders a national economy more sensitive to its international context. The success of domestically-oriented policies becomes increasingly dependent upon sympathetic external conditions. Indulgence in free trade may thus have a quasi-narcotic effect, similar to its apparent, protectionist antithesis. The difficulties of effective economic policy within either policy disposition may often be overcome, at least in the short term, only by the adoption of more of the same.

The reality of the Advanced Industrial Economies is, however, that while all are involved in international trade and in the shipment of exports, their involvement has always been highly variable, as Table 6.6 indicated. Amongst the 'high income economies', exports ranged in 1991 from 7 per cent of GDP in the case of the United States of America to a massive 62 per cent in the case of the Irish Republic. There is, moreover, no close correlation between wealth, measured in terms of GDP/capita, and the proportion of exports to GDP. Table 6.6 illustrated the highly variable relationship between levels of exports as a proportion of GDP and a country's level of Gross National product (GNP) per capita. Indeed there appear to be clear sectoral distinctions, with modest levels of positive correlation for members of the Low Income Group turning, by stages, into a modest level of negative correlation as wealth per capita increases.

Such caveats notwithstanding, the export trades of many Advanced Industrial Countries are of considerable significance to their immediate well-being, as attested by Table 6.6. The value of exports, as a percentage of GDP, exceeds 50 per cent in the case of the Irish Republic and Belgium; is greater than 40 per cent for the Netherlands; 30 per cent for Denmark; and falls in the range between 20 and 30 per cent for New Zealand, Austria, Canada, Germany, Sweden, Finland and Switzerland.

Moreover, Advanced Industrial Countries that have developed substantial balance-of-trade surpluses with other large market economies may also find themselves in a delicate position. While the achievement of such a balance-of-trade surplus may have contributed to the loss of domestic industrial capacity in the partner country, that very surplus may also signal the sensitivity of many firms' profitability, local employment prospects and the general prosperity of the domestic economy to any disruption of their export market(s). Japan's substantial trade surpluses with the United States of America, the United Kingdom and the European Community, while signifying competitive success, can also be seen as a source of strategic weakness. Thus, by 1990 Japan had achieved a balance-of-trade surplus of some £24,190 million ($36,446 million) with the United States of America, £17,627 million ($26,558 million) with the European Community, and £4,356 million ($6,563 million) with the United Kingdom.[12] Sensitivity to any potential loss of her markets, particularly in the USA, has left Japan vulnerable to US pressure on a range of issues of economic and political significance.[13]

The combination of specific areas of industrial specialisation with high levels of involvement in specific foreign markets can produce additional sensitivities of potential significance to exporting countries. A number of Western economies are heavily involved in the production and sale of advanced forms of weaponry. The markets for such products are relatively limited and therefore highly prized. The significance of any one such market may, however, assume considerable importance for major industrial enterprises in arms-producing economies, as evidenced by the anxieties over the potential loss of a Saudi Arabian order for British weapons' systems, in early 1994.[14]

The net value of exports as a promotion of GDP is a clear indication of the general importance of exports to any national economy. This *general export dependence* provides an important key to the likely consequences of a number of possible developments at the level of macro-economic life and policy. Developments such as changes in currency values, or world-wide alterations in the level of economic activity, may have a wide-ranging effect upon a heavily trade-dependent economy. However, a country's general export dependence will not provide much information about the complex range of sensitivities and vulnerabilities that are likely to be encountered by traders, and policy-makers, on a day-to-day basis. Greater insight into these complexities will be provided by measures of the geographical concentration of an economy's exports and the level of its product-concentration.

Geographical concentration

Advanced Industrial Economies do not, in general, experience the same problems of export over-concentration, both geographical and sectoral, that are still suffered by far too many Less Developed Countries. This general statement, however, obscures considerable variation in the geographical concentration of export markets amongst the AICs. Some members of this group of more-favoured economies do exhibit considerable concentration in the countries to which they direct the bulk of their exports. Chart 6.7 provides the percentage of exports directed by the seven leading AICs to their four largest export markets (states or regional groupings of states).

Noticeable in the pattern of geographical concentration of exports is the significant level of regional concentration. This will be discussed in a later section, but it is significant to note at this stage that the regions that absorb the bulk of AIC exports are, themselves, composed of AICs. Such a concentration of exports in the markets of complementary economies stands in marked contrast to the situation of the great majority of the LDCs.

Product and sector concentration

Advanced Industrial Countries also differ from the majority of Less Developed Countries, in two further respects. First there is the relatively low contribution made by basic commodities to the total value of AICs' exports. Many of the AICs were major exporters of primary commodities during the early stages of their industrialisation. A combination of developments rapidly converted them into net importers of a range of important commodities. Prominent amongst such developments were the rising demands for primary commodities of a rapidly growing industrial system, and expanding population, and the depletion of some domestic sources of raw materials and energy. The combination of a deteriorating balance of trade in primaries with a rapid increase of exports of manufactured goods and advanced services lies behind the relatively low contribution of primary commodities to the total value of the exports of the majority of contemporary AICs.

The second difference between the AICs and the LDCs is the former group's low level of reliance upon a restricted range of export goods. Table 6.14 demonstrates the prominence of machinery and equipment, and 'other' items in the export structures of most AICs. Foodstuffs, minerals and fuels, in contrast, make a modest contribution. Table 6.15

Chart 6.7 Geographical concentration of exports — leading market economies (Group of 7)

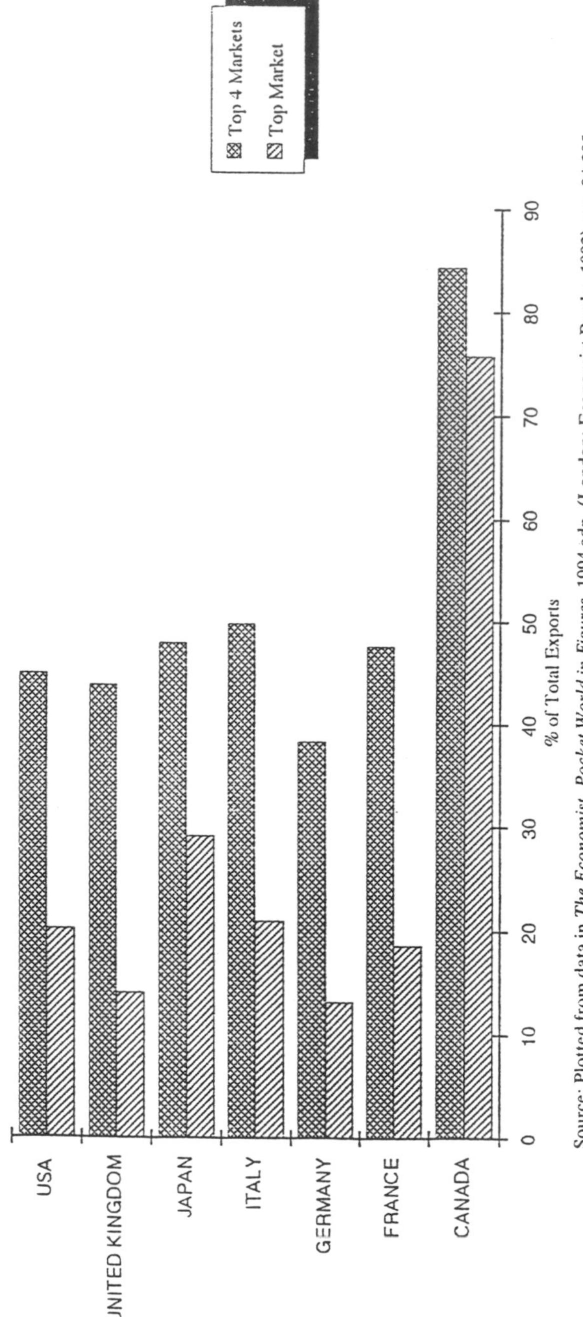

Source: Plotted from data in *The Economist*, *Pocket World in Figures*, 1994 edn. (London: Economist Books, 1993), pp. 84-205

reveals the consistently high number of 'commodities' exported in notable quantities. With the exception of the small, island economies of the Faroe Islands and Iceland, the AICs continue to export some two hundred or more commodities.

Table 6.16 shows the relatively low percentages of export income that the AICs derive from any one of their major exports. This again is in marked contrast to the situation confronting many LDCs. Even where a primary commodity is an AIC's major export, it does not, with the exception of the Faroe Islands and Iceland, make a dominant contribution to export earnings and is usually balanced by a range of quite different exports.

It is the geographical and product range of the exports of the majority of the AICs that cushions them against many of the external shocks that have derailed the development, and undermined the prosperity, of the LDCs and that proved particularly damaging during the 1980s. The AICs are not immune from the disruptive effects of 'external' difficulties, however, as the experience of the recessionary early 1990s demonstrated. The growing concentration of the AICs upon markets in other AICs and, in some cases, within their local geographical regions, has generated a considerable sensitivity to unfavourable developments in the general level, or specific pattern, of economic and industrial life in these target areas. This is an issue which will receive further consideration in the section on intraregional trade and dependencies.

The export dependence of the Less Developed Countries

The characteristic difficulties of the Less Developed Countries are reflected in, and are partly caused by, their peculiar patterns of export dependence. Revenues from exports provide the foreign currency with which to purchase a wide range of necessary commodities, goods and services from the international economy. The stability of these revenues, and the security of the trade from which they are derived, remains, however, vulnerable to external disruption. This vulnerability is a product of the continuation of overdependence upon a narrow range of exports and a limited number of major foreign markets.

The catastrophic declines in earnings received from exports of many primary commodities during the first half of the 1980s exemplified the acute over-concentration of exports of many LDCs and the great sensitivity to changing world economic conditions to which they were therefore condemned. Such sensitivity, itself, embraced real vulnerabilities in the areas of development finance and imports of many basic resources, including foodstuffs.

Table 6.14 EC, exports by commodity class, 1990 (millions of European Currency Units)

Exporting Country	Total exports	Food, beverages and tobacco	Mineral, fuels, lubricants, etc.	Crude materials, oils and fats	Machinery & equipment	Other
EUR 12 (intra plus extra)	1,081,428	105,851	39,350	32,798	419,136	484,293
percentages	100	10	4	3	39	45
EUR 12 (extra)	419,814	30,595	11,185	8,846	169,749	199,439
percentages	100	7	3	2	40	48
EC (12)						
1. Belg/Lux	92,962	8,366	3,284	2,691	25,355	53,302
2. Denmark	27,848	7,170	917	1,406	7,438	10,917
3. W.Germany	317,238	14,263	4,079	6,353	156,923	135,620
4. Greece	6,350	1,625	461	596	265	3,403
5. Spain	46,175	5,977	2,047	2,119	17,565	18,467
6. France	174,499	24,794	3,868	5,915	70,287	69,635
7. Ireland	18,638	4,149	115	658	5,809	7,907
8. Italy	133,773	7,953	2,992	1,963	50,176	70,689
10. Holland	107,188	20,809	10,414	6,744	25,361	43,860
11. Portugal	12,847	854	462	1,200	2,493	7,838
12. UK	143,912	9,891	10,748	3,152	57,464	62,657
Non-EC AICs						
14. Norway	26,565	1,804	12,725	973	3,707	7,356
15. Sweden	45,158	873	1,363	4,041	19,421	19,460
16. Switzerland	49,891	1,353	35	597	15,717	32,189
17. Austria	32,190	1,058	330	1,725	12,266	16,811
18. Finland	20,857	495	307	2,120	6,446	11,489
20. USA	308,596	28,436	9,512	22,012	134,783	113,853
21. Canada	99,636	7,769	9,898	13,826	36,898	31,245
22. Japan	225,407	1,259	995	1,597	158,542	63,014

Source: Basic Statistics of the Community (29th edn., Luxembourg: EUROSTAT, 1992), Table 6.13, p. 288

Table 6.15 Export ranges of the Advanced Industrial Countries

Country	1980 Number of commodities exported	1989 Number of commodities exported
Faroe Islands	12	11
Iceland	44	11
Norway	216	215
Finland	215	209
Australia	230	228
New Zealand	199	192
South Africa	231	224
Japan	224	222
Ireland	226	224
Canada	219	236
Greece	191	204
Gibraltar	57	61
Sweden	230	229
Belg/Luxembourg	235	235
Spain	231	235
Portugal	210	214
Switzerland	222	225
USA	236	235
Germany	236	235
Denmark	229	228
Netherlands	230	236
Austria	223	224
UK	237	235
France	238	237
Italy	233	235
Average =	202	202

Source: Table 4.5, *Handbook of International Trade Statistics* (New York: UNCTAD, 1992), pp. 241-4

Table 6.16 Export concentration of the AICs, 1988/9

Country	Top four exports	% of Country's total
Faroe Islands	Fish — fresh	44.91
	Fish — processed	17.6
	Shellfish — frozen	14.83
	Ships and boats	9.28
Iceland	Fish — fresh	39.15
	Fish — processed	17.18
	Aluminium	11.82
	Shellfish — frozen	7.49
Norway	Crude petroleum	27.76
	Gas — nat. and refined	9.29
	Aluminium	8.09
	Ships and boats	4.05
Finland	Paper and paperboard	25.68
	Pulp and waste paper	5.19
	Wood shaped/sleepers	4.6
	Ships and boats	4.4
Australia	Special transactions	16.87
	Wool	12.45
	Coal, lignite, peat	11.02
	Gold	6.34
New Zealand	Meat	16.29
	Wood	12.55
	Milk and cream	6.2
	Aluminium	5.54
South Africa	Gold	13.18
	Silver	12.99
	Coal, lignite, peat	10.06
	Pig iron, etc.,	6.15
Japan	Motor cars, etc.	14.34
	Telecom. equipment	5.51
	Transistors	4.9
	Data processing equip.	4.19
Ireland	Data processing equip.	10.21
	Office equip. parts	8.94
	Meat — fresh	5.65
	Edible products	4.51

Canada	Motor cars, etc.	12.13
	Paper and paperboard	6.19
	Motor vehicle parts	5.68
	Pulp and waste paper	4.94
Greece	Knitted outwear	6.06
	Knitted underwear	5.26
	Fruit and nuts	5
	Refined petrol products	4.69
Belgium	Motor cars etc.,	10.5
	Pearls and precious stones	7.11
	Iron and steel plate	4.2
	Polymerisation products	3.68
Sweden	Paper and paperboard	10.17
	Motor cars, etc.	5.77
	Pulp and waste paper	4
	Motor vehicle parts	3.97
Portugal	Footwear	7.11
	Knitted outwear	6.81
	Pulp and waste paper	5.83
	Mens' clothing	4.74
Switzerland	Watches and clocks	6.9
	Medicinal products	6.48
	Pearls and precious stones	4.76
	Textile & leather machinery	3.9
USA	Special transactions	7.6
	Aircraft, etc.,	6.62
	Motor vehicle parts	3.71
	Data processing equip.	3.53
Germany	Motor cars, etc.,	10.34
	Motor vehicle parts	4.18
	Polymerisation products	2.35
	Machine parts	2.08
Denmark	Meat — fresh	6.74
	Special transactions	4.98
	Furniture parts	3.75
	Medicinal products	3.15
Netherlands	Petroleum products	6.15
	Special transactions	3.49

	Polymerisation products	3.35
	Meat — fresh	3.3
Austria	Paper and paperboard	5.16
	Petrol engines	4.2
	Iron and steel plate	3.1
	Polymerisation products	2.77
UK	Crude petroleum	4.63
	Data processing equip.	4
	Ships and boats	2.81
	Motor vehicle parts	2.76
France	Motor cars, etc.	6.1
	Motor vehicle parts	3.55
	Aircraft, etc.,	3.24
	Alcoholic beverages	3.12
Italy	Footwear	3.88
	Furniture parts	3.3
	Motor cars, etc.,	3.29
	Specialised machinery	2.97

Source: Table 4.3, *Handbook of International Trade and Development Statistics, 1991*, (New York: UNCTAD, 1992), pp. 196-218

The geographical concentration of the exports of the Less Developed Countries

The ending of empire has not eliminated the overdependence of many Less Developed Countries on the export markets of a small number of Advanced Industrial Countries. The poles of 'attraction' for such LDC exports are exercised by former colonial 'masters', the world's biggest industrial countries, or regionally prominent industrial economies. Thus Algeria's main four export markets are to be found in Italy (15.3 per cent of Algeria's exports), the United States of America (16.8 per cent), France (15.1 per cent) and Germany (8.3 per cent), to a combined total of 61.9 per cent of Algeria's annual exports.[15] Bangladesh's four main export partners are the United States of America (28.9 per cent), Germany (9.6 per cent), the United Kingdom (7.7 per cent) and Italy (5.5 per cent), taking 51.7 per cent of her exports, overall.[16] Colombia sends 38.5 per cent of her exports to the United States of America, 7.5 per cent to Germany, 4.3 per cent to the Netherlands and 3.2 per cent to Japan; a total of 53.5 per cent of her overall exports.[17] The Ivory Coast sends 14.1 per cent of her exports to France, 8.5 per cent to Italy, 7.7 per cent to Germany and 7 per cent to the Netherlands: 37.3 per cent of exports in total.[18] Pakistan exports 10.8 per cent to the United States of America, 8.9 per cent to

Germany, 8.3 per cent to Japan and 7.3 per cent to the United Kingdom; these four absorbing 35.3 per cent of her total exports.[19]

Commodity concentration of the exports of the Less Developed Countries

The Less Developed Countries also remain overly dependent upon the export of a narrow range of exports. The standard measure of such overdependence is the Hirschmann Index of Commodity Concentration, ranging from 0 to 1, with 1 representing the extreme case of concentration (or overdependence).[20] Table 6.17 provides the Hirschmann Indices for the exports of a selection of Less Developed Countries.[21] The average of the Hirschmann Indices for the Advanced Industrial Countries (excluding the exceptional cases of the Faroe Islands and Iceland) is 0.09. For the LDCs, excluding the Newly Industrialised Countries, the Hirschmann Index remains at 0.5 (down marginally from 0.55 in 1980); ranging from Nauru's massive 0.962 to Morocco's 0.173.[22]

Export dependence of the Newly Industrialised Countries

The Newly Industrialised Countries (NICs), as they have come to be called, constitute some of the world economy's most interesting phenomena during the late 1970s and 1980s. A range of domestic and international economic policies, and conditions, contributed to a remarkable rate of industrialisation and economic expansion. The contributory conditions varied amongst the NICs, as did the contribution of exports to the stimulation of economic growth.

Given the variety of economic conditions and experiences, it is unsurprising that the proportion of exports to Gross Domestic Product amongst the NICs varies massively, from Brazil's 7.63 per cent to Singapore's 147.24 per cent, as indicated in Table 6.6. Singapore's capacity to export more than the value of goods and services produced domestically, indicates the role of re-exporting and entrepôt trade to some of the smaller, trading economies amongst the NICs. The significance of imports for the NICs is broadly in line with the level and salience of exports.

The overall significance of exports to the NICs, and thence their export dependence, thus varies considerably. It is for this reason that the level of correlation between the growth of exports for the NICs, between 1979 and 1991, and that of GDP is very low, as was indicated earlier in Table 6.6.[23]

Regional interdependence

The discussion of interdependence and dependencies has conventionally been conducted in global terms. The major exceptions to this were

Table 6.17 Export commodity concentrations of selected Less Developed Countries

Country	1980 Commodities exprtd. No.	1980 Concentration Index (2)	1989 Commodities exprtd. No.	1989 Concentration Index (2)
Nauru	3	0.995	7	0.962
Nigeria	147	0.948	102	0.918
Guinea	23	0.905	28	0.9
Iraq	83	0.99	93	0.884
Iran	88	0.814	82	0.875
Libya	42	0.961	56	0.814
Zambia	49	0.717	55	0.813
UAE	197	0.87	190	0.721
Seychelles	11	0.571	6	0.705
Saudi Arabia	183	0.942	128	0.678
Liberia	42	0.534	28	0.575
Algeria	49	0.82	105	0.552
Malta	145	0.223	23	0.551
Venezuela	153	0.674	175	0.515
Central African Rep.	15	0.415	17	0.494
Ghana	55	0.729	54	0.472
Ecuador	80	0.547	78	0.462
Zaïre	62	0.45	43	0.421
Solomon Islands	17	0.484	15	0.394
Chile	181	0.406	168	0.372
Tanzania	83	0.286	55	0.371
Panama	136	0.255	74	0.342
Peru	176	0.264	141	0.281
Egypt	80	0.575	147	0.279
Morocco	113	0.31	147	0.173

Source: Table 4.5, *Handbook of International Trade and Development Statistics 1991* (New York: UNCTAD, 1992), pp. 241-4

Note: for the Hirschmann Index see Appendix 6.1 at the end of this chapter.

the many references to the importance of trade with members of the European Economic Community as a justification for continued, or prospective, membership of that regional economic association during the 1970s and 1980s. Since the period of formation and expansion of the European Community, the importance, actual or potential, of intraregional trade has become a matter of increasing attention and association with arguments in favour of the institutionalisation of regional economic associations.

The evidence for regionalisation within the international political economy is, however, complex and varied.[24] Moreover, such potential regionalisation is an outstanding example of self-realising prediction, or prescription, in human affairs. The more political leaders herald increasing regionalisation, the more the policies of their governments and the behaviour of their countries' enterprises will reinforce regionalising tendencies.

Clear 'regions' within the international economy will exhibit some, or all, of a number of characteristics. Trade amongst the central participants will be of significantly greater value than that with other regions or countries. The region, and its dominant economies in particular, will exercise an attractive force upon the exports of its closest geographical neighbours. The significance of the region's markets for such neighbouring economies may, moreover, be far greater than the significance of those neighbouring economies' markets for exports from the region's core. It is also possible that the decisions of Transnational Corporations on investment, location of production and managerial structures, will increasingly reflect the influence of any established, or emergent, region. Finally, a region may manifest a measure of institutionalisation, in treaties and/or formal, administrative institutions.

The overall picture of regionalisation during recent decades, provided by statistics on intraregional trade, is highly varied. Table 6.18 indicates the steady advance of regionalisation within the European Community, the steady dissolution of the Soviet block's CMEA (Council for Mutual Economic Aid — otherwise known as COMECON) and the mixed message provided by trade between the United States of America and Canada. However, further regionalisation will be as much a product of the views of influential actors about the likely future pattern of international economic development, as of the effect of impersonal forces. Evidence that Transnational Corporations (TNCs) are increasingly organising their companies' activities along regional lines is thus highly significant.[25] Evidence for such a regional focus in the outlook of prominent TNCs is also provided by the surge of investment within the European Community by US-based companies during the run-up to the Single European Market (on 1 June 1992).[26]

A significant source of the 'regionalisation' of economic and trade patterns reflects the lower transport, and allied transaction, costs associated with relative geographical proximity. This, however, merely demonstrates the persisting influence of spatial as well as structural influences in the political economy[27] and on regional dynamics.

The European Community as a regional economic block

The development of the European Community as a regional economic block has been clear and relatively steady. Table 6.19 shows the growth of intra-EC trade from 51.6 per cent of its members' exports in 1981-3 to 60.7 per cent by 1990. The EC is also exercising a growing pull on the exports of its fellow European states within the rump of the European Free Trade Association (EFTA), the majority of which have now joined

Table 6.18 Intraregional trade of the Industrialised Countries as a percentage of total group exports

Region	1960	1975	1985	1990
EEC (6)	34.6	..	..	..
EFTA	15.7	..	..	..
EEC (12)	-	52.5	54.7	60.7
USA/Canada	-	8	12.5	9.6
CMEA	62.3	57.4	53.7	38.2

Source: Table 1.12, *Handbook of International Trade and Development Statistics, 1991* (New York: UNCTAD, 1992), p. 38

.. = not applicable } change of EEC calculational base from 6
- = not applicable } to 12 'members'.

Table 6.19 The European Community as a regional magnet for exports (% of regional exports directed to the EC (12))

Source of exports	1981-3	1984-6	1987-9	1990
EEC (12)	51.6	52.8	59.1	60.7
EFTA	51.2	52	55.8	57.6

Source: Table 3.1,D, *Handbook of International Trade and Development Statistics, 1991* (New York: UNCTAD, 1992), p. 68-9

Note: encompasses all 12 members from 1980 onwards

the new European Economic Area. Non-European neighbours also feel the attractive force of the European Community's economy.

Table 6.20 indicates the proportion of the exports of the EC's neighbours within the Mediterranean area that are drawn into the Community. Some of this pattern of exports can be attributed to the ties established between these Mediterranean economies and former colonial powers that are now members of the European Community. It also demonstrates that the attractive force of the European Community has been sufficient to draw back exports from its neighbours after a degree of diversion elsewhere during the era of Southern 'radicalism', with its emphasis upon an elimination of colonial residues and a general reduction of overdependence upon a narrow range of Northern markets.

The North American economic region

A belief that the North American area constitutes an economic region of considerable, and growing, importance to its members lies behind the pressures for the institutionalisation of the relationships amongst participating members through the North American Free Trade Agreement (NAFTA).[28] As with so many relationships between economies of markedly different sizes and influence, there is an asymmetry in the relations between the United States of America and her two immediate neighbours, Canada and Mexico. The USA absorbs the predominant share of the exports of her NAFTA partners, while the USA's pattern of exports is far more diverse. The USA took over 70 per cent of the exports of both Canada and Mexico in 1990, as Table 6.21 reveals. Canada, in contrast, took only 20 per cent of the USA's exports in 1991 and Mexico a mere 9 per cent.[29]

The interests of Canada and Mexico in the conclusion of the NAFTA, while not uncontested, are easy to understand in the light of such figures. The USA's position is based upon wider, and more complex, calculations about the potential for complementary patterns of economic growth, and industrial development, particularly in the face of intensifying competition from the low wage, and increasingly high skilled, economies of South East Asia. The combination of an expanded 'domestic' market, with new opportunities to fuse low-cost labour with high-technology production, should, according to this vision, provide the North American region with a singular opportunity to revive its international competitiveness.

The United States of America, however, stands at the apex of a wider economic region, as indicated by the pattern of export absorption from non-NAFTA economies within the American continent and Caribbean area. Table 6.22, of the exports of the USA's non-NAFTA 'neighbours', reveals a number of interesting political, economic and geographical influences. The economies that export very little to the USA do so for predominantly political reasons: their past, or present, political estrangement from the USA, or, as in the case of the Caribbean departments of France, their close political association with major economies outside the American continent.

Political influences aside, the dominance of the USA in any Latin American or Caribbean economy's export pattern generally reflects the size of that economy and its relative proximity to the USA itself. Thus a small economy that is close to the USA, like Guatemala, sent 50.8 per cent of its exports to the USA in 1989, while far larger and more distant economies, such as those of Chile and Argentina, sent only 19.3 per cent and 13.4 per cent respectively. This relationship is far from exact, but enjoys some support from the data. Moreover, recognition of the significance of the USA as the fulcrum of a new continental economic regional block, has stimulated renewed interest in a plethora of lesser economic association agreements, many of which are seen as potential stepping stones to a wider American free-trade area, once the promise of NAFTA

Table 6.20 Percentage of country's exports sent to the European Community

Origin Country	1970	1975	1980	1985	1989
Algeria	81	55.1	39.8	68.7	70.6
Cyprus	74.8	43.7	30.7	27.6	54.7
Egypt	14.2	11.8	45.6	41.1	42.5
Israel	41.7	37.4	39.9	30.6	35.2 **
Jordan	..	4.9	1.7	4.5	8*
Lebanon	10.5	12	7.3	10.4 ***	..
Libya	91	51.7	39.3	69.2 ***	78.3 ****
Malta	78.7	73.4	78.3	69.4	75.8
Morocco	72.8	54.1	55.7	49.5	65 **
Syria	35.5	47.5	63.3	42.9	31.3
Tunisia	62.1	47.8	71.7	64.6	77.8 **
Turkey	50	43.9	43	39.4	53.2 **
Yugoslavia	41.2	22.8	26.4	24.6	45.7 **

Source: Table 3.4, *Handbook of International Trade and Development Statistics, 1991* (New York: UNCTAD, 1992), pp. 112-25

Note:
* = 1988
** = 1990
*** = 1986
**** = 1987
.. = not available

Table 6.21 NAFTA partners — percentage of exports sent to the USA (USA & Canada for Mexico)

Country of origin	1970	1975	1980	1985	1990
Canada	65.4	65.7	63.4	77.8	75.8
Mexico	71.2	63.1	66	66.8	71.3

Source: Table 3.4, *Handbook of International Trade and Development Statistics, 1991* (New York: UNCTAD, 1992), pp. 112-25

has been realised, its virtues impressed upon its citizens and enthusiasm fostered for the further development of this experiment.

The picture presented by the economies of the American Continent, that are not currently associated with NAFTA, is, however, rather uneven. Some economies, like that of Bolivia, are heavily committed to export trade with their regional neighbours. Others, like Venezuela, exhibit a progressive decline in the level of their exports to their Southern American and Caribbean neighbours. Indeed, as Table 6.28 shows, later in this chapter, intra-trade within the subregional trade associations that have been formed within Southern America and the Caribbean has been a somewhat uneven experience.

South and South-East Asia and the Pacific Rim

The third major area of potential regionalisation within the contemporary international political economy is located in the general area delimited by South and South-East Asia and the Pacific Rim. The precise embrace of this potential region is imprecise, in a manner akin to the uncertain encompassment of the eventual American economic area. Indeed, the ambiguous role of the United States of America is a major, complicating factor in the designation of any economic region associated with the Pacific 'area'. Japan also plays a major role in the economic life of the Western side of the Pacific.

The Association of South East Asian countries has often been identified as the core of a potential South/South-East Asian economic region. However, the volume of trade amongst these economies remains limited. Intra-trade as a percentage of ASEAN states' exports has fluctuated from 21.7 per cent in 1960, to 13.9 per cent in 1976 and 18.5 per cent in 1990.[30] This is to be compared with exports to the overseas, Advanced Industrial Countries of 32.8 per cent of total exports in 1960, 30.3 per cent in 1976 and 38.3 per cent in 1980. The markets of extra-regional Developed Economies thus remain a powerful attraction to ASEAN's exporters. As many of the economies of South and South-East Asia have industrialised at a rapid pace, however, they have exerted a growing attraction for the exports of other economies within the Pacific region, as Table 6.23 indicates.

ASEAN, alone, thus presents a mixed picture on regionalisation.[31] However, the Pacific area does constitute an area of considerable levels of economic growth and steadily increasing mutual trade. The key actors in this putative region revealed themselves at the Seattle summit of 17-21 November 1993, on the creation of an Asia-Pacific Economic Co-operation forum (APEC). Consisting of the USA and Canada, Japan, China, South Korea, Australia, New Zealand, Hong Kong, Taiwan, Malaysia, Singapore, the Philippines and Indonesia, APEC encompasses areas of rapid industrialisation, technological innovation, extensive natural resources and substantial markets. It is unsurprising, therefore, that trade within this embryonic region absorbs an increasing proportion of the exports of many of its more prominent members.

Table 6.22 USA's regional partners (non-NAFTA) — percentage of country exports sent to the USA (countries ranked by decreasing proximity to the USA)

Country of origin	1970	1975	1980	1985	1989
Bermuda	10.5	23.9	14.7	28.3	34.4
Cuba[1]					
Haiti	60.5	76.3	..	81.2	77.1
Dominican Rep.	81.8	70	63.9	78.3	83.7 **
Jamaica	61.1	41.3	40.2	52.5	49.6
St Kitts and Nevis	1.7	..	..	70	50.3
Guadeloupe	24	0.8	0.8	4.2	0.2
Dominica	6.2	0.6	5.3	4.8	7.7
Martinique[3]	0.1	0.2	0.3	0.4	0.7
St Lucia	0.8	2.3	24.1	..	..
St Vincent & Grenadines	11.1	..	4.8	..	..
Barbados	28.5	43.2	46.8	84.9	15.9 ***
Grenada	..	5.8	6.4	5	13.6
Netherlands Antilles	66.6	63.4	52.2	46.9	34.4
Trinidad & Tobago	49.3	70.7	60.6	63.4	58.2
Guatemala	28.9	25.5	29.1	37	50.8
Belize	57.9	46.7	61	63.4	44.2
El Salvador	22.1	27.5	30.5	33.2	38.9
Honduras	54.6	51.9	53.2	49.1	51
Nicaragua[2]	33.5	28.2	39.1	16.7	7.5 *
Costa Rica	43.1	42.2	35.3	40.9	46.9
Panama	66.5	59.8	50.2	64.5	47.4
Colombia	38	33.1	28.6	33.9	44.7
Venezuela	48.6	51.8	37	49.7	60.6
Guyana	46.3	28.1	27.7	28.2	28.3 ***
Surinam	41	37	26.3	..	..
French Guiana[3]	78.2	45.6	26.2	37.9	3.2 ***
Ecuador	43.2	46.9	32.5	55.8	60.7
Brazil	26.2	17	18.6	28.8	25.9
Peru	32.4	24.4	33.3	29.5	32.2
Bolivia	34.8	31.2	29.8	14.1	13.2
Paraguay	14.5	8.1	5.5	1.3	4.3 ***
Chile	14.4	9.8	11.5	23.4	19.3
Argentina	9.3	7	9.5	12.9	13.4
Uruguay	14.9	12.8	10.6	8.2	10.8 ***

Source: Table 3.4, *Handbook of International Trade and Development Statistics, 1991* (New York: UNCTAD, 1992), pp. 112-25

Notes:
1. US embargo since inception of the Castro regime in 1959
2. Economic relations with the USA disrupted by US embargo during the Sandanista period of rule
3. Technically *départements* of France and therefore furnished with unrestrained access to the EC market.

* = 1986
** = 1988
*** = 1990

Table 6.23 Pacific region economies — percentage of exports sent to South and South-East Asia (& South China Sea)

Country of Origin	1970	1975	1980	1985	1990
Australia	10.4	13.8	14.8	17.6	23.8
China	..	32.6	33.1	39.2	53.8
Fiji	2.5	8.3	13.3	12.3	8.2 *
French Polynesia	..	..	..	4.4	..
Hong Kong	6.3	17	17.6	13.1	14
Indonesia	20.7	14.3	16.7	18.7	24.6
Korea (S)	7	8.7	14.6	13.7	17.3
Macao	20.5	11.8	12.7	18.5	13.7
Malaysia	31.8	31.3	31.7	39.8	38.7 *
New Zealand	3.8	8.2	10.8	9.8	16.8
Papua New Guinea	0.3	0.3	2.7	8	14.2 *
Philippines	7.2	6.5	15.7	19.5	19.1 *
Samoa	..	0.6	..	..	1.7 *
Singapore	13.2	37.6	39.4	37.4	40.2
Solomon Islands	0.6	1	2.1	11	22.2 *
Taiwan	20.3	19.1	17.7	15.9	25.8
Thailand	30.7	32.3	24.8	25	20.8
Tonga	1.2	0.1	12.6	..	..
Vanuatu	..	..	4.6	2.6	5.5

Source: Table 3.4, *Handbook of International Trade and Development Statistics, 1991* (New York: UNCTAD, 1992), pp. 112-25

Note:
* = 1988
.. = not available

Table 6.24 Japanese exports to South and South-East Asia

Year	% of total exports
1970	21.8
1975	22.5
1980	23.8
1985	19
1990	28.8

Source: Table 3.4, *Handbook of International Trade and Development Statistics, 1991*
(New York: UNCTAD, 1992)

Japan's exports to South and South-East Asia have, with a slight blip in the mid-1980s, risen steadily throughout the past two decades. The region had absorbed some 25 per cent of Japan's total exports by 1990, as Table 6.24 shows. In return, exports to Japan have also remained substantial for many APEC members, as Table 6.25 indicates. The United States of America has also increased its exports to the region, slowly but steadily, as Table 6.26 demonstrates. Again, the proportion of exports being sent by APEC members to the USA and Canada has, with some divergences and variations, also risen, or remained high, during the period between 1970 and 1990, as Table 6.27 suggests. Whatever the periodic ebbs and floods of export volumes, the general significance of trade within the APEC region remains high for all participants, with claims, by late 1993, that 40 per cent of the USA's exports were now being directed towards APEC members, compared with less than 25 per cent being shipped to the whole of Europe.[32]

The shape and stability of a new international economic region formed around APEC is, however, far from clear or certain. Part of the justification for the conclusion of the North American Free Trade Agreement lies in its potential as a bulwark against competition from many of the very economies that lie at the very heart of APEC. North American participation in deliberations on APEC might, therefore, be little more than a delaying tactic; an insurance policy, while the shape, and operating principles, of the emergent international political economy make themselves clear. Whatever the motives and expectations of United States' negotiators, the compatibility between a dynamic, and expanding, NAFTA and an APEC association of any real substance must remain inherently problematical.

Latin America and the Caribbean as a potential subregion in the international political economy

Latin America and the Caribbean presents a mixed picture as an actual, or potential, region, or subregion, within the international political economy. There have been many attempts to form more local trading associations to stimulate greater trade amongst close neighbours but these have met with limited success, with intra-trade as a proportion of group exports in 1990 amounting to only 15.8 per cent for the Central American Common Market (CACM); 4 per cent for the Caribbean Community (CARICOM); 10.4 per cent for the Latin American Integration Association (LAIA); and 3.3 per cent for the Andean Group.[33]

More generally, however, the proportion of exports that the Latin American and the Caribbean economies have directed towards their fellow regional states has varied enormously, as Table 6.28 makes clear. However, for all but those that are denied normal trade relations with their fellows by political constraints, intraregional exports are generally of substantial significance for the region's economies. The centripetal effects of an expanding NAFTA region, with its growing potential for

Table 6.25 Asia-Pacific Economic Co-operation forum economies — percentage of exports sent to Japan

Country of Origin	1970	1975	1980	1985	1990
Australia	27.7	30.4	25.1	26.4	26.8
China	-	23.3	22.9	22.2	14.5
Hong Kong	4	6.4	4.6	4.2	5.3
Indonesia	33.3	43.9	49.3	46.2	42.7
Korea (S)	27.7	25.3	17.3	15	19.4
Malaysia	18.3	14.5	22.8	23.8	16.1
New Zealand	10	13.5	12.9	14.9	16.7
Philippines	39.6	37.4	26.5	19	20.3
Singapore	7.6	8.7	8.1	9.4	8.7
Taiwan	15.1	13.2	11	11.3	12.4
Thailand	26.3	28.1	15.3	13.4	17.2
Tonga	-	-	-	0.2	8.8

Source: Table 3.4, *Handbook of International Trade and Development Statistics, 1991* (New York: UNCTAD, 1992), pp. 112-25

Note:
- = not available

Table 6.26 United States of America, exports to South and South-East Asia and Japan

	Exports to:	
Year	S and SE Asia (% of US total)	Japan (% of US total)
1970	8.5	10.8
1975	9.5	8.9
1980	10.8	9.5
1985	11.2	10.5
1990	14.2	12.4

Source: Table 3.5, *Handbook of International Trade and Development Statistics, 1991* (New York: UNCTAD, 1992)

Table 6.27 Asia-Pacific Economic Co-operation (APEC) forum economies — percentage of exports sent to the United States of America and Canada

Country of origin	1970	1975	1980	1985	1990
Australia	15.8	12.5	11.9	8.6	13.6
China	:	3.2	6.6	9.4	9
Hong Kong	45.2	29.2	28.1	33.2	31.8
Indonesia	14.1	26.3	19.8	22	13.7
Korea (S)	49.4	34.2	28.4	39.7	32.6
Malaysia	14.9	17.2	16.8	13.7	19.4
New Zealand	20.7	13.6	15.3	16.5	15
Philippines	42	30.6	28.8	37.5	37.4 *
Singapore	12.3	14.9	13.4	21.9	22.2
Taiwan	43.4	38.1	36.6	51.5	34.8
Thailand	13.6	10.9	13.2	21	24.1

Source: Table 3.4, *Handbook of International Trade and Development Statistics, 1991* (New York: UNCTAD, 1992), pp. 112-25

Note:
* = 1989

complementary patterns of economic development, might, however, further encourage subregional and wider regional association and intra-trade.

Sub-Saharan Africa and the structural impediments to effective regionalisation

As a continent-wide region, and an area of local trade agreements, sub-Saharan Africa has had a disappointing history. A primary obstacle to effective regionalisation within Africa has been the legacy of geographical dependence upon markets in Advanced Industrial Countries and particularly those of former colonial economies and the wider economic areas of which they are now members. These North-South trade flows have effectively inhibited the emergence of buoyant South-South exchanges within the subcontinent. Moreover, many sub-Saharan African economies remain critically dependent upon the earnings of foreign currency derived from the export of their primary products to markets outside the region. Without even these receipts, however meagre, all hopes of development, and even of the physical survival of much of their populations, might be placed in considerable jeopardy.

The variation in the proportions of their exports that sub-Saharan African countries send to their continental 'neighbours' is thus considerable; ranging from the 1.1 per cent of Liberia to the 54.7 per cent of Chad. Most African states, however, cluster at the lower end of the range. As Table 6.29 indicates, twenty-one of the thirty-six states reviewed send less than 10 per cent of their exports to their other African economies; five are in the range of 10 to 20 per cent; and only five export more than 20 per cent to their fellow states. These figures contrast markedly with the high proportions of exports that these economies send to the Advanced Industrial Countries. Indeed, the geographical poles of attraction for many African exports are dramatically demonstrated, in Table 6.30, by a comparison of the levels of exports sent by the Mediterranean countries of North Africa to other African states, with those sent to the European Community.[34]

However, it is the generally low level of wealth and demand for imports that underlies the overall weakness of Africa's demands for her own exports. Proportional to their low level of imports, the countries of the African continent actually exert as strong an attractive force upon exports from other African economies as do the Western European economies upon one another.[35]

The failure of sustained and sustainable development throughout much of sub-Saharan Africa is thus reflected in its high level of dependence upon export markets in the Advanced Industrial Countries. This is a product of limited success in economic and industrial diversification, weaknesses in penetrating new markets, and a generally low level of growth or prosperity, and hence the 'domestic' market, throughout much of the region; the effects of which have often been reinforced by the attractive force exercised by the European Community's General System of Preferences, with its 'preferential' market access terms for many African economies.

Financial Dependencies

Students of North-South economic relations often give considerable emphasis to the flow of fees, premiums and profits from many 'Southern' economies to private enterprises and governmental bodies, within the rich 'North'. This financial flow is far from trivial, and clearly contributes substantially to the prosperity of some sectors of the economies of many Advanced Industrial Countries. The level and significance of overseas investments is indicated, rather imprecisely, by the figures for Overseas Direct Investment (ODI) from the European Community during the period 1984-8 quoted in Table 6.31. These indicated the very low ration of ODI to regional GDP and the relatively small proportion (11.29 per cent by 1988) of EC ODI that was directed towards the 'Third World'. The significance of these patterns of

Table 6.28 Developing America — percentage of country exports sent to other developing American economies (countries ranked by increasing distance from the USA)

Country of origin	1970	1975	1980	1985	1989
Bermuda	0.7	9.5	19.2	1.7	8.1
Cuba	..	..	..	0.7	1.1
Haiti	2.2	2.1	..	4	4
Dominican Rep.	1.2	1.1	16	3.7	3.6 *
Jamaica	7.1	6.7	9.6	11.7	9.8
St Kitts and Nevis	7.9	..	..	25	26.2
Guadeloupe	2.1	11.6	21.9	28.5	18.2
Dominica	6.9	63.2	44	26.7	31.9
Martinique	6.8	25.9	50.5	30.1	31.3
St Lucia	32.2	39	42.2	50.8	40
St Vincent & Grenadines	19.2	..	44.5	31.2	22.1 **
Barbados	8.2	19.9	31	3.6	32.9 ***
Grenada	7.3	..	13.8	36.9	23.1
Netherlands Antilles	15.5	19.9	26.2	35.7	48.2
Trinidad & Tobago	22.6	13.9	19.1	18.8	25.3
Guatemala	36.7	30.1	30.4	34.4	18.3
Belize	0.7	17	7.7	6.4	12.5
El Salvador	32.9	30.2	42.5	35	36.6
Honduras	18.9	22.9	13.5	7.9	6.3
Nicaragua	28.3	26.1	19.8	21.4	12.2
Costa Rica	23.5	29.4	35.1	27.3	17.7
Panama	8.8	8.6	19.8	15.3	20.6
Colombia	14.2	21.7	17.7	14.2	16
Venezuela	36.7	34.5	37.2	10.7	9.6
Guyana	15.4	15.4	24.4	17.1	14.7 ***
Surinam	2.2	14.9	13.8	..	..
French Guiana	13.2	29.6	20.7	20.9	19
Ecuador	11.1	37.8	43.2	10.7	18.2
Brazil	11.7	15.8	18.1	9.7	11.7
Peru	6.5	18.6	22.3	17.3	15
Bolivia	8.5	35	35.7	60.2	63.7
Paraguay	38.5	36.1	45.8	37.1	53.6
Chile	11.5	23.8	24.7	15	10.9
Argentina	21.1	31.2	24.5	22.1	24.6
Uruguay	12.8	28.8	37.3	28	40.6

Source: Table 3.4, *Handbook of International Trade and Development Statistics, 1991* (New York: UNCTAD, 1992), pp. 112-25

Notes:
* = 1988
** = 1987
*** = 1990
.. = not available

Table 6.29 Developing Africa (non-Mediterranean) — percentage of country exports sent to other developing African economies and the AICs

Country of origin	% to	1970	1975	1980	1985	1989
Angola	Africa	4.6	3	4	2.6	1.8
	AICs	92.4	95.8	69	76.7	81.5
Benin	Africa	18.3	12.6	18	..	..
	AICs	80.9	66.2	74.7	..	..
Burkina Faso	Africa	49.2	57.9	43.1	23.7	16.9
	AICs	47.1	40.4	42.4	40.7	65
Burundi	Africa	3.3	3.2	2	19.2	3.6
	AICs	95.8	93.3	91.3	74.1	86.6
Cameroon	Africa	8.3	14.4	2.8	10.5	22.3
	AICs	86.2	74.1	95.7	86.2	67.5
Cent. African Rep.	Africa	6.5	8.2	1.7	3.6	4.3
	AICs	91.6	89.3	97.6	96.3	95.1
Chad	Africa	28.6	-	27.2	..	54.7
	AICs	71	..	72.8	..	37.2
Congo	Africa	12.5	3.9	1.1	3.4	2.2
	AICs	80.6	86.5	76.2	94.7	96.1
Côte d'Ivoire	Africa	7.8	16.3	..	15.6	28.5
	AICs	89.8	76.7	..	72.4	56.3
Ethiopia	Africa	6.2	19.3	13.4	6	3.2
	AICs	81.2	58.4	61.5	71.1	78.3
Gabon	Africa	9.4	1.4	..	8.9	6.4
	AICs	71.8	81.6	64.8	70	68.2
Gambia	Africa	0.6	2.7	24.8	43	14.8
	AICs	99.4	97.2	74.6	45.8	82
Ghana	Africa	0.7	2.6	0.8	3	6.4
	AICs	71.2	77.5	76.2	78.1	75.3
Kenya	Africa	12	16.4	24.8	24.5	23.9
	AICs	64	54.7	46.3	56.9	64.9
Liberia	Africa	1.3	1.4	1.9	2.4	1.1
	AICs	98	95.7	93.5	93.2	97.9
Madagascar	Africa	19.6	14.8	8.8	3.9	8
	AICs	69.6	58.7	76.8	78.9	83.2
Malawi	Africa	19	16.3	14	11.8	11.4
	AICs	76.6	82.8	83.8	86.6	82.8
Mali	Africa	62.2	48.5	23.1	22.5	30.8
	AICs	28.8	28.5	65.6	28.8	27.6
Mauritania	Africa	6	4.6	4	7.4	9.6
	AICs	93.9	94.3	94.9	87.1	72.6
Mauritius	Africa	1.1	1.5	1.8	2.7	2.7
	AICs	98.4	97.7	97.8	95.6	93
Niger	Africa	34.6	29.9	18.7	20.4	..
	AICs	65.1	70	79.4	79.1	-
Nigeria	Africa	0.7	2	-	4.1 *	7.2
	AICs	88.7	82.5	-	90.8 *	89.8
Réunion	Africa	1.1	2.4	5.4	7.5	9.5 **
	AICs	96.6	97.5	94	89.3	89.6
Rwanda	Africa	17.9	13.1	5.3	38.7	4.8
	AICs	81.8	70.2	94.7	45	89.7

Senegal	Africa	21.7	17.7	30.9	29.6	20.1
	AICs	74.9	70.7	54.8	43.4	55.6
Sierra Leone	Africa	1.6	0.5	..	1.2	8
	AICs	95	89.6	100	76.2	79.9
Somalia	Africa	3.2	3.2	1.1	0.2	..
	AICs	30.2	8.4	16.2	26.7	..
(South Africa)	Africa	..	12.9	10.4	7.6	8.2
	AICs	74.5	78.3	79	84.4	73.8
Sudan	Africa	5.5	8.6	2.6	3.4	8.3
	AICs	49.2	56.5	52.1	56.5	45.4
Togo	Africa	3.1	6.2	26.3	16	14
	AICs	90.9	92.3	67.1	66.5	62.3
Tunisia	Africa	16.3	10.6	3.2	5.2	8.8
	AICs	67.2	75.6	87.8	83.7	79.7
Uganda	Africa	3.8	9.4	14.1	10.6	7.8
	AICs	77.3	81.5	78.7	85.2	88.5
Tanzania	Africa	9.6	6.8	16.3	4.2	9.6
	AICs	59.7	54.9	58.4	79	71.4
Zaïre	Africa	23.5	3.3	..	1.8	3.5
	AICs	75.9	63.9	..	96.5	85.2
Zambia	Africa	1	2.7	..	1.4	1.2
	AICs	87.3	91.1	..	85.6	65.7
Zimbabwe	Africa	..	..	6	12.6	17.2 **
	AICs	..	60.8	74.9	74.8	73.4

Source: Table 3.4, *Handbook of International Trade and Development Statistics, 1991* (New York: UNCTAD, 1992), pp. 112-25

Notes:
* = 1986
** = 1990
.. = Not available

Table 6.30 North African countries (Mediterranean) — comparisons of percentages of exports sent to other developing African economies and the EC

Country of origin		1970	1975	1980	1985	1989
	%					
Algeria	to Africa	3.8	2.6	0.8	1.5	2
	to EC	81	55.1	39.8	68.7	70.6
Egypt	to Africa	6.1	5	1	0.8	2.3
	to EC	14.2	11.8	45.6	41.1	42.5
Libya	to Africa	..	1	0.1	0.9	0.9
	to EC	91	51.7	39.3	69.2	78.3
Morocco	to Africa	5.6	4.7	3.5	5.1	7.8
	to EC	72.8	54.1	55.7	49.5	65

Source: Table 3.4, *Handbook of International Trade and Development Statistics, 1991* (New York: UNCTAD, 1992), pp. 112-25

Notes:
.. = not available

Table 6.31 European Community overseas investment in AICs and LDCs (millions of ECU)

	1985	1986	1987	1988
GDP of EC 12	3,340,300	3,546,700	3,736,800	4,054,800
Total of ODI*	15,459	22,164	30,780	30,711
Investment in AICs	11,656	19,634	27,418	26,001
Investments in LDCs	3,535	2,167	3,017	3,466
ODI as % of GDP	0.46	0.62	0.82	0.76
LDC investment as % of total ODI	22.87	9.78	9.80	11.29

Source: Table 4 - EUR-1, *European Community Direct Investment, 1984-88* (Luxembourg : EUROSTAT, 1991), p. 86; and Table 2, *Basic Statistics of the Community (29th edn.;* Luxembourg : EUROSTAT, 1992), p.39

Note:

* ODI — Overseas Direct Investment.

investment to the overall prosperity, rather than sectorally specific profitability, of the European Community's economies was thus relatively low.

In the international political economy, multiplier effects can substantially magnify the effects of relatively modest initial disturbances. It is possible that the loss of substantial overseas investments by Advanced Industrial Countries would have serious domestic consequences. Such dangers were at the heart of the anxieties that surfaced during the 'debt crisis' of the early 1980s, when the general economic well-being of the 'Northern' economies was believed to be vulnerable to the proliferating consequences of the default of one, or more, of the major debtors amongst the Less Developed Countries.[36]

Many states, in all categories, are also dependent upon the international financial system for short and medium-term funding of balance-of-payments deficits, arising from imbalances between imports and exports of goods and services. The ratio of balance-of-payments deficits to Gross Domestic Product is far higher in the case of many Less Developed Countries than for the NICs or the AICs. Inflows of official economic aid, private lending and private investment contribute substantially to bridging this payments' shortfall and thereby maintaining the LDCs' ability to pay for necessary imports of food, commodities and capital equipment.

Nothing better illustrates the continuing dependence of many of the LDCs upon foreign financial support than their regular receipt of official economic assistance from direct donors or from such multilateral institutions as the World Bank (International Bank for Reconstruction and Development — IBRD). Official Development Assistance (bilateral and multilateral) in 1991 was equivalent to some 130 per cent of the balance-of-payments' deficits of the world's low-income countries, and near 80 per cent of those of the lower-income economies that continued to suffer from substantial deficits.[37] The central point here is that the source of such ODI, whether bilateral or multilateral, is ultimately the economies of the rich 'North' and hence indicates a substantial form of 'Southern' dependence upon that sector of the international political economy.

The delicacy and dependence in the financial relations of many Less Developed Countries with their external environment is further illustrated by the continuing, and in many cases deepening, levels of indebtedness. The so-called 'Debt Crisis' of the early 1980s may have been 'resolved' to the satisfaction of the creditor countries and their financial institutions but the 'Debt Crisis' of the world's poorer countries has continued unabated. As Table 6.32 shows, levels of indebtedness as proportions of exports and GNP have risen for all groups of the Less Developed Countries, except the 'upper-middle income' group. Moreover, it is only the impressive export performances of a number of the 'upper-middle income' and East Asian economies, throughout the 1980s, that have moderated their ratios of debt service and interest payments to exports. For the other groups of Less Developed Countries, increasing indebtedness has meant commensurate increases in the

Table 6.32. External debt of the Less Developed Countries, by income groupings

	Total external debt as percentage of				Total debt service as		Interest Payments as	
	Exports of goods and services		Gross National product		percentage of exports		percentage of experts	
Economies	1980	1991	1980	1991.	1980	1991	1980	1991
Low income	105.5	225.7	16.6	44.6	10.1	21	5	9.4
Lower-middle income	100.2	157.6	28.7	53.2	16.7	19.5	8	8.3
Upper-middle income	173.1	162.2	34.4	33.2	33	21.1	17.5	10.4
Sub-Saharan African	96.6	329.4	28.6	107.9	10.9	20.8	5.7	10.5
East Asia and Pacific	89.8	96.2	16.9	28.2	13.5	13:3	7.7	5.9
South Asia	160.4	287.1	17	35.6	11.9	26	5.1	11.5
Middle East and N. Africa	114.4	185.8	31	58.8	16.1	25.9	7.3	8.4
Latin American and Caribbean	195.5	256	35.1	41.3	37.1	29.2	19.6	15.8
Severely indebted	176.6	285.9	34	46.4	34	30.8	17.1	14.1

Source: Table 24, *World Development Report, 1993* (New York/Oxford: World Bank/Oxford University Press, 1993), pp. 284-5

growth of their dependence upon aid, and other financial flows, from the Advanced Industrial Countries, to maintain some semblance of international solvency.[38] Sensitivity to changes in the climate affecting such North-South financial transfers is thus acute for many LDCs and may well indicate the serious vulnerabilities of their economies.

Conclusions

Once interconnections, interdependencies and their contributory dependencies have been defined with some clarity, it is necessary to put some flesh on the conceptual bare bones. Much of this chapter has been devoted to a review of the diversity of contemporary patterns of interconnections, dependencies and interdependencies. Much of the evidence on such patterns derives from data on the conditions of individual states or the sets of bilateral relationships within which they find themselves. Some of the data is also suggestive of structural conditions obtaining in the international political economy, which have a general influence upon the structure of opportunities and constraints bearing upon sets of individual states.

The material survey suggests the diversity within contemporary conditions and supports the judgement of one eminent observer that, at this level of analysis at least:

> Globalisation is a term used too loosely, characterising finance rather than production and trade. There is global management of production by some companies, but what is surprising, given modern technology, is how little production is organised on this basis — and how firmly national most economic variables remain.[39]

Patterns of interconnectedness are highly variable, as was shown in the earlier part of the chapter. This seriously qualifies notions of globalisation, when these are constructed aggregatively from the range of contemporary conditions. Such empirical data reinforce the notion that the international political economy resembles a multi-layered set of diverse, if interconnected, domains of activity, with some exhibiting marked levels of globalisation while others remain highly localised or regionalised. They do not, however, pose a direct challenge to some of the holistic presumptions of some models of contemporary globalisation.

In the realms of interdependence, the picture is frequently that of substantial asymmetry. Large economies are, for example, able to exploit the importance of their domestic markets to others by imposing 'optimum tariffs' which force down the prices charged by smaller exporters, while capturing the resultant gain for the national budget.[40] It is rare that any individual measure of dependence can establish a serious vulnerability for any national economy. Reflection upon a range of potential conditions can, however, suggest situations in which a statistical dependence might constitute a serious vulnerability. Most of these measures do, moreover, indicate sensitivities which, if situationally combined with adverse developments in other areas of sensitivity, could also expose, or precipitate, situations of serious vulnerability. Thus, levels of basic food import dependencies and aid dependencies might be no more than moderately serious for many LDCs, when the condition of the others remains relatively benign. Adverse developments in two or more areas of dependence simultaneously, as with a situation of rising international food prices and an 'aid famine', could, however, prove extremely serious for a number of LDCs, thereby exposing a situation of significant, real dependence.

Important as such specific sensitivities and vulnerabilities clearly are, the full significance of contemporary international interdependence cannot be appreciated solely from a survey of the situations of specific states or sets of bilateral interdependencies. Questions of considerable significance for the nature and prospects of the international political economy turn around the sources of contemporary patterns of 'interdependence'; the appropriate form and level of their conceptualisation; and their diverse, potential consequences for the future peace and prosperity of the world's peoples. It is to these issues that the subsequent chapters in this section are addressed.

Appendix 6.1 The Hirschmann Index

$$\mathrm{Hj} = \frac{\sqrt{\sum_{i=1}^{239}\left(\frac{x_i}{X}\right) - \sqrt{1/239}}}{1 - \sqrt{1/239}}$$

x = product category

i = each individual product category

$$X = \sum_{i=1}^{239} x_i$$

Notes and references

1. See 'China's government in a jam', *The Economist*, 15 January 1994, pp. 63-4; 'Next in line', *The Economist*, 23 January 1993, pp. 70-5.
2. See, especially, Richard Rosecrance *et al.*, 'Whither interdependence', *International Organization*, Vol. 31 (1977), pp. 425-71; Richard Rosecrance and W. Gutowitz, 'Measuring interdependence: a rejoinder', *International Organization*, Vol. 35, (1981), pp. 553-60.

3. See, for instance, the report of related world-wide movements of share prices: 'Markets reach global highs', *The Guardian*, 1 February 1994, p. 14.
4. Calculated from data on overnight interest rates for 1984-93, from various sources.
5. Ibid.
6. See 'Dodgy diversification', report in *The Economist*, 20 November 1993, p. 128.
7. World Bank Data on export growth and GDP growth between 1979 and 1991 produces a correlation of only 0.3821 for those countries on which reliable data are available; sources: *World Development Report*, 1981 Table 3, pp. 138-9 and Table 8, pp. 148-9; *World Development Report*, 1993, Table 3, pp. 242-3 and Table 14, pp. 264-5 (New York: World Bank, 1981 and 1993).
8. Ibid.
9. W. Brandt (ed.), *North-South : A Programme for Survival* (London: Pan Books, 1980); and see also W. Brandt, *Common Crisis, North-South: Cooperation for World Recovery* (London: Pan Books, 1983).
10. The AICs are defined, here, as the group of high-income members of the Organisation of Economic Cooperation and Development (OECD — see the list in the World Bank *Annual Reports* (World Bank, New York)).
11. On which concept see R.J. Barry Jones, *Conflict and Control in the World Economy: Contemporary Economic Realism and Neo-Mercantilism*, (Brighton: Harvester/Wheatsheaf, 1986), esp. pp. 30-5 and 50-5.
12. Calculated from Tables 6.6 and 6.8, pp. 280 and 282, *Basic Statistics of the Community* (29th edn., Luxembourg: EUROSTAT, 1992). Exchange rates as at 5 February 1994.
13. See, for example, the report 'The good news from Japan', *The Economist*, 29 January, 1994, pp. 63-4.
14. See the report 'Saudi budget cuts threaten British jobs', *The Guardian*, 8 January 1994, p. 11.
15. *The Economist, Pocket World in Figures, 1994 edition* (London: Economist Books Ltd., 1993), p. 85.
16. *Ibid.*, p. 93.
17. *Ibid.*, p. 107.
18. *Ibid.*, p. 109.
19. *Ibid.*, p. 161.
20. See *Handbook of International Trade and Development Statistics, 1991* (New York: UNCTAD, 1992), p. 244.
21. For the full table see Table 4.5, *Handbook of International Trade and Development Statistics* (New York, UNCTAD, 1992), pp. 241-4.
22. Ibid.
23. Calculations of correlation for such a small sample must, however, be treated with considerable caution.
24. For a succinct review see Robert C. Hine, 'Regionalism and the integration of the world economy', *Journal of Common Market Studies*, Vol. XXX, No. 2 (June 1992), pp. 115-23.
25. See, in particular, the survey 'Multinationals; back in fashion', after p. 86 in *The Economist*, 27 March 1993, esp. pp. 16-19; and for a review of the effects of the European Community on Japanese Foreign Direct Investment, see V.N. Balasubramanyam and D. Greenaway, 'Economic integration and Foreign Direct Investment: Japanese investment in the EC', *Journal of Common Market Studies*, Vol. XXX, No. 2 (June 1992), pp. 175-93.
26. See Edward M. Graham, 'Strategic responses of US multinational firms to the

Europe–1992 initiative', in G. N. Yannopoulos (ed.), *Europe and America, 1992* (Manchester; Manchester University Press/Fulbright Commission, 1991), pp. 177-205, esp. pp. 180-2.
27. For a vigorous argument on which see Paul Krugman, *Geography and Trade* (Leuven and Cambridge, Mass.: Leuven University Press and MIT Press, 1991).
28. For a review of the background on regional association in the American Continent see J. Whalley, 'CUSTA and NAFTA: can WHFTA be far behind', *Journal of Common Market Studies*, Vol. XXX, No. 2 (June 1992), pp. 125-42.
29. *The Economist, Pocket World in Figures, 1994 edition* (London: Economist Publications, 1993), p. 197.
30. *Handbook of International Trade and Development Statistics, 1991* (New York: UNCTAD, 1992), p. 39.
31. See A. Bollard and D. Mayes, 'Regionalism and the Pacific Rim', *Journal of Common Market Studies*, Vol. XXX, No 2 (June 1992), pp. 195-209.
32. See the report 'Booming Asian economies take a cool look at themselves', *The Guardian*, 17 November 1993, p. 9.
33. See Table 1.13, *Handbook of International Trade and Development Statistics, 1991* (New York: UNCTAD, 1992), p. 39.
34. For a review of the European Community's impact on African export trade see: M. Davenport, 'Africa and the unimportance of being preferred', *Journal of Common Market Studies*, Vol. XXX, No. 2 (June 1992), pp. 233-51.
35. See Andrew Walter, 'Regionalism, Globalisation and World Economic Order', Table 2, in L. Fawcett and A. Hurrell (eds.), *Regionalism and International Order* (Oxford: Oxford University Press, (forthcoming) 1995).
36. For an early review of such dangers see H. Lever and C. Hune, *Debt and Danger* (Harmondsworth: Penguin Books, 1985).
37. Calculated from Tables 3, 18 and 20 of the *World Development Report, 1993* (New York: World Bank, 1993), pp. 242-3, 272-3 and 276-7.
38. For evidence of the deepening debt crisis of the poorest group of states see 'African debt deepening says Bank', *The Guardian*, 16 December 1993, p.19.
39. Will Hutton, 'Markets threaten life and soul of the party', *The Guardian*, 4 January 1994, p.13.
40. See, for a recent discussion of this, and its problematical consequences, John A. Kroll, 'The complexity of interdependence', *International Studies Quarterly*, Vol. 37 (1993), p. 321-47, esp. pp. 338-40.

CHAPTER 7

The sources of international economic interdependence and globalisation

The patterns of contemporary international interdependence, and globalisation processes, are complex and varied. Asymmetry and imbalance characterise all but a few of the more specific forms of interdependence. Moreover, dependencies and interdependencies rarely spring into being immaculately. While a few arise from the structure of a given situation or relationship, as with mutual strategic interdependence between nuclear adversaries, most result from the activities of economic and political actors. The variety of actors and actions that can generate significant interdependencies, however, opens up a number of important questions about the sources of economic interdependence in the modern world.

Such questions encounter central issues concerning the nature and sources of major developments within human affairs. Contrasting views of the course of human evolution contend with one another, here. One approach attributes a central role to self-conscious, and purposeful, human agents. The opposing perspective identifies impersonal forces and processes as the basic engine of change in human affairs. This interpretative conflict is particularly pertinent to discussions of the development of international economic interdependence and globalisation, given the frequency with which it is presented as an irresistible and irreversible process. This, as will be seen later in the chapter, is particularly true in respect of the significance attributed to modern technology.

Differential resource endowments and contemporary international economic interdependence

The simplest view of international economic interdependence is that it reflects, and has arisen from, differing patterns of endowments of a range of basic resources and capabilities amongst the states of the world. This basic notion of 'natural' interdependence has much in common with earlier theories of international economics that attributed the existence and direction of international trade to the patterns of *absolute advantage* amongst economies. According to this interpretation, economies exchanged goods and services that were readily producible at home for commodities that could not be produced domestically. However, patterns of actual trade within the world economy proved to be far more complex than could be explained by the theory of absolute advantage and a more sophisticated interpretation was required.

The theory of *comparative advantage* emerged to fill the explanatory gap left by the inadequacy of the theory of absolute advantage. This theory, while not denying the limited influence of absolute advantage, sought to explain the greater part of international trade in terms of the relative efficiencies with which different economies could produce a wide range of goods and services. In the simplest of terms, while one society might be more efficient at producing every kind of good and service than any other society, it might still find it beneficial to specialise in the production of export of those goods and services in which its relative efficiency was at the highest level, while withdrawing from the domestic production of the goods and services in which its greater efficiency was not quite as great. Demand for goods and services no longer produced domestically could then be satisfied from imports from other societies that had continued with their production.[1]

Such a notion of comparative advantage is vulnerable to a degree of empirical circularity: its existence being identifiable through the condition that it is supposed to explain. The explanation for the fact that some societies prove able to specialise successfully in the production and trade of certain goods and services is constructed in terms of the possession of comparative advantage, but the existence of that comparative advantage cannot be established independently of the patterns of successful production and trade that it is supposed to explain. An attempt to break this potential circularity in the principle of comparative advantage was made through reference to the differing endowments of the *factors of production* necessary for the production of the goods and services traded internationally.[2] Factor endowments theory, however, is still confronted by two serious difficulties.

The first problem for factor endowments theory is that relatively few goods and services can be produced by only one combination of factors of production. The volumes, and relative costs, with which a range of potentially pertinent factors of production may be available in a number of societies may vary sufficiently to make it far more difficult than might be imagined to plot, with precision, those that should be able to produce and trade any good or service with a clear, competitive advantage.

The second, and ultimately greater, difficulty facing the theory of factor endowments is that such endowments are not immutable for the great majority of goods and services. Rather than being 'given' by situation, or circumstance, for all time, most of the more significant factors for the production of advanced goods and services are very much 'man-made'. The construction and accumulation of capital equipment is clearly responsive to time and circumstance. The development and deployment of skilled work-forces is also highly alterable with the implementation of suitable social, educational and training policies. Even the natural environment is open to some modification. Dams can transform the possibilities for agricultural irrigation and power generation. Policies for the clearance of forests, or the drainage of water-logged land, can enhance capacities for agricultural production. Energy-poor lands can be transformed through the introduction of power generation by nuclear fission and breeder reactors, or other forms of 'renewable' energy generation.

The implication of the alterability of many critical factor endowments is that many patterns of international dependence and interdependence are themselves the consequence of actions taken, or not taken, by societies in the past and the present. Most dependencies and interdependencies, in short, are created by those, or the forebears of those, who are their subjects. Few international dependencies or interdependencies can thus be deemed to be either natural or inevitable. They may be desirable, or a consequence of desirable developments, but they have not been 'given' by conditions external, or prior, to the activities of human societies. *Revealed* comparative advantage is thus the most that can often be identified by way of a snapshot of an ever changing pattern of competitiveness and productive advantage.

A contemporary variant of the emphasis given by 'liberal' perspectives to the impersonal forces of the market is the proposition that contemporary technologies are exerting automatic and irresistible pressures towards intensifying interdependence and progressive globalisation in the international economy. Modern technologies have been ascribed a central role in facilitating, and possibly driving, both the economic interconnections associated with the continuing spread of TNCs and the growth of financial 'integration'.[3] The emphasis upon the role and influence of technology, however, again highlights central questions about the relative roles of human agents and impersonal forces in basic developments in world affairs. The problem here is to establish the extent to which any technical condition, or possibility, translates automatically into a readily attainable opportunity for, or an irresistible constraint upon, any society upon which it impacts directly, or indirectly.

Technology clearly exerts a considerable influence upon the structure of opportunities and constraints confronting societies.[4] Its overall impact will, however, be a function of a wide range of factors. The uneven development and application of industrial technologies underlay the pattern of uneven growth within the world economy which intensified dramatically in the nineteenth and early twentieth centuries. The military applications of many of the newer technologies also reinforced the capacity of the rapidly industrialising economies to translate economic preponderance into a remarkable level of political and military domination throughout the non-industrial world. New patterns of interdependence were forged by the technologically-supported expansion, and intensification, of economic and political contacts amongst many of the separate societies of the world; and the seeds of contemporary tendencies towards globalisation sown.

The diffusion of increasingly advanced technologies has, however, also played a significant role in the subsequent relocation of production to formerly less developed regions of the international economy. The 'globalisation' that has begun to result from this changing international division of labour is not that of asymmetrical interdependence amongst industrial and non-industrial economies, but a new form in which the increasingly similar productive profiles of an increasing number of economies generates ever intensifying competitive pressures. The consequence of such rising competitive intensity is, in turn, increasing sensitivity to economic, and industrial, conditions and developments elsewhere. Convergence in conditions of production and employment and homogenisation in the output of industrial systems are the perceived implications of such a pattern of globalisation. The level of such globalisation, and the extent of its effects, is easy to exaggerate, however, as has often been contended in this study. Pressures in such directions are evident; it is merely their level and force that are questionable, given the range of factors that condition their practical effects.

While technological possibilities clearly provide humanity with a range of powerful opportunities, these possibilities may not always be unidirectional, or even complementary, in their implications. Thus the great advance in human mobility, resulting from the development of the modern aircraft, can be deployed with equal ease to promote direct contact between formerly separated peoples or to unleash mass destruction upon previously inaccessible populations. The advent of the personal computer and world-wide electronic networks can both facilitate direct, and immediate, contacts amongst individuals internationally, and enhance the armoury of those who would seek to centralise information about, and ultimately control of, the entire membership of societies and/or economic enterprises. The balance of effects of any given technology will thus be a product of a complex set of contextual factors including, critically, the political and ideological dispositions of the peoples that are to deploy the technology in question.

The question thus arises as to the sources of the patterns of dependence, interdependence and globalisation that characterise the contemporary international political economy. This question leads directly into some central, and often controversial, issues concerning the nature and central experiences of the modern international system: its experiences of industrial transformation, imperialism, war, peaceful 'management', the emergence of Transnational Corporations and continued structural differentiation.

Development and dependence

The first paradox to be noted in any consideration of contemporary dependence and interdependence is the increasing levels of dependence upon the external economy exhibited by most economies as they grow, develop and industrialise. Far from increasing autarky, growth and development often entails reduced independence from the international economy. Reflection reveals this outcome to be no paradox, for a developing and industrialising economy is likely to expand its range and volume of exports, while its industrial system places ever greater demands upon its own finite resources and, hence, generates a steadily increasing need for imports.

Industrialising economies have often been transformed from exporters of basic foods and materials into major importers of such commodities, as was Great Britain during the nineteenth and early twentieth centuries. Even resource-rich economies, like the United States of America, have moved from being major exporters of primary commodities like oil, into major importers during the twentieth century. For a resource-poor industrialising economy, such as that of Japan, there was never any choice but to accept chronic import dependencies from the early days of its industrialisation process.

The relationship between industrialisation and dependence is neither simple, nor unidirectional, however. Industrialisation may actually reduce an economy's dependence upon the international economy in a number of respects. The acquisition of greater technical competence and productive capability at home will reduce the economy's dependence upon the expertise of foreigners and the import of more advanced goods and services. Greater local knowledge and technical capacity might also assist with the location, development and exploitation of local sources of basic commodities and energy. The growth of the domestic market should also reduce the economy's dependence upon export markets and, hence, sensitivity to externally generated economic dislocation.

The development of the economy of the United States of America during the eighteenth and nineteenth centuries exemplifies just such a pattern of declining dependence upon the international economy. Initially a supplier of raw materials to its British colonial master, the young USA embarked upon an industrialisation process in which European technicians and European capital played a significant role. With the establishment of domestic competencies, a dynamic of indigenous capital formation and the emergence of a rapidly growing domestic market, the United States of America acquired a largely self-sustaining mechanism of growth and development, to which exports, while valuable, actually contributed little more than the 'icing on the cake'.

The development of economies with quite different characteristics of size and indigenous resource base can, in direct contrast, increase external dependencies substantially. Modern Singapore, as data in the last chapter indicated, is highly dependent upon both exports and imports. Indeed, her level of exports exceeds local GDP, with goods and commodities flowing through her ports for transhipment to markets overseas. The level of transhipment, when combined with her heavy commitment to the export of locally produced goods and services, renders Singapore massively dependent upon the external economy as a source of an extensive range of inputs and as a market for exports and shipments.

The longer term pattern of an economy's dependencies upon the international economy may thus be highly changeable. In the case of

Great Britain, as has been indicated, an exporter of primary commodities became, with the progress of the industrial revolution, a major exporter of manufactured goods and an increasing importer of a wide range of foodstuffs and commodities. As the competitive pressures from later industrialisers increased in international markets for manufactured goods, Great Britain then became increasingly dependent upon receipts from overseas investments and the 'export' of financial services, for the foreign revenues with which to pay for her ever rising levels of primary, and increasingly manufactured, imports.

Whatever the particular benefits brought to any individual economy by its international trade and, indeed, whatever role that trade has played in its economic development, it is difficult to establish any general propositions about the relationship between the overall level of industrialisation of an economy and the range and intensity of its *dependencies* upon the international economy or any of its member states. The range, quantitatively and qualitatively, of the dependencies associated with different societies at different levels of development is too great for any such simple generalisations, save for the proposition that true autarky is probably possible only for the most economically undeveloped of economies.

The material surveyed in Chapters 5 and 6 indicates much of the variety exhibited within the contemporary international political economy and, hence, the need for a discriminating analysis of the relationship between industrialisation and development, on the one hand, and developments in patterns of national economic dependence, on the other. It also leads into the complex question of the relationship between international trade, economic interdependence and globalisation: whether trade *reflects* the existence of revealed, or immanent, interdependencies; or whether international trade is a *cause*, and possibly the prime cause, of the dependencies that arise amongst national economies. This question highlights the significance of the concept of interdependence in discussions of the effects of international trade and of the feasibility, and limits, of neo-mercantilist policies in the contemporary international political economy.

Economic interdependence and globalisation: cause or consequence of international trade?

A major issue in the interpretation of core developments in the international political economy is, as has already been suggested at a number of points in this discussion, that of the relationship between economic developments and other forces that may shape the pattern of relations, political, military and economic, amongst the 'nations' of the world. Economistic perspectives on central developments in the international political economy, whether they be of the 'liberal' or 'Marxist' variant, here come into direct conflict with 'Realist' interpretations.

Economistic propositions about the influence of economic developments upon the wider character of the international political economy have long exerted a considerable influence. As was seen in Chapter 2, 'liberal' interpretations identified, in a Functionalist manner, the benign and progressive effects of a burgeoning international free-trade system. Once governments withdrew, in a spirit of enlightened self-interest, from undue interference with economic developments in general, and international trade in particular, a dynamic force for good would be unleashed upon the world stage. The new global division of labour, and 'national' specialisation of production, would increase prosperity, promoting ever higher levels of mutual advantage and harmony amongst the peoples of the world. Benign interdependence and a beneficial form of globalisation would thus be generated automatically by an emancipated free-trade system.

The theory of benign interdependence has remained popular since its heyday in the late nineteenth century. A more recent variant of this disposition is to be found, as was suggested in Chapter 3, in the Functionalist theory of European integration. Again the proposition was that, left to their own devices, economic processes would exert a constructive influence upon the political arena. Within Europe, if closer economic associations were allowed, and even encouraged, amongst the separate states, the beneficial results of that association would encourage further association, while the requirements for the regulation of the resulting patterns of economic interaction would generate requirements for new, Europe-wide political institutions, thereby laying the foundations of a new political community.

Such interpretations of the origins of, and prospects for, movement towards further European integration have been found wanting by critics of various persuasions. Critics of modern capitalism have tended to highlight the neglect of the influence of major capitalist actors in Functionalist interpretations of European integration. Neo-Functionalists have judged classical Functionalism as being far too simplistic in its hopes for automatic 'spill over' from the economic realms and, hence, neglectful of the more complex interaction between economic developments and political initiatives in such a complex process.[5] Economic Realists have contended that Functionalism completely reverses the causal relationship actually revealed in the history of relations between economic and political developments.

The Economic Realist assault upon the doctrines of benign interdependence and Functionalist integration highlights the negative as well as the positive aspects of economic association amongst societies. Economic associations actually involve many sources of friction and structural strain, which prompt caution before entry into closer relationships and which, when established, can generate considerable economic and political difficulties. Considerable prior political determination is therefore necessary before any set of economic societies will increase their openness to mutual trade and/or initiate measures of economic integration. Such prior political determination will sometimes reflect the influence of a dominant political and economic actor; it will sometimes, as in the case of a number of European states in the post-Second World War era, result from the commitment of influential political leaders in a number of countries to construct a new political and economic framework within which to conduct, and shape, their future relations.[6]

Global liberalisation and regional integration may both, therefore, require a high measure of political determination. Great Britain, in the nineteenth century, and the United States of America, in the post-Second World War era, were both able to exercise considerable, though often diffuse, influence upon a world economy that moved in an increasingly, albeit imperfectly, liberal direction. Both periods of 'hegemonic' influence permitted the substantial growth of international trade. The growth of trade, in turn, generated new patterns of international interdependence and trends towards increasing 'globalisation' that would not have been possible in the absence of a structure of 'political' influence in favour of peaceful, and increasingly open, relations amongst the states involved. Political determination, along the central Franco-German axis, within the immediate post-Second World War era provided a similarly nourishing environment for the growth of economic relations amongst the states of Western Europe and the resulting growth of new patterns, and levels, of interdependence.

Eras lacking 'benign' regional or 'global' politico-economic leadership demonstrate the quite different patterns of international economic association and 'interdependence' that may result. An increasingly fragmented political system inhibits the growth of patterns of international economic exchange and interdependence and may in the extreme destroy those that have been established in the past, as the case of the former Yugoslavia demonstrated, so tragically, in the early 1990s. Worse, the promotion of closer patterns of international economic association, and possible interdependence, in a fragmenting political order may be malevolently motivated. Nazi Germany, during the years immediately preceding the outbreak of the Second World War, directed her trade relations towards the progressive subordination of her neighbours in Central and Eastern Europe: to create a quasi-empire within the region.[7] Major patterns of international trade, interdependence and globalisation are thus constructed within a sympathetic political context but, in being constructed, may be equally directed towards benign or malign ends.

Exploitative and malignant patterns of interdependence and globalisation are certainly identified by 'Marxist' critics of the *laissez-faire* economic system. As was seen in Chapter 2, in the classical version of Marxism-Leninism, political actions, nationally and internationally, were determined by developments in the economic infrastructure. Cyclical developments and instabilities within the metropolitan capitalist economies drove the outward expansion of capitalist investment, exploitation and imperialism. The consequence was a world remade to the requirements of capitalism and its dominant class. While economic determinism may have fallen from fashion amongst many later 'Marxists', most continue to emphasise some degree of 'fit' between hegemonical political and ideological forms and the interests of socio-economically dominant classes. If the world exhibits growing economic interdependence and globalisation, critical 'Marxist' analysts would continue to identify the economic interests that lie behind, and are served by such developments.[8]

For Marxists of all varieties, contemporary interdependencies and globalisation are a direct product of the voracious expansionism of modern capitalism. Competitive specialisation and trade, imperialist acquisition and, more latterly, the global reach of Transnational Corporations have all been driven by the irrepressible pressures for the pursuit of profit and capital accumulation. Two of the characteristic features of the contemporary international economy have, in particular, been the products of this capitalist dynamic: the chronic asymmetries and imbalances of North-South economic relations; and the role, influence and structural impact of Transnational Corporations.

Structuralists, and some Economic Realists, would share some of Marxists' views of the role and persisting impact of modern imperialism and Transnational Corporations. However, these views remain methodologically possibilistic or mildly probabilistic and thus lack the degree of determinism associated with classical Marxist-Leninists and contemporary Dependency Theorists. The modification of prevailing structural conditions, and the functioning of TNCs, would thus be judged to be possibilities that obviated against the need for wholesale revolution, or Southern disengagement from involvement in the international capitalist system.

Imperialism

The historical impact of Western imperialism is, however, widely recognised to be a major source of the contemporary division of labour globally. Analysts of many persuasions are able to acknowledge the transformational impact wrought upon many of today's Less Developed Countries by their economic and political dominance by European powers, particularly during the latter half of the nineteenth century. With territorial divisions, transport patterns and the economic organisation of considerable swathes of the globe being wholly determined by the economic and administrative interests of the occupying powers, much of the modern 'Third World' provides clear testimony of the dramatic effects of colonialism.

Whether imperial control induced the positive underdevelopment of the colonies, or whether it merely accelerated the transformational effects of exposure to an increasingly differentiated, and fast changing, world economy, is a question to be answered primarily in terms of personal intellectual taste and political disposition. Whatever the source and effect of such a transformation, it secured its undeniably dramatic character largely from the pace at which it took place and this, for areas that were previously fairly remote from the centres of rapid economic change, was largely a consequence of the colonial experience.

The character of imperial political economy was also to be seen in a wider patterning of the international economic system, with its subordination to the 'needs' of a relatively small number of the more advanced industrial economies. Patterns of economic incentives were often sufficient to attract local elites, in areas free of formal imperial control, towards productive activities that complemented those of the industrial metropoles.[9] The elites of these areas were often attuned to international developments by their past associations with metropolitan areas, as with the Iberian connections of the elites of the Latin American countries, and/or contemporary educational, cultural and social experiences. 'Informal empire', in the words of neo-Marxists, was a ready option under such conditions of complementary elite outlooks and perceptions of self-interest.

Transnational Corporations

Transnational Corporations (TNCs) were also able to complement the processes of imperialist transformation in the world economy. A number of TNCs were born from colonial trading companies. Others arose to manage investments in primary production in those nominally independent economies that were being drawn, increasingly, into a complementary relationship with the industrial metropoles. A close relationship between the managers of the TNCs and local elites often resulted, with mixed consequences for the local economies. For good, or ill, the characteristic fate of an economy that was drawn into a colonial relationship with a capitalist metropole, was to become the producer and supplier of one, or a small number, of basic commodities that were of particular interest to the metropolitan economy and an importer, in turn, of a wide range of goods and services from its more developed partner: a pattern that a number of Less Developed Countries have found difficult to reverse, or even modify substantially, as was seen from the empirical evidence surveyed in Chapter 6.

The retreat of colonialism has not, itself, transformed the structure of the international political economy. The persisting role of the TNC has provided one major element of continuity. Indeed, to theorists of neo-colonialism, the Western TNC constituted the primary agent for the perpetuation of economic imperialism, in the aftermath of formal decolonisation.[10] Theories of neo-colonialism, however, remain inherently controversial and turn upon prior judgements about the intrinsically exploitative character of all relations of production and exchange within the capitalist order and negative judgements of the role of foreign economic interests and activities in the majority of Less Developed Countries.

The impact of TNCs upon patterns of production and exchange in the contemporary international economy is clear, however. Contentious prior theoretical judgements are not required to identify the transformation that TNCs have wrought upon patterns of manufacture and supply in many industries during recent decades. While imperialism and 'informal empire' may, in the past, have generated the LDCs' characteristic dependence on primary exports, modern TNCs are continuing to promote transnational patterns of production for manufactured goods and advanced services. Manufactured products that were formerly produced primarily within one industrial economy are increasingly assembled from components and sub-assemblies manufactured in subsidiaries in other countries. The consequence of such developments is to increase the volume, and change the content, of cross-border shipments. The 'dependencies' of individual economies have, in turn, been altered significantly by the rise of the TNCs' transnationally integrated systems of production, for they now no longer reflect past patterns of 'comparative advantage', but are now directed by the strategic interests and calculations of parent companies. The resulting 'interdependencies' are thus decreasingly 'natural', in any sense of that term, and are increasingly forms of *induced interdependence:* induced in the interests, and at the behest, of Transnational Corporations.

Technology, TNCs, international finance and globalisation

The intra-firm shipments, arising both from transnationally integrated production and traditional TNC shipments, now constitute a significant proportion of nominal international trade. Their nature and impact are, however, noticeably different from that of conventional trade, as will be seen further in Chapter 9. The scale of intra-firm trade is, however, one of the developments that some observers take to be a clear indicator of the progress of globalisation in the world economy. When the effect of such intra-firm shipments is added to that of the ever increasing scale of international financial flows and interactions, then the appeal of globalisation concepts can be readily understood.

The growth of the Transnational Corporations has been much encouraged by a range of contemporary technologies. Such technologies have, however provided opportunities; only rarely established imperatives. The disposition of TNCs to exploit the opportunities offered by modern technologies has been prompted, as much, by the opportunities and pressures arising from: the framework of policy generated within a politically fragmented international system; the appearance of possible tendencies towards regionalisation within the international political economy; the general increase of competitive forces within the international economy; and the global distribution of resources and markets. Technology exerts a discernible influence on each of these factors, but remains an analytically distinct, and ultimately secondary, factor.

A major, although often neglected, motive for the transnational mode of production is the range of opportunities presented by a world fragmented into nominally sovereign states. The existence of such states, each jealous of it own legal and regulative automony, has created a major obstacle to effective joint regulation and control of the activities of those enterprises that operate across 'national' frontiers. The age-old principle of 'divide and rule' applies directly to the relations between TNCs and the states in which they operate: the TNC as a centrally co-ordinated, unitary actor confronting a chronically divided set of self-regarding states.

The capacity of TNCs to act cohesively and strategically in their dealings with poorly co-ordinated states endows them with a number of potentially decisive advantages. In direct negotiations, or confrontations, a TNC can often threaten to relocate its operations in another country. The TNC also retains unique knowledge of its own operations: only it knows the strategic importance, or profitability, of its operations in any particular country; only it knows the details of its costings, accountancy procedures, investment plans and market strategies.

Those TNCs that operate transnationally integrated production systems are also able to take maximum advantage of the possibilities of transfer pricing.[11] When TNCs ship materials or components between their various subsidiaries in different countries they are able to 'price' those shipments, for reporting to national authorities, in ways that suit range of strategic purposes. The value added by the operations of a subsidiary in a country that charges relatively high levels of value-added tax can be made to disappear, only to reappear on the books of a subsidiary in a country with lower rates of value-added tax. Such magic can be made through the simple device of 'overpricing' the components sent to the subsidiary in the high tax country by the subsidiary in the low tax country. Alternatively, shipments from the subsidiary in the high tax country can be underpriced. In the extreme, value added by a subsidiary in a high tax country can be squeezed at both ends by overpricing incoming shipments and underpricing outgoing shipments.

Evasion of tax is not the only motive for manipulative transfer pricing. A TNC might wish to evade the exchange controls introduced by a country that wishes to protect the stability of its currency. Transfer pricing would allow the effective transfer of funds from the country in question, in a manner that remains invisible to all but the most discerning eyes. The movement of investment funds into, or out from, any economy, can also be orchestrated via suitable patterns of transfer pricing. Complexity, secrecy and the proliferation of national jurisdictions all combine to make transfer pricing, and its effects, extremely difficult to monitor and, therefore, regulate. California's 'unitary taxation' initiative marked one imaginative, but ultimately much troubled, response to the difficulties faced by separated political authorities when confronting transnationally integrated, and strategically cohesive, business enterprises.

The expansion of TNCs has not only been encouraged by the negative effects of political fragmentation within the international system, however; it has often been seen to serve the particular interests of specific states. The exploitation and control of valuable resources was one of the most significant, early motives for governmental support for the foreign operations of home-based companies. This was particularly true in the case of oil during the early years of the twentieth century and found its ultimate expression in the British government's acquisition of a significant stake in a major oil company — British Petroleum — and active support for its activities.[12] Here, the technology of the internal combustion engine generated an emergent dependence of central strategic significance which motivated, in turn, support for the expanding role of a TNC. This was the reverse pattern to that of a TNC orchestrating new patterns of international dependence for its own purposes.

State-sponsored expansion of TNCs may not always assume such a dramatic form as in the case of British Petroleum. However, a range of considerations has often prompted governments to smile upon the activities of TNCs. The balances of payments of many countries have been substantially aided by the receipts of earnings from the overseas operations of 'national' TNCs. Indeed, a number of more mature industrialised countries have found that earnings from the foreign investments and operations of such TNCs have filled a substantial part of the balance-of-payments' gap created by declining competitiveness in manufactured goods.

Governments have also been concerned to ensure the continued competitive strength of national firms, often through the development of new foreign associations. Some such associations have assumed the form of strategic alliances with established firms in other countries. More frequently, TNCs have been formed, or expanded, through the acquisition of existing foreign enterprises or the establishment of new subsidiaries in foreign countries. Acquisition and new construction can both serve the purposes of matching, or even defeating, emergent, or established, competition from firms in the countries into which the TNC expands its operations.

It is also possible that TNCs may be encouraged to expand their foreign operations by the unintended, and unexpected, consequences of governmental policies introduced with quite different motivations. Much of the expansion of US TNCs during the post-Second World War era has been attributed to the effects of a number of policies undertaken for a variety of strategic and economic reasons, including the wish to revive Europe after the devastation of war and the wish to subject US corporations operating abroad to equitable tax treatment, by such measures as allowances against taxes paid abroad on the operations of foreign subsidiaries.[13]

The policy framework created by the governments of the countries into which TNCs seek to expand their operations will influence decisions on the nature and extent of such expansion. Many governments have traditionally obstructed the absorption of existing enterprises by foreign-owned firms and/or required local equity participation in any enterprises that seek to operate within their areas of jurisdiction. Many Less Developed Countries were deeply suspicious of, and maintained hostile policies towards, TNCs until relatively recently. However, something of a sea change in attitudes towards TNCs occurred during the late

1980s with governments in both mature industrial countries, and many of the Less Developed Countries, converting to a more welcoming approach, with incentives and assorted inducements being deployed in the pursuit of inward investment and the perceived contribution that it might make to national industrial development.

The pattern of state policies will determine whether a TNC deems direct investment in a country to be worthwhile and, if so, the precise character and extent of that investment. The influence of policies may, however, be enhanced by a state's participation in a wider regional association. If a regional association of states is perceived to be set upon a course that is discriminatory against imports from external competitors, then firms based in that competitor country may judge it judicious to establish productive facilities within the frontiers of that region. Much of the recent Japanese interest in new plant within the European Community is believed to reflect just such concerns about the future course of European Community policies towards imports of manufactured goods.[14] The nature, extent and durability of patterns of interdependence, and globalisation, associated with the activities of Transnational Corporations may thus be substantially influenced by the evolving policy framework within which they find themselves operating.

Such policy influences upon TNCs complement traditional explanations of TNC activity, and expansion, in terms of 'offensive' oligopolistic behaviour against potential competitors, or 'defensive' responses by innovative firms to the progress of the product cycle, with its threat of declining competitiveness in the face of new centres of competition.[15]

Strategic partnerships may also be developed amongst large firms, many of which are Transnational Corporations. The purpose of these arrangements may range from market control through to burden sharing in costly areas of research and development. Whatever the motives, such partnerships generate new, and higher, levels of interconnections and 'interdependencies' amongst the economies in which these companies operate. These new levels and forms of association are, however, driven by the logic of the firms in question and *induce* the subsequent changes in the patterns of 'international' economic relationships.[16]

Financial integration

The interconnections and interdependencies that are commonly associated with the expansion of international financial transactions have many of the features in common with the activities of TNCs within the contemporary international political economy and are, in part, their corollary. Technological 'progress' has clearly facilitated an unprecedented level of international financial transactions and formal integration. Trading in shares across national frontiers, on a twenty-four hour basis, is one, new possibility. Funds can now be transferred internationally by purely electronic means. All manner of information pertinent to international financial transactions is available almost instantaneously, on a global basis.[17]

The technologically-based vision of contemporary international financial integration can be dazzling. It remains important, however, to disentangle those features of the contemporary situation which reflect a policy framework created by the past decisions, good and bad, and errors of governments and international institutions, those which continue only on the tolerance of political authorities and those that could survive even in the face of outright governmental opposition.

To address the last category first, it is clear that modern telecommunications have reduced the ability of governments, acting singly at least, to disrupt international communication flows and, hence, financial transactions. Where financial resources can be held 'off-shore', and where satellite communications remain functional, complex international transactions can now be conducted even by an inhabitant of a state with otherwise close frontiers. Satellite telephone calls from Kuwaitis, during the brief era of Iraqi occupation, demonstrated the difficulty of severing such channels of communication. However, such channels of communication could be disrupted by a sufficiently determined regime, in possession of more advanced jamming equipment. Moreover, the availability of external locations through which to orchestrate financial arrangements, and transactions, is crucial to an ability to evade any of the constraints imposed by governments.

Effective joint action by the governments of a number of the world economy's more influential states would substantially reduce the ability of other actors to maintain, and further develop, a highly integrated financial system. The establishment of such regulation would generate its own costs, but so will the further progress of a minimally regulated system. That most of the relevant governments have shown little interest in establishing joint regulation and control, thus far, and that such collaborative action would encounter intrinsic difficulties and costs, does little to qualify the general argument about the significance of governmental and contextual influences within the international financial system.

The past decisions and non-decisions of the governments of a number of influential states have, for good or ill, contributed substantially to the growth of the international financial system and its current level of integration. Governments, acting singly or severally, cannot secure the automatic compliance of the international financial operators. Post-war attempts to construct, and sustain, a fixed exchange rate system, under the auspices of the International Monetary Fund, faltered and failed in the early 1970s. However, the extent to which the collapse of an ordered international exchange rate regime was an inevitable consequence of the irrepressible increase of the volume and volatility of international monetary movements is a matter of continuing controversy. Susan Strange has propounded a plausible, alternative account of the international financial turbulence of the 1970s, 1980s and early 1990s in terms of the cumulative effects of policy failures by governments, such as those of the

United States of America, that occupied a position of central importance in the management of the international financial system.[18]

Strange's argument turns on five key 'non-decisions' that ultimately contributed to the financial turbulence of the 1970s onwards. These key 'non-decisions' came against a background of failings in the upper echelons of the international political economy since the 1950s: the failure of NATO allies to shoulder a fair share of the costs of European defence in the early 1950s, thus leaving the USA with a disproportionate financial burden and a major source of a persisting balance-of-payments deficit;[19] a collective failure to devise a standard procedure for handling bad international debts;[20] the spread of subsiding exports through tied aid and export credits and guaranties;[21] the failure to institutionalise restraints upon the ever growing mega-corporations of the USA and other leading industrial powers;[22] and, finally, the decision to reopen the London commodity markets for international trading and, hence, revive London as a centre of activity for international financial operators.[23]

Against such a background, five key 'non-decisions' were then to have a dramatic effect. The first of these 'non-decisions' was the failure to establish any authority over the foreign exchange markets after the failure of the Smithsonian Agreement on monetary stabilisation of 1971.[24] The second was the failure to return, eventually, to some modified form of gold-exchange standard for major currencies and, hence, the inability to develop new rules for international economic and financial adjustment, holdings of monetary reserves and general exchange rate management.[25] The third and fourth were the inability to establish a new *modus vivendi* with the major oil-producing countries, or to take seriously the plight visited upon the non-oil-producing Less Developed Countries, during the phase of major oil price rises in the 1970s.[26] The final international 'non-decision' of the period was the failure to establish a new 'lender of last resort' for the international 'community'.[27]

The consequence of this series of critical 'non-decisions' was to reinforce the effects of earlier domestic policy decisions made by the governments of some of the most influential members of the international financial system. The British government's decision to allow British banks to accept deposits and make loans in dollars in 1958 opened the door to the emergence of the eurodollar market from the early 1960s onwards. This was subsequently reinforced by the US government's permissive attitudes towards those overseas branches of US banks that also engaged in dollar deposit-taking and lending; its restrictive attitude towards lending practices within the USA; tax support for US banks competing in overseas financial markets; and a generally relaxed attitude towards the burgeoning of the eurodollar market, and its wider international financial implication.[28]

The combined effect of such a series of 'non-decisions', permissive policies and other contributory conditions, was to enhance substantially the scale and speed of international financial transactions, with the ratio of financial transactions in the London eurodollar market to the value of annual world trade increasing from 6:1 in 1979 to 25:1 by 1986.[29] That, in turn, substantially increased international financial volatility, the vulnerability of national currencies to speculative pressures and the availability of funds for (ultimately risky) loans to Developing Countries. Many of the roots of the Less Developed Countries' 'Debt Crisis' of the early 1980s, the dramatic stock market gyrations of October 1987 and the tribulations of the European Exchange Rate Mechanism (ERM) during 1992 and 1993, can thus be identified in a series of political decisions and 'non-decisions' made in, and by, the major economies during the preceding decades.

Many of the origins of the current condition of the international financial system may be clearly 'political'. This does not mean, however, that they may be readily modified, or even reversed, by even the clearest and most cogent of political decisions. Politicians often find disasters far easier to perpetrate than to resolve. The level of integration that has been permitted in international financial markets certainly increases the costs of effective regulation or reversal. Advanced technology has also found a fruitful home in the international financial system and that, too, will increase the difficulties of constraint and control. Governments also continue to face the problems of effective collaboration, where the costs of compliance are likely to be high and the short-term advantages of 'free-riding' may be considerable.

Such difficulties aside, the current level of integration in the international financial system, the 'dependencies' that it has spawned and the measure of globalisation that it has sustained, remains the product of a 'favourable' political context. Major disruption through widespread military conflict or significant measures of international regulation could both transform the level and nature of the bulk of current international transactions. Unlikely though either of these developments might be, their potential implications illustrate the basically conditional character of financial, and many other forms of interconnectedness, interdependence and globalisation.

Conclusions

Interpretations of the primary sources of contemporary interconnectedness, interdependence and globalisation are highly varied. A measure of automaticity is ascribed by those who see the growth of interdependence as an inevitable product of an universal tendency for the market system to expand its range and deepen its effects upon the economic affairs of humanity. A variant of such a perspective rests upon the identification of technological imperatives and opportunities as a primary source of ever closer connections amongst the peoples of the world, individually and collectively.

Such interpretations of the growth of contemporary interconnections, interdependence and globalisation contrast, markedly, with those that entertain more voluntaristic and political interpretations of the sources of the international political economy. At the initial level of analysis, such interpretations identify the effects of sequences of political decisions, and 'non-decisions', that have contributed critically to the shaping of the contemporary international order and its constituent relationships. Voluntarist and political interpretations are secure at this level of analysis. At the second level of analysis, however, more problematical questions arise as to whether the critical decisions and 'non-decisions' are, themselves, determined by deeper forces, and interests, within the prevailing economic order. Responses to such questions turn upon prior theoretical perspectives and personal dispositions. Such analytical persuasions are, however, central to the subsequent issue of whether it is more appropriate to view contemporary interdependencies and globalisation in terms of sets of discrete relationships in distinct 'issue areas', or whether they can be analysed effectively only in holistic terms.

Notes and references

1. For a further, and more formal, outline of the theory of comparative advantage see R.J. Barry Jones, *Conflict and Control in the World Economy: Contemporary Economic Realism and Neo-Mercantilism* (Brighton: Harvester/Wheatsheaf, 1986 (Humanities Press, in USA)), pp. 30-5 and 50-4; or, R.J. Barry Jones (ed.), *The Worlds of Political Economy: Alternative Approaches to the Study of Contemporary Political Economy* (London: Pinter Publishers, 1988), pp. 34-6 and 47-8.
2. Ibid.
3. See Andrew Walter, *World Power and World Money: The Role of Hegemony and International Monetary Order* (Hemel Hempstead: Harvester/Wheatsheaf, 1991), esp. p. 201.
4. For one of the seminal discussions of the economic implications of technology, see Harry G. Johnson, *Technology and Economic Interdependence* (London: Macmillan, for the Trade Policy Research Centre, 1975); and for a further discussion of the relationship between technology and the international political economy see: R. Williams, 'The international political economy of technology', in S. Strange (ed.), *Paths to International Political Economy*, (London: George Allen and Unwin, 1984), pp. 70-90.
5. See, for example, Robert O. Keohane and Stanley Hoffmann, 'Institutional change in Europe in the 1980s', in Robert O. Keohane and Stanley Hoffmann (eds.), *The New European Community: Decisionmaking and Institutional Change* (Boulder, Colo: Westview Press, 1991), pp. 1-39.
6. For a discussion of such a pattern of determination, see Barry Buzan, 'Economic structure and international security: the limits of the liberal case', *International Organization*, Vol. 38, No. 4 (1984), pp. 597-624.
7. For the classic analysis of which, see: Albert O. Hirschmann, *National Power and Structure of Foreign Trade* (Berkeley: University of California Press, (expanded edition), 1980 (originally published, 1945)).
8. See, for example, the work of Stephen Gill: S. Gill, *American Hegemony and the Trilateral Commission* (Cambridge: Cambridge University Press, 1991); and S. Gill (ed.), *Gramsci, Historical Materialism and International Relations* (Cambridge: Cambridge University Press, 1993).
9. A thesis fully explicated by Andre Gunder Frank, *On Capitalist Underdevelopment* (Bombay: Oxford University Press, 1975).

10. Kwame Nkrumah, *Neo-Colonialism: The Last Stage of Imperialism* (London: Heinemann, 1965); and Jack Woodis, *Introduction to Neo-Colonialism* (London: Lawrence and Wishart, 1967).
11. For a discussion of transfer pricing and allied practices see Robin Murray, *Multinationals Beyond the Market* (Brighton: Harvester, 1981).
12. See Anthony Sampson, *The Seven Sisters: The Great Oil Companies and the World They Made* (London: Hodder and Stoughton, 1975); and Daniel Yergin, *The Prize: The Epic Quest For Oil, Money and Power* (New York: Simon and Schuster, 1991).
13. See Robert Gilpin, *US Power and the Multinational Corporation: The Political Economy of Direct Investment* (New York and London: Basic Books/Macmillan, 1975), esp. pp. 128-34.
14. See, for example, V.N. Balasubramanyam and D. Creenaway, 'Economic integration and Foreign Direct Investment: Japanese investment in the EC', *Journal of Common Market Studies*, Vol. XXX, No.2 (June 1992), pp.175-93.
15. Gilpin, *US Power and the Multinational Corporation: The Political Economy of Direct Investment*, op. cit. pp. 118-26.
16. For a brief discussion of such strategic partnerships see Duncan Campbell, 'The globalizing firm and labour institutions', in P. Bailey, A. Parisotto and G. Renshaw, *Multinationals and Employment: The Global Economy of the 1990s* (Geneva: ILO, 1993), pp. 267-91, esp. pp. 278-81.
17. For a recent survey of finance and the international political economy see P.G. Cerny (ed.), *Finance and World Politics: Markets, Regimes and States in the Post-Hegemonic Era* (Aldershot: Edward Elgar, 1993).
18. Such interpretations are particularly associated with Susan Strange; see especially Susan Strange, *Casino Capitalism* (Oxford: Basil Blackwell, 1986).
19. Ibid., p. 31.
20. Ibid., pp. 32-3.
21. Ibid., pp. 33-6.
22. Ibid., 36-7.
23. Ibid., pp. 37-8.
24. Ibid., pp. 38-41.
25. Ibid., pp. 41-3.
26. Ibid., pp. 34-5.
27. Ibid., pp. 45-6.
28. Ibid., pp. 47-8.
29. Andrew Walter, *World Power and World Money*, pp. 196-7.

CHAPTER 8

Globalisation and levels of interdependence

The contemporary idea of globalisation highlights a fundamental theoretical and methodological issue in the study of the international political economy: that of atomistic versus holistic approaches. This issue also overlaps with the related agent-structure controversy in the study and analysis of human affairs.

Much of the data surveyed in Chapter 6 related to the circumstances of individual economies and their involvement in bilateral relationships with other economies or groups of economies. These data can also indicate more complex patterns of international interdependence and globalisation. However, the move from propositions about the conditions of individual states, or their bilateral relationships, to holistic forms of analysis constitutes a major step, theoretically and methodologically. Questions arise about the 'reality' of complex aggregates and the bases upon which they, and their characteristics, can be analysed. The answers to these questions remain profoundly controversial and intensely contested within the 'social sciences'.

The claims of atomistic modes of analysis

Atomistic approaches to the study and analysis of various aspects of human affairs rest upon simple and straightforward foundations. At the social level, individual human beings clearly exist; at the level of international relations, states, while they are not sentient human beings, exist in the eyes of their beholders and the myriad institutions that give them shape and 'reality'. States are thus real and significant for reasons that are more substantial than the fact that they are definitionally central to an international (or, properly speaking an interstate) system.

Established states also conduct economic, political and military relations with one another. Only the most extreme of philosophical idealists, or literary deconstructionists, would deny the physical reality of trade flows, international diplomatic relations or the many acts of war that have disfigured the bulk of human history. Such international interactions, while often posing considerable practical problems of measurement, are also amenable, in principle, to straightforward documentation and charting.

It is the basic simplicity of the behaviour of the central actors, and their bilateral interactions, that commends them as the most appropriate basis of studies of, and theories about, international relations and international political economy. A major controversy within international studies in the 1960s was stimulated by an assertion of the methodological primacy of unit-level analysis. The advocacy of the 'foreign policy decision-making' approach to the study of international relations, in the seminal work by R.C. Snyder, H.W. Bruck and B Sapin,[1] rested upon such a repudiation of the claims of international systems' analysis. The argument was that notions of an international system, that went beyond mere linguistic convenience, were unfruitful and inherently misconceived. All that 'really' existed, according to Snyder, Bruck and Sapin, were the discrete actors who were directly responsible for behaviour in the international arena. Indeed, even the identification of *states* as the primary actors in international relations might constitute an unwarranted measure of reification. Those who actually acted, and reacted, in international relations were the identifiable foreign policy decision-makers, individually or collectively, who determined, and authorised, the external actions that would subsequently be undertaken in the name of each 'state'.

Models of the international system might be constructed on either of two distinct methodological, and ontological, foundations. The first — purely *analytical* approach – makes no claims to the existential reality of an international system, but is based merely upon the proposition that useful analytical models can be based upon orderly selection from, and simplified descriptions of, the complexities of the prevailing patterns of international relations. The second — *concrete* conception of the international system — takes a further methodological step to claim existential reality for the international system and, therefore, a causal influence upon the behaviour of its constituent parts.

Both approaches to the study of international systems fell foul of serious methodological pitfalls, in the view of Snyder, Bruck and Sapin. The analytical approach to international systems was suspect because the need to produce intellectually manageable models of a highly complex reality led, inevitably, to a damaging, and ultimately unwarranted, level of simplification. The second — concrete view of international systems — rested upon the dubious proposition that the 'whole was greater than the sum of the parts' or, more specifically, that the complexities of the experienced world both generated, and overlaid, the existence and influence of a smaller set of forces or processes that were identifiable by, and only by, the analytically acute.

The defence of atomistic approaches to international relations thus rests upon the rejection of the claims of holistic perspectives, of all types. The relationship between empirical data and description is also straightforward within such an approach, for no explicit use has to be made of prior theoretical notions or any reference made to non-observable factors or processes. The atomistic approach is thus secure within its own terms of reference.

The holistic critique of atomistic approaches to international phenomena

Atomistic approaches to international relations and, hence, to the study of international interdependence, have been assailed from many quarters. The common element to all such critiques, however, is that atomistic forms of analysis miss a vital component of reality: the way in which complex patterns of interaction within human affairs assume a momentum and a force that exert a far more powerful influence upon development than any set of discrete actions and interactions, however varied and frequent.

Kenneth Waltz's Realist Structuralism

In the mainstream of international relations' theory, one of the most trenchant attacks upon atomistic forms of analysis was that of Kenneth Waltz, in his highly influential *Theory of International Politics.*[2] Condemning all such approaches to international relations as inherently *reductionist*, Waltz advocated an analytical approach that emphasised the centrality of distribution of capability, and potential 'power', amongst the member states of an international system. The particular patterns of interconnectedness in the political and military domain were thus both definitive of any international system and a major influence upon its internal developments.

Only such a 'structuralist' approach could, in Waltz's view, constitute a truly systemic approach to the study of international relations; and such an approach was, as presented by Waltz, quintessentially holistic, with the opportunities and constraints of individual actors being determined largely by their location within the system-wide distribution of capabilities and potential 'power'.

Waltz's advocacy of what came to be known as 'neorealism', and latterly 'Structural Realism',[3] evoked an intense debate within the international relations' profession. Interestingly, few of the more vigorous critics of Waltz's position advocated a simple reversion to an atomistic approach. In this reaction to a purportedly theory of the international *political* system, there were strong echoes of a similar, and often earlier, critical response to simpler models of the structure of power and influence within the international political economy. Marxist and post-Marxist resonances were thus to be detected in a number of the reactions to Waltz[4] as they were clearly present in a number of earlier critical approaches to the international political economy and, in particular, critiques of the theory of benign hegemony.[5]

The elusive point about holistic approaches to the international political economy is that their foundations lie in the same complex sets of actions and interactions that are analysed by atomistic approaches. Nothing in atomistic forms of analysis denies the range and complexity of the empirical world that is being studied. What holistic theories do, however, is to claim that 'reality' encompasses more than is to be seen at first glance. Complexity thus configures into definitive patterns of influence and development, which can be appreciated properly only through the prism of the appropriate theory.

The agent-structure issue

A parallel expression, of the complex and problematical relationship between the behaviour of individual actors and the holistic phenomena that they may collectively create, is to be found in the 'agent-structure' issue, that has recently attracted considerable attention within the study of international relations.[6] This is more than merely a matter of 'levels of analysis' for it confronts the issue of the ontological status of both 'individuals' and aggregate entities in human affairs. The problems here can be illustrated by two extreme arguments. The first possible argument is that it is only individuals that really exist and that all other conceptions of the human condition involve unwarranted invocation of imagined collectivities: that, in the view of some ultra-liberals 'there is no society!'. The opposing argument contends that holistic phenomena exist and are capable of exerting a causal influence upon human developments that transcends the volition and expectations of any of the human beings involved. Both positions offer considerable attractions to those who are psychologically disposed towards their respective appeals, but both leave substantial problems unresolved.

Extreme individualism leaves the question of the origin of human ideas and understandings in an unsatisfactory backwater. The acquisition of such intellectual equipment might be attributed to spontaneous, and unaided, development by each individual, but this bears no correspondence to the patterns of language acquisition and intellectual development of most human infants. The alternative is to acknowledge the 'social' character of intellectual development and cultural acquisition, but simply evade its wider implications for the analysis of human affairs.

Extreme holism, in contrast, drifts dangerously close to metaphysical determinism. All human volition, let alone the influence of any individuals, is now denied a significant role in human developments. Some feature, force, compulsive process or extraterrestrial influence is identified as decisive. Human consciousness can only be a derivative, and an imperfect reflection, of the determining force that is intrinsic to the aggregate reality of the human condition. The most to which the individual can aspire is an appreciation of the imperatives inherent in the human system: any ambition for their modification or reversal would clearly be futile.

The problematical relationship between individual action and the nature, and development, of aggregate human phenomena has been a matter of more than academic interest. The issue confronted revolutionary Marxists with acute difficulties, and dilemmas, during the later years of the nineteenth century and the early years of the twentieth. Marxist revolutionaries wondered whether they could merely sit back and await the arrival of the inevitable socialist revolution passively, or whether the inevitable socialist revolution would be 'inevitable' only if they initiated appropriate actions.[7] The debate over this issue was one of theoretical ferocity and practical anxiety. It has, moreover, remained a problematical issue for those who continue to identify themselves as Marxists.

Structuration and the construction of complex systems of human activity

A systematic resolution of the agent-structure issue would thus be most helpful for students of human affairs. The discussion towards the ends of Chapters 1 and 2 suggested the contribution that could be made by a *constructionist* perspective. This approach starts from the proposition that human behaviour is, in the first instance, determined by the beliefs, understandings and expectations of the individual human actor. Such beliefs, understandings and expectations are, in turn, derived primarily from the 'society' within which the individual is educated and further influenced by his, or her, lifetime set of experiences. Most significantly, however, the individual actor interacts with other actors who, by virtue of a common 'culture', share many of the same beliefs, understandings and expectations. Each individual's set of beliefs, understandings and expectations is thus likely to be reinforced by the behaviour of all those other members of the same society whose own behaviour is directed by a comparable set of beliefs, understandings and expectations. The actions of each individual thus contribute to a pattern of broadly similar actions by other individuals. Moreover, dissonant behaviour by any individual is challenged, and ultimately constrained, by the adverse or uncomprehending reactions of others. A collective 'reality' is thus created and recreated constantly by the complementarity amongst the actions of individuals and the sets of shared beliefs, understandings and expectations upon which they rest. Cohesive societies thus rest upon sets of mutually supporting intersubjectivities amongst their members and constitute a 'reality' that is more than, and has greater durability and force than, the behaviour of its individual members, but which remains a product of the sum of complementary behaviours.

Such a perspective upon human conduct and institutions corresponds to Anthony Giddens' concept of 'structuration'.[8] This perspective, while still controversial, finds ready application at the level of well-established, and widely recognised, societies. The 'fit' between the actions of individuals and the explicit beliefs, understandings and expectations of other members of a society is readily observable, where it exists, and dramatic by its absence, where it does not. The fate of individuals who find themselves trying to function in unfamiliar societies illustrates the point with considerable force.

The appropriateness of concepts of structuration to international relations is, however, a little more problematical. The actors in international relations are not sentient human beings like the members of normal societies. This difference lies at the heart of the difficulties encountered by the concept of 'international society'.[9] Structuration remains a valid concept at the international level, however, if it is recognised that the processes involved will be more complex than those of domestic societies, will operate at a number of 'levels' and be mediated by a range of complex institutions including state bureaucracies, political structures and information systems. The complexity and distance from most sentient human beings of much that takes place at the international level of activity reinforces Margaret Archer's wider contention that it is necessary to maintain, and operate, an analytical distinction between the levels of agent and structure in the analysis of social developments.[10] The explanation of fundamental change reduces, in Archer's view, to one of spontaneous changes of collective outlook unless the mechanisms operative at the structural level can be accessed.

The theories that are required for the description and analysis of complex, holistic phenomena in human affairs thus operate at two levels. The validity of holistic notions has to rest upon appropriate philosophical and methodological foundations; foundations that sometimes sail close to metaphysics, but that always involve basic propositions about the 'realities' that underlie the complexities of life that present themselves to the senses. Such fundamentals of any holistic approach remain essentially 'meta-theoretical', in that they furnish a broad interpretative framework, rather than propositions about reality that are, in any precise manner, testable against that reality.[11] All holistic theories of international relations and the international political economy ultimately rest upon some such 'meta-theoretical' foundations, with the Platonic form[12] of 'scientific realism' frequently filling this role.

Holistic approaches to international relations also involve substantive levels of theory, however. Such theories conventionally embrace primary propositions about the fundamental factors or forces that drive international relations and/or the international political economy and secondary propositions that identify a number of empirical phenomena that are deemed to be shaped by those fundamental factors or forces. The structure of such theories is akin to that of Noam Chomsky's theory of the deep structural foundations of all human languages. The theory rests upon basic propositions about the implications of the human nervous system for the basic structures of all languages and, hence, the argument that all human languages, despite their superficial diversity, could be reduced to, or derived logically from, the deep structure if only the 'transformational rules', whereby deep structures are actually translated into surface languages, could be identified.

The example of Chomsky's structural theory of language illustrates the difficulties that commonly attend holistic theories of human activity. Day-to-day 'realities' are highly diverse. Without an ability to specify appropriate transformational rules, attributions of causal force to deep structural factors and forces remain merely a matter of interpretative plausibility. Evidence will be readily found to 'support' the propositions of the favoured theory, but the same empirical 'reality' will invariably provide evidence for alternative approaches.

A number of criteria can be identified to assist judgements between contending, substantive theories of complex phenomena in human affairs. The range of the theories is one such criterion: how wide a range of phenomena can be accommodated without strain. The ability to deal effectively with change is also important for an acceptable theory. A capacity to provide a plausible account of theory generations is also highly valuable: a capacity that should include both self-explanation and an explanation of the emergence of contending theories. However, in the absence of any means of 'testing' such theories conclusively, their acceptance will remain, to a degree, an act of faith.

Holistic theories of the contemporary international political economy: complex interdependence and the radical critiques

The study of the international political economy has witnessed the rise of a number of popular perspectives that are, to a greater or lesser extent, holistic. These perspectives, themselves, throw into sharp relief the range of issues encountered by holistic approaches to the study of human affairs, including: the role of Functionalist influences; the problematical relationship between rationalistic and reflective forms of theory and analysis; and the meta-theoretical character of most genuinely holistic theories of international relations.

Complex interdependence

One of the more influential forerunners of the contemporary notion of globalisation was the concept of complex interdependence. An evaluation of the nature and significance of this concept, however, goes to the heart of many of the issues raised by holistic approaches to international relations and the international political economy.

As presented by Robert Keohane and Joseph Nye, the idea of complex interdependence was seen as signalling a new, and highly significant, condition within the international system: a condition in which, as was shown in Chapter 3, the traditional hierarchy of policy issues has been dissolved, multiple channels of contact amongst peoples have been established and the utility of force has been dramatically reduced. Patterns of interdependence were clearly central to such a 'condition': their density and salience configuring a new set of constraints and opportunities for the states that interacted in the contemporary system.

Keohane and Nye presented complex interdependence as an 'ideal type', with no necessary, simple correspondence in reality. However, with such statements as: 'we shall argue that complex interdependence sometimes comes closer to reality than does realism',[13] they left the door sufficiently ajar for those who were so minded to proclaim complex interdependence as *the* model of the new international reality. Later attempts to clarify the concept of complex interdependence as a clearly heuristic, and ideal type, model,[14] could not halt the deepening hold of such a view of the international condition. Indeed, in a later paper with Stanley Hoffmann on developments within the European Community, Robert Keohane, himself, employed the concept of complex interdependence as a signifier of an empirical condition: 'Boundaries are difficult to draw in a world of complex interdependence'.[15]

The concept of complex interdependence thus exemplifies the problems of holistic concepts of interdependence and globalisation. It is often unclear as to whether the idea is intended to serve as a mere metaphor or a statement about a real condition. To the extent that complex interdependence is maintained as an empirical condition, it lies on the cusp between aggregative notions of a complex international 'reality', in which the condition reflects the simple density and salience of a multiplicity of interactions and interdependencies, and genuinely holistic theories of the international political economy, with central significance attributed to underlying, and often non-observable, factors and forces. This problem is widespread throughout the study of international relations, specifically, and of human affairs, generally. A model that is nominally heuristic in its nature and intent, constitutes a series of suppositional statements about the world: statements of what *might* be expected to take place *if* specific conditions prevail. The elaboration of such a model takes place through a series of rationalistic arguments. It is, however, all too easy for such rationalistic arguments to metamorphose from a suppositional into an imperative form: that certain consequences *must* follow upon specific conditions or developments because the logic of the analysis requires that they do so. The imperative drift in rationalistic modes of analysis is, as will be seen, a common tendency within most holistic approaches to international relations

Many notions of globalisation are effective extensions of the earlier notion of complex interdependence and perpetuate its inherent ambiguities. Moreover, they also share its strong echoes of Functionalism, in the expectation of the clear and consistent implications of the growth of economic interconnectedness and interdependencies.

Radical holistic conceptions of contemporary interdependence and globalisation

Radical theories of hegemony and dependency in the international political economy are both examples of substantive, holistic theories that encounter the difficulties outlined in the preceding section of this chapter. Their acceptance thus, involves some 'act of faith'; but an act of faith that does not automatically discount their value or impact.

Radical theories of global hegemony reject the benign account of international hegemony provided by those 'liberals,' and the many Economic Realists, who are interested in the orderly management of a free-trade international economy. The purpose of the critics of such comfortable conceptions of hegemony is to craft a critical analysis of the contemporary international political economy that exposes its exploitative character while avoiding the mechanistic character of much of the traditional Marxist critique of the capitalist economic order.

Gramscian hegemonical holism

Critical theories of international hegemony often give considerable emphasis to concepts, and analytical perspectives, associated with the Italian revolutionary, Gramsci. The resultant perspective combines a number of central theoretical and methodological propositions: a rejection of methodological individualism; an abandonment of the excessively deterministic materialism of earlier 'Marxisms'; and a central focus upon the complex sources, and dynamics, of dominant hegemonic 'blocs' and anti-hegemonic reactions. One of the central points, here, is that hegemony in the international political economy is not be equated simply with the dominant managerial role of a leading state, or small group of states: the hegemony in question is really that of dominant 'class' or 'bloc', encompassing the leading roles in the economic, social and political lives of the dominant states and, thereby, the maintenance of a complementary global structure of 'knowledge', production and exchange.[16]

Critical perspectives upon international hegemony thus make central reference to a complex set of interconnections amongst a number of dimensions of the human experience that are often viewed separately by more empiricist 'social sciences'. These interconnections do not entail vulgar conspiracies, or even require continuous recognition by their participants. The world of such 'hegemonies' is a holistic world in constant evolution, in which developments are not narrowly determined by conditions within the economic infrastructure, but are, rather, constrained by a more complex set of social, political and economic circumstances, and their interactions. This is not an entirely voluntaristic world, but a world that encompasses more possibilities than those allowed by many traditional interpretations of 'Marxism'.

Much of the appeal of Gramscian analyses of the contemporary international political economy is its evasion of the apparent simplicities and undue determinism of earlier versions of Marxism. Of particular value is the identification of the pivotal role of prevailing ideas; their complex origins in the economic, social and political domains of human life; and their capacity to spread internationally in a manner conducive to the interests of dominant groupings.

The incorporation of an emphasis upon the central role of the ideological component of the struggle between hegemonic and anti-hegemonic forces also leaves it suspended across the divide between rationalistic and reflective approaches to human affairs.[17] Traditional 'Marxism' rested upon clear rationalistic foundations, with analysis presenting the findings of omniscient observers about the realities that underlie, and must underlie, day-to-day empirical 'realities' and developments. Approaches that identify the ideational foundations of human action, in contrast, derive from more 'reflective' foundations. The Gramscian approach straddles these two contending perspectives in a manner that offers the best of both worlds to some enthusiasts, but that appears dangerously over-extended to more critical commentators. It is possible, however, that purity in a rationalistic or a reflective direction is impossible in analysis that seeks to grapple with the intrinsic complexities, and multidimensionality, of international relations. Holistic approaches that do not remain determinedly pure in their presumptions and procedures are certainly likely to encounter a difficult transition from rationalistic to reflective perspectives, or vice versa, at some point, or points, in their analytical progress.

The general broadening of the analytical perspective, and widening of the empirical embrace, of a Gramscian approach to the international political economy moves it further into the realms of elusive holism and 'untestable' meta-theory. Indeed, a perspective that necessarily involves movement across the rationalistic-reflective divide inevitably assumes meta-theoretical characteristics and revives the agent-structure issue, raising central questions about the precise relationship between human volition and 'structural' influences in any specific situation or development. Acceptance of such a theoretical view of the contemporary condition thus rests less upon clear empirical verification or falsification, and more upon acceptance of a long and complex set of interpretative arguments. This does not invalidate such an approach, but does increase the psychological element in judgements about its acceptability, or otherwise. It also highlights many of the problems characteristically associated with holistic views of the international system and the international political economy.

The holism of World System of Capitalism and Dependency (Dependencia) Theories

Related, although in many ways distinctive, holistic perspectives upon the modern global political economy are those of World System of Capitalism[18] and Dependency (or Dependencia) Theory.[19] The central concept of these initially rationalistic analytical perspectives is, as was suggested in Chapter 2, that of a world system of capitalism which subjects its member economies to a set of constraints and opportunities that go beyond the constituents of any given bilateral relationship within the capitalist world system. The historical experiences of capitalist 'progress', and of underdevelopment, through interactions within the evolving world capitalist system, has driven the Advanced Industrial Countries towards ever greater prosperity, while leaving the Less Developed Countries in a condition of chronic structural weakness.

The characteristically narrow export-based, distorted socio-economic structure, and fragile, and ultimately dependent, political system are all seen to be the direct consequences of the underdeveloping impact of the capitalist system upon Less Developed Countries. The influence of such a disastrous historical experience carries itself forward into the contemporary world, in which the damaged Less Developed Countries struggle, vainly, against the entrenched economic and political bastions of the Advanced Industrial Countries: bastions built upon, or much reinforced by, their past ability to exploit the Less Developed Countries. It is in the enduring, structural character of this unequal, world-wide struggle between the beneficiaries and the victims of past imperialism, both formal and informal, that the holistic nature of the contemporary global political economy is seen by Dependency Theorists.

The dynamic of capitalism domestically and globally, and the influences of major structural differentiation amongst national economies, is also the major source of the behaviour of individuals and groups within the various categories of states in the international political economy. The owners and managers of capital in the Advanced Capitalist Countries sustain exploitative patterns of economic production and exchange in a virtually amoral manner. The non-owning groups in Advanced Industrial Countries have, according to Dependency Theory, collaborated with this structure 'voluntarily', because of the disproportionate benefits that they also receive from an internationally exploitative economic system. The local elite groups within dependent societies are effectively co-opted by the international capitalist order and collaborate in the continued exploitation of their own societies and their fellow citizens. The exploited masses in the dependent societies have little choice, locally or internationally, but to accept their exploited and systematically disadvantaged lot until such time as the general structure of their societies relationships with the wider capitalist order can be transformed in some way.

Both World System of Capitalism and Dependency Theory are thus critical holistic perspectives, with clearly rationalistic foundations, that identify structural conditions and dynamics that have a substantial conditioning influence upon the behaviour of participating human individuals and groups. Less reflective in their methodological foundations than Gramscian perspectives upon global hegemony, they also limit the range of feasible human responses to the conditions identified with such critical force. The extensive empirical and explanatory embrace of World System of Capitalism and Dependency Theory, however, places them firmly in the realms of meta-theory, with all the difficulties of substantiation thus entailed. However, they are meta-theories upon which the recent experiences of the Newly Industrialising Countries and the mixed fortunes of many Advanced Industrial Countries have cast some challenging rays of light.

Conclusions

Atomistic approaches to international interconnectedness and interdependence are relatively straightforward from a methodological point of view. They work with the data of the observable world and are content to construct models of the contemporary condition in a purely aggregative manner. No worries are entertained about the precise extent to which the set of contemporary international interactions might constitute something more than the sum of their parts; complexity, and density, of interactions remains no more than simple complexity and density. Similarly, there are no concerns over the existence and effects of non-observable factors or forces; for atomists, in human affairs, 'what you see is what you get!'

Holists are fundamentally critical of the simplistic empiricism of atomistic approaches to the study of human affairs, of all forms. Holists, however, encounter, to a greater or lesser extent, a range of serious methodological and philosophical problems that profoundly affect their acceptability. Rationalism is prevalent throughout the range of holistic theories and approaches. Indeed, it is probably the case that rationalism is an essential ingredient of any holistic propositions about any aspect of human activity. Thus the 'reflective' features of the Gramscian approach to global hegemony rest upon strongly rationalistic foundations; a complication that raises serious questions about the sustainability of pure 'reflective' approaches. The danger of all such rationalistic perspectives is that the persuasiveness of the internal argument dominates, and ultimately displaces, the complexities and curiosities of the empirical world, that is nominally being examined. The meta-theoretical character of holistic theories both promotes such a tendency and preserves them from subsequent challenges from the realm of empirical experience.

The rationalism of holistic approaches to international relations and the international political economy are also often prone to Functionalist tendencies. Concepts of complex interdependence and benign globalisation reveal strong Functionalist currents. Strains of a 'critical Functionalism' can be also detected in the Gramscian, World System of Capitalism and Dependency Theory critiques of the correspondence between many contemporary conditions, and arrangements, and the 'requirements' of global capitalism.

The problems posed by some holistic approaches for any simple division between rationalistic and reflective approaches to the study of the international realm are paralleled in the difficult questions posed for any neat solution to the agent-structure issue. Holism commonly entails structural notions, but has to specify with great care the relationship between any structures and the activities of participants, be they states, enterprises or real individuals.

Holism thus highlights the problems of determinism in theories of human activity; an issue that is closely related to that of agent-structure. If structures are held to have a life and an impact 'of their own', how far can sentient human beings influence developments? World System of

Capitalism and Dependency Theory tend towards such a form of structural fatalism, envisaging significant change only on the basis of cataclysmic developments which may, themselves, be primarily shaped by 'objective' disorders in the World System of Capitalism.

If, in contrast, the activities of sentient and self-volitional individuals are all-important, then how far can structures be held to enjoy any enduring reality? Gramscian theory remains seriously hesitant here. Perspectives upon human activity and institutions that are based upon such notions as social and political construction, or structuration, offer a methodological resolution to the issues of determinism and voluntarism questions by moving analysis into the more modest realms of possibilism and probabilism. The resolution offered by the perspectives of constructionism and structuration theory, however, postpones, rather than incorporates, the examination of many issues concerning substantive developments, and their theoretical appreciation.

The range of methodological and theoretical issues raised by the contrasting claims of atomistic and holistic approaches to the study of international interdependence and, where appropriate, globalisation do not minimise the appeal or importance of the contending perspectives. The tastes and dispositions of each student, or analyst, will ultimately determine the choice of general level of approach. Both, however, require an appreciation of the range and complexity of the empirical material concerning the current pattern, and development, of international interactions and exchanges. Both also lead into unresolved issues concerning the ultimate impact of various patterns of interconnectedness or interdependence upon the international system and its central participants.

Notes and references

1. R.C. Snyder, H.W. Bruck and B. Sapin, (eds.), *Foreign Policy Decision-Making: An Approach to the Study of International Politics* (New York: Free Press, 1962).
2. Kenneth Waltz, *Theory of International Politics* (Reading, Mass.: Addison-Wesley, 1979).
3. On which term, see B. Buzan, C. Jones and R. Little, *The Logic of Anarchy: Neorealism to Structural Realism* (New York: Columbia University Press, 1993), esp. Ch. 1.
4. See, in particular, Robert W. Cox, 'Social forces, states and world orders: beyond international relations theory', in R.O. Keohane (ed.), *Neo-Realism and Its Critics* (New York: Columbia University Press, 1986), pp. 204-54.
5. See, for example, S. Gill and D. Law, *The Global Political Economy: Perspectives, Problems and Policies* (Hemel Hempstead: Harvester/Wheatsheaf, 1988), esp. pp. 76-80.
6. For the seminal discussion of which see Alexander Wendt, 'The agent-structure problem in international relations theory' *International Organization*, Vol. 41, No. 3 (Summer 1987), pp. 335-70; and see also Alexander Wendt, 'Bridging the theory/meta-theory gap in international relations', *Review of International Studies*, Vol. 17, No. 4 (October 1991) pp. 383-92; and Alexander Wendt, 'Levels of analysis vs. agents and structures: part III', *Review of International Studies*, Vol. 18, No. 2 (April 1992), pp. 181-5.

7. G.V. Plekhanov, *The Role of the Individual in History* (London: Lawrence and Wishart, 1940).
8. Anthony Giddens, *The Constitution of Society: Outline of the Theory of Structuration* (Cambridge: Polity Press, 1984).
9. See, on these, Roy E. Jones, 'The English School of international relations: a case for closure', *Review of International Studies*, Vol. 7, No. 1 (January 1981), pp. 1-13; and R.J. Barry Jones, 'The English School and the political construction of international society', in Barbara Allen Roberson (ed.), *The English School Revisited* (forthcoming).
10. Margaret S. Archer, *Culture and Agency: The Place of Culture in Social Theory* (Cambridge: Cambridge University Press, 1988), esp. Preface and Chs. 1 and 9.
11. On the concept of 'meta-theory' see F.G. Castles, *Politics and Social Insight* (London: Routledge and Kegan Paul, 1971).
12. As exemplified by Plato's doctrine of the 'shadows in the cave'. See Plato, *The Republic* (various editions).
13. R.O. Keohane and Joseph S. Nye, *Power and Interdependence: World Politics in Transition* (Boston: Little, Brown, 1977).
14. R.O. Keohane and J.S. Nye, '*Power and Interdependence* revisited', *International Organization*, Vol. 41, No. 4 (Autumn 1987), pp. 725-53.
15. Robert O. Keohane and Stanley Hoffmann, 'Institutional change in Europe in the 1980s', in Robert O. Keohane and Stanley Hoffmann (eds.), *The New European Community: Decisionmaking and Institutional Change* (Boulder, Colo.: Westview Press, 1991), pp. 1-39.
16. See, in particular, S. Gill and D. Law, *The Global Political Economy: Perspectives, Problems and Policies* (Hemel Hempstead: Harvester/Wheatsheaf, 1988); S. Gill, 'Historical materialism, Gramsci, and international political economy', in C.N. Murphy and R. Tooze, *The New International Political Economy* (Boulder, Colo.: Lynne Rienner Publishers, 1991), pp. 33-75; S. Gill, *Gramsci, Historical Materialism and International Relations* (Cambridge: Cambridge University Press, 1993); E. Augelli and C.N. Murphy, *America's Quest for Supremacy and the Third World* (London: Pinter Publishers, 1988).
17. The distinction drawn by Robert O. Keohane, in 'International institutions: two approaches', *International Studies Quarterly*, Vol. 32 (1988), pp. 379-96.
18. See especially: Immanuel Wallerstein, *The Capitalist World-Economy*, (Cambridge: Cambridge University Press, 1979); and Robert W. Cox, *Production, Power and World Order: Social Forces in the Making of History* (New York: Columbia University Press, 1978).
19. See, for the most succinct account, Andre Gunder Frank, *On Capitalist Underdevelopment* (Bombay: Oxford University Press, 1975).

CHAPTER 9

The consequences of international interdependence and globalisation

For some observers, the development of complex forms of international interdependence, and the continued advance of globalisation, has profound and wide-ranging implications for the human condition. Contemporary developments in many patterns of international interactions generate a range of important effects within the international system and the international political economy. However, the depth and breadth of these effects, and their durability and even potential reversibility, are issues that require further interrogation.

A major issue is immediately encountered in any consideration of the consequences of international interdependence or globalisation. This concerns the difficult question as to whether international interdependence, or globalisation, is a *cause* of a range of significant conditions or primarily their *consequence*. Thus, in some discussions, developments in the patterns of international trade are identified as a major source of growing international interdependence. In other accounts, the intensification of complex forms of interdependence, and globalisation, constitutes a major pressure for individual states to develop and intensify their trade relations. Again, in some discussions of globalisation, the phenomenon is seen as a consequence of the joint 'decisions' of major states and enterprises; while in others it is identified as a compelling constraint upon the actions of both states and private economic interests.

The apparent confusion over interdependence and globalisation as causes or consequences of other significant conditions stems from the nature of complex forms of interdependence, and any tendencies towards globalisation. Such phenomena are both consequences of the actions of states and major economic enterprises and significant influences upon their future behaviour. In many respects, therefore, complex forms of international interdependence and/or globalisation demonstrate the nature and effect of structuration processes in the international arena.

The Janus-faced character of complex international interdependence, or globalisation, is thus an abiding difficulty and a considerable source of potential confusion. Any review of the supposed effects of interdependence, or globalisation, has to handle this intrinsic ambiguity with considerable care. There are, however, many areas in which the development of these conditions, whatever their origins, may have considerable potential implications, whether they be upon the effectiveness of 'national' economic policies; the role of non-state economic actors; the limits of democracy within separate states; the shaping of foreign and defence policies; or the future prospects of global peace and prosperity. Conflict rather than consensus may thus be the ultimate effect of many forms of growing international economic association.

Interdependence, globalisation and the effectiveness of 'national' economic and industrial policies

Richard Cooper outlined the classic case for the impact of international interdependence upon 'national' economic policies. Cooper defined interdependence in somewhat different manner from that adopted in this discussion. For him, interdependence denoted 'the *sensitivity* of economic transactions between two or more nations to economic developments within those nations'.[1] Such a definition of interdependence locates it closer to interconnectedness, in a manner akin to that of Richard Rosecrance and his associates, than to the dependence-based notions of Robert Keohane and Joseph Nye, David Baldwin, or this study. This definitional difference does not diminish the pertinence of the consequences of interdependence identified by Cooper, for interconnectedness is often associated with true interdependencies and constitutes, in itself, a major ingredient of globalisation.

Richard Cooper's central view is that the growth of international interdependence 'by joining national markets, erodes the effectiveness of... policies and hence threatens national autonomy in the determination and pursuit of economic objectives'.[2] National autonomy, which is conceptually distinct from either economic autarky or political sovereignty,[3] is a measure of a government's 'ability to frame and carry out objectives of domestic economic policy which may diverge widely from those of other countries...'.[4] The growth of interdependence, primarily through increases in interconnectedness in trade and finance that erode the former fragmentation of markets, will then reduce national autonomy in the fields of monetary policy,[5] tax policy,[6] the regulation of business enterprises,[7] domestically redistributive programmes[8] and policies aimed at influencing an economy's external balance of trade and payments.[9]

Three features of the interdependent world, of Cooper's model, are particularly pertinent to the diminishing effectiveness of policy instruments in these policy areas: international financial integration; the increasing globalisation of the market for a wide range of manufactured goods; and the scale and range of operation of Transnational Corporations. International financial integration facilitates the rapid international movement of funds in response to changes in national economic conditions, real or imagined. Real alterations in the relative interest rates available in various economies can precipitate rapid and substantial flows of money in pursuit of higher short-term returns. Perceived changes in the economic prospects of respective countries can stimulate precautionary flights of capital from 'weaker' to 'stronger' economies. The policies of states that maintain financial openness are increasingly constrained by an awareness of such reactions to a wide range of initiatives and developments.

The globalisation of the market for a wide range of manufactured goods and services has been complemented by the increasing speed of technological diffusion. This has steadily enhanced the sensitivity of many economies to conditions elsewhere and increased their exposure to external constraints. The combination of lower wages and increasingly sophisticated productive technology by foreign competitors places local producers under increasing pressures to reduce unit costs by decreasing labour costs and/or introducing ever more productive equipment. Official policy is also increasingly constrained to complement such reactions by business enterprises rather than to pursue policies that might threaten, or retard, the local competitive response.

Transnational Corporations (TNCs) contribute both to international financial volatility and to alterations in the manner, and location, of production and the flow of goods, and services, across 'national' frontiers. TNCs now dispose of a considerable proportion of liquid funds internationally and are constantly attuned to risks of loss or opportunities for financial gain. Movements of considerable funds are also necessitated by the business activities of TNCs and the major investments undertaken at their behest. Strategic decisions on investments, the location of production and the acquisition of resources are also influenced by the policies of governments, and by national economic conditions. Such decisions, in turn, exert a powerful effect upon the global division of labour, the fate of individual economies and, hence, the deliberations of 'national' governments.

In Richard Cooper's view, the responses of governments to such reductions of autonomy can assume one of five forms, in each of the affected policy areas. The response may be essentially *passive*, with the pursuit of independent policies being largely abandoned.[10] Some governments may attempt to develop an *exploitative* response by taking advantages of the new opportunities presented by increasing interdependence, through such devices as offering flags of convenience to footloose maritime operators.[11] *Defensive* responses offer an alternative, with efforts to restore the fragmentation of markets upon which the potency of so many national economic policy instruments rested.[12] *Aggressive* actions may also result when some countries seek to extend national control of mobile economic factors and resources, whether through legal restrictions or physical restraints.[13] Finally, some governments seek to deal with the growth of interdependence, and the attendant threats to national autonomy, through *constructive* engagements with other governments, aimed at increasing collaborative responses to the increased international mobility of critical factors of production.[14]

Globalisation embraces, and reflects, many of the sources of the form of interdependence analysed by Richard Cooper and carries many of the same implications for national autonomy and governmental responses. All but the passive forms of these possible patterns of response to the growth of international interdependence and globalisation reflect the seriousness of the attendant decline of effectiveness of a range of central economic policies and its profound implications for many important objectives of domestic policy.

Globalisation and domestic economic transformation

The constraints upon the effectiveness of economic policy at the state level are compounded by changes in the structures and prospects of the domestic economies, and industrial systems, of many of the members of the contemporary international economic system. The emergence of long-term unemployment within many of the Advanced Industrial Economies is often held to be as inevitable a consequence of the new global economic order as is the imperative upon developing countries to embrace the market with unrestrained enthusiasm.[15] Moreover, such globally-induced structural unemployment is believed to further circumscribe the range of policies that are available to governments as they endeavour to combine domestic socio-economic well-being with international economic competitiveness. The resultant tensions underlie many of the contemporary challenges to the vitality and viability of democratic institutions that will be examined later in this chapter.

As with so many other aspects of the nature and effects of contemporary globalisation, discussions of domestic economic transformation and its supposed consequences, have been simplistic, indiscriminate and unduly fatalistic. As with the varied patterns of dependence in the modern international system, the economies of contemporary states exhibit considerable diversity in condition and potentiality. The simple scale of unemployment within the leading industrial economies ranged, in 1991, from the 16.1 per cent of the Irish Republic down to the 1.2 per cent of Switzerland, as Table 9.1 illustrates. This demonstrates that unemployment within Advanced Industrial Economies is not exclusively, or even primarily, a result of exposure to a globalising international economy.

Discriminating amongst the various sources of unemployment within Advanced Industrial Countries, and of other constraints upon industrial and economic performance, is complicated by the interconnections among a number of nominally distinct factors. Globalisation both encourages and reflects the impact of modern technologies and the activities of Transnational Corporations. The result is a complex of globalising impulses.

Technology has long been heralded as a potent force for the transformation of economies and industrial systems. The emergence of the micro-electronics revolution in the 1970s was accompanied by dire warnings of mass unemployment as one industrial occupation after another was rendered redundant by computer controlled machinery.[16] Where workers were not entirely displaced, there were fears that modern technology would reduce many jobs to deskilled and demoralising drudgery. However, technological innovation has always taken place in the Advanced Industrial Economies, from the onset of the industrial revolution, if not well before. It is essentially the speed and scale of the adoption of new procedures and processes that has been stimulated by enhanced competition from an increasingly globalised market-place.

Table 9.1 Unemployment within the Advanced Industrial Countries – 1991

Country	Unemployment Rate – Percentage
European Community (12)	8.9
Belgium	8.3
Denmark	8.6
W. Germany	4.3
Spain	15.9
France	9.7
Irish Republic	16.1
Italy	10.3
Luxembourg	2.0
Holland	7.5
United Kingdom	9.4
Norway	5.5
Sweden	2.7
Switzerland	1.2
USA	6.7
Canada	10.2
Japan	2.1

Source: Basic Statistics of the Community, (29th edition, Luxembourg, EUROSTAT, 1992), Table 3.22, p. 136.

Technological innovation and changes in employment patterns have not, however, taken place in an institutional vacuum. Government policies and the activities of Transnational Corporations have influenced both the rate and nature of much innovation. Governmental support for the development and introduction of new technologies into national or regional industries has both reflected a perception of intensifying competition within the international economy and made a direct contribution, intentionally or unintentionally, to the accelerating process of technological transformation in the industries of the leading industrial countries. Japan's Ministry of International Trade and Industry (MITI) has a long, if somewhat controversial record, of close interest in the technologies of 'tomorrow', and was instrumental in Japan's ill-fated programme for the development of Fifth Generation computers.[17] The European Community has spawned a myriad of programmes directed towards technology and industrial innovation, while the US administration of President Bill Clinton has sought to institutionalise the forms of official support for innovation that were previously the indirect effect of massive financial support for the military and aero-space industries.

Transnational Corporations (TNCs) have played no less a role in the processes and patterns of international technological innovation.[18] The general relocation of production by TNCs has contributed substantially to contemporary globalisation and the increased level of apparently international competition facing many national economies. However, the immediate impact of TNCs' international investments is not to stimulate technological innovation in all regions of the world economy. A major motivation of a substantial amount of foreign investment by TNCs is to take advantage of the low wages available in less developed economies. The low wage costs that result allow profitable production to be undertaken with relatively unsophisticated technologies. Overseas investments by some TNCs may thus actually preserve the life and profitability of obsolescent and labour-intensive technologies. Competition for producers in higher-wage economies will, however, intensify as a result of such investments and compel either the adoption of more efficient productive technologies, and practices, or the eventual cessation of production.

Competitive globalisation may face all economies with challenges, but the response to such challenges will vary according to a range of industrial, social and political conditions. Dynamic and self-confident industrial societies have responded with considerable energy and success to intensifying international competition. Those, in contrast, that have found themselves endowed with ageing industries and antique attitudes among managers and workers have found recent challenges difficult to meet.[19] Governments, both national and regional, have sought to preserve competitiveness and promote innovation through many means. Different cultures have demonstrated quite different patterns of response to the challenges of sustaining, or creating, industrial competitiveness. The substantial variations among national rates of unemployment reflect just such diversities of domestic circumstance.[20] Globalisation, technology and Transnational Corporations may form the common context for contemporary economies, but it is in their own domestic conditions that the variations in their recent responses and experiences are largely to be found.

The growth of interdependence and globalisation thus has effects upon states of all sizes and kinds. The nature of such effects is, however, substantially influenced by the size, structure and general strength of the economy in question. Structural differentiation within the international political economy thus underpins a differential impact upon its diverse members.

Interdependence, globalisation and 'North-South' relations

The impact of growing interdependence and globalisation is, as has been suggested previously, particularly marked for the Less Developed Countries. The force and character of this impact is, however, a matter of persisting controversy, as has been indicated at a number of points in this discussion. The critical conditions in the international political economy are an increasingly interconnected world trade system, and the continued growth of a range of strategic dependencies. It is the significance of these two conditions that is the subject of intense debate amongst the disputants over the dynamic of the contemporary system.

An increasingly interconnected world trade system has been heralded as *the* outstanding opportunity for those economies that would seek growth and development through the promotion of their exports of manufactured goods. With ever expanding international markets for an extensive range of manufactured goods, societies that abjure import substitution in favour of a promotion, maintain a stable and appropriate exchange rate and avoid damaging domestic economic policies, could, according to some analysts, replicate the encouraging experiences of the Newly Industrialised Countries of South-East Asia.[21]

Less sanguine analysts, however, identify the progress of interdependence and globalisation with the intensification of the adverse structural features of the prevailing international economic order that have long subordinated the needs and interests of the Less Developed Countries. As was suggested in Chapters 2 and 7, Dependency Theorists view the prevailing international capitalist order as profoundly damaging to the developmental prospects of the 'dependent' economies. Positively underdeveloped by their historical impact of imperialism, both formal and informal, such societies can only be condemned to perpetual subordination within a fundamentally exploitative international political economy. The intensity of competition amongst Advanced Industrial Countries and some of the Newly Industrialised Countries; continuing problems of irregular growth in the world economy; and protectionist currents amongst the major importing economies, may continue to damage and ultimately destroy the prospects of many of the Less Developed Countries. Only through increased attention to, and reliance upon, their domestic regeneration, can the majority of the Less Developed Countries find a promising and prosperous future.[22]

The scale and significance of increasing dependencies amongst the Advanced Industrial Countries are also matters of controversy amongst those interested in the prospects of the Less Developed Countries within the contemporary international economic order. Much of the optimism of the countries of the 'South', and their many supporters, during the latter half of the 1970s was founded upon a belief that the 'balance of power' in the international political economy might be tilting in favour of the Less Developed Countries. If, as was widely believed, the 'North' was becoming increasingly dependent upon supplies of vital resources from the 'South', then the latter countries might be able to exploit this new source of strength to secure advantageous changes in a range of the principles and practices that prevailed within the international economy.

The confidence with which representatives of the 'Southern' economies approached the negotiations for a New International Economic Order, during the later 1970s, reflected such an analysis of the changing balance of interdependencies within international economic relations. However, the overall picture of relative dependencies between 'Northern' and 'Southern' economies, individually and in aggregate, was, and remains, far more complex than was popularly imagined. LDCs that lacked the ability to feed their populations, sustain their industrial systems from domestic resources, or pay for their necessary imports, were ultimately in a very weak position in any confrontations with those Advanced Industrial Countries upon which they were often dependent for succour and supply.

The complexities of contemporary international interdependencies, as illustrated by the data presented in Chapter 6, added their effects to the considerable difficulties encountered by those states that sought to translate the strategic economic advantages that they enjoyed into effective international negotiating 'power'. The cartels that sought to control the supply of a range of basic commodities, and hence exert influence upon the prices paid, or the policies adopted, by importing Advanced Industrial Countries, commonly foundered in the face of the difficulties confronted in the supply of many such 'collective goods'.[23] When confronted by the determined 'divide and rule' strategies adopted by their AIC adversaries, Less Developed commodity exporters could hardly be expected to prevail in bilateral or multilateral negotiations.[24]

The range and complexity of patterns of contemporary international interdependencies is thus such as seriously to qualify any simple expectations about the distribution of decisive strength. Certainly, the expectations entertained by many Southern advocates in the late 1970s proved to be highly premature, at best, and dangerously misleading, at worst. The dependencies of much of the South upon the North have proved to be more substantial and enduring, at least in the short and medium term, and have shown themselves to have perverse effects. It was, in large part, a wish to escape from some of their more pressing dependencies that persuaded a number of Less Developed Countries to undertake substantial loans from the international financial system in the 1970s. The unfortunate consequence of this process, however, was the massive 'debt crisis' of the early 1980s which, itself, increased the exposure of many of the indebted Less Developed Countries to the influence of the richer members of the international system. Continued dependence upon aid, and other financial support, contributed substantially to the willingness of the affected debtor states to accept the dictates of their patrons amongst the Advanced Industrial Countries.

The widespread movement towards increased 'liberalisation' of the policies and economies of many Less Developed Countries, during the late 1980s and early 1990s, reflects, in part at least, such a balance of politico-economic power and influence. The longer-term development of dependencies and interdependencies, and their impact upon national policies and North-South relations, will be a function of the complex interactions amongst technological innovations, national and international economic developments and widespread responses at the level of 'national' and international policy-making.

Non-state actors, interdependence and globalisation

Non-state actors occupy a critical position in the contemporary debate about interdependence and globalisation.[25] To some critics, such non-state actors as Transnational Corporations are identified as a major, if not *the* major, source of tendencies towards increased international interdependence and globalisation. To other analysts, many non-state actors are seen to be the prime beneficiaries of a world that is characterised by enhanced opportunities for international movement, shipment and communication, but that continues to be fragmented into a set of nominally sovereign states.

The role of Transnational Corporations as major sources of induced interdependence in the contemporary international political economy and, through their promotion of enhanced communications, homogenised tastes and accelerated change, as primary promoters of globalisation, was considered in Chapter 7. They and a number of other non-state actors are, however, greatly assisted in a number of areas of activity by the fragmentation of political sovereignty and legal authority within the contemporary international system. Chapter 7 also indicated some of the decisive advantages that TNCs secure from their ability to operate ever more complex patterns of internationally integrated production, intra-firm trading[26] and, in tandem, transfer pricing practices. The advantages so secured by TNCs in their dealings with geographically constrained 'national' governments are difficult to exaggerate and have frequently permitted malpractices of a scale that is matched only by their remarkable invisibility.

Tendencies towards globalisation within the contemporary international political economy are not only promoted by TNCs, and their behaviour, they also encourage a favourable climate for the continued expansion of the role and influence of such enterprises. The acquisition of a cloak of normality by transnational business operators eases their wider acceptance and increased toleration for their activities. Criticism of TNCs, or resistance to an expansion of their role, is increasingly marginalised from the mainstream of thought in the most influential of policy-making, and academic, circles. The thought that the world could function and prosper in the absence of such world-bestriding mammoths becomes increasingly 'unthinkable' outside all but the most radical circles. A major plank of an ideological hegemony, favourable to TNCs and all their doings, is thus fostered by the increasingly 'commonplace' nature of their activity in, and impact upon, the societies in which they conduct their affairs.

The loss of tax revenues, and general economic control, that governments experience as a result of the existence and operation of TNCs merely illustrates the range of difficulties generated by international political fragmentation. Businesses that are able to straddle state boundaries in their operations are not confined to the suppliers of natural resources and manufactured goods, however. Modern technology has massively enhanced the capacities of financial institutions to transfer funds and conduct financial transactions, internationally. The ultimate significance of this development is hotly debated, but far from clear. There have been claims that the advanced level of international financial integration has, itself, transformed the international political economy. The scale and intensity of international financial flows has brought national economic autonomy to an end, and fundamentally circumscribed the freedom of manoeuvre of governments. However, there are others who believe that the impact of this international financial volatility is readily exaggerated.

The volumes of funds flowing around the international system are not disputed, and their sensitivity to some developments in the real economy are clear. There are, however, grounds for scepticism about the weight of the impact of international finance upon the non-financial sectors of the world economy. Prior to 1987 conventional wisdom attributed profound, potential consequences to any major dislocation in the international financial system, be they the results of default by Less Developed Country debtors or other shocks to confidence and liquidity. However, the muted consequences of the great financial crash of October 1987 suggested a degree of disconnection between the real world economy and the world of international finance: a disconnection that is clearly not absolute, but that can be effected more readily than might previously have been supposed. Globalisation there may thus be, but a form of globalisation with implications that have yet to be fully clarified.

Communications' media have also benefited enormously from the dramatic technological innovations of recent years. Here, again, devotees herald a new, and irresistible force for, and form of, globalisation. Communications' satellites have clearly facilitated forms of direct interpersonal communication across state boundaries that were impossible, and largely inconceivable, until recently. The satellite-linked telephone calls that Kuwaiti nationals were able to make to foreign contacts during the period of occupation by Iraq bear vivid testimony to this new, and unprecedented, facility. The translation of such technological possibilities into the irresistible force of global cultural homogeneity, that some observers identify in satellite-based international television broadcasting, is, however, a rather more contentious matter. The pressure for global common taste, driven by increasingly international producers of goods, services and processed foodstuffs, encounters the substantial, and often highly intentional, force of local cultural identity. Many countries, and regions, in the modern world have exhibited the waxing and waning of the forces of cultural homogenisation: as the dramatic experience of the Iranian revolution against the pro-Western Shah evidenced. History may ultimately be on the side of a common culture, driven by the needs and values of Western capitalist society, but that history is unlikely to be one of steady and uninterrupted 'progress'.

The forms of association that mark, or are facilitated, by contemporary trends towards globalisation are not only those promoted by dominant interests, of one form or another. Terrorist groups (or freedom fighters according to taste and circumstances) that have developed the ability to operate across state frontiers are also able to exploit political fragmentation in a way that imposes considerable potential costs upon the populations of the states against which they direct their activities. The mobility of many modern terrorists and the multiplicity of their sources of deadly supply within the modern international system marks a pernicious form of 'globalisation' that actually exploits, and partially depends upon, the continuing divisions amongst states. To the extent that states surrender a measure of sovereignty, in the name of effective anti-terrorist policies, a perverse form of globalisation gives way to a more constructive form of co-operative internationalism.

Interdependence, globalisation and the limits to democracy

One consequence of any erosion of national economic autonomy, and increasing pressures for closer international political and policy co-operation, is increasing constraints upon the scope for democratic action within affected states.[27] David Held has surveyed the argument succinctly, attributing to the growth of international interconnectedness, and the increasing permeability of state frontiers, five central areas of difficulty facing contemporary governments: (1) the reduction of the range and effectiveness of policy instruments available to governments in the face of increasing global interconnectedness; (2) the restriction of influence of governments over their citizens resulting from the expansion of transnational forces and interactions; (3) the increasing requirement for traditional state responsibilities to be fulfilled through international co-operation; (4) the resulting pressure for increasing levels of formal integration amongst states; and (5) the consequential, substantial growth of international institutions, organisations and regimes.[28]

Numerous disjunctions of power and authority are deemed to derive from such contemporary conditions. The common theme of such disjunctions is of the growing inability of problems to be solved, or even contained, by democratic procedures, if their operation is to be confined solely to the 'national' level. These have added their effects, in limiting the area of manoeuvre for democratic institutions, and practices, to those that have prevailed throughout much of the post-war era, including the hegemonical roles enjoyed by the USA and the USSR within their Cold War spheres of influence. Democratic principles could be preserved in the face of such pressures by the development of a suitably restrained international arena which permits democratic practices within a more complex set of national and international politics, with overlapping authority structures.[29] The dangers exist, however, that a failure to develop appropriate responses to the challenging developments in the international arena will encourage the emergence of antagonistic, and ultimately anti-democratic, reactions.

A paradox of the contemporary condition, however, is that at the very time that the freedom of manoeuvre of democratic polities has become circumscribed, the international pressures for the democratisation of previously authoritarian regimes are considerable and rising.[30] Such pressures reflect contemporary interdependence and globalisation tendencies, which have added their force to primarily domestic pressures for democratisation. Interdependencies, of various forms, have left many regimes, particularly within the Third World, vulnerable to pressures for increased democracy from their various patron states in the Advanced Industrial West.[31] Enhanced transnational communications have also eased the passage of demonstration effects and other diffusion processes favouring democratic principles and practices.[32] The problem is that democratic credentials may readily be assumed by those opposition political movements that, for a variety of reasons, seek the greater assertion of national autonomy. The domestic success of such movements, when they have been legitimised by democratic victories, might make the subsequent confrontation with an increasingly overweening international system all the more frustrating and embittered. The inherent contradiction between the continuing promotion of democracy and the increasing constraint of its practical effect, might prove extremely difficult to resolve and keep within manageable limits.

Interdependence, globalisation, foreign policy and security

A central tenet of notions of complex interdependence and globalisation is that the context within which states now act has been so transformed by a variety of developments that the central problems, and possibilities, for both foreign policy and security policy have been changed profoundly, if not irreversibly.

There has been a series of propositions about the influence of external constraints upon the foreign policies of states. Substantial dependence upon one or more states has been identified as a major determinant of the foreign policies of 'dependent' states.[33] The general increase of complexity in general patterns of interdependence, or globalisation, has been seen to extend, and/or intensify, the set of constraints under which all states operate. The advance of many forms of common fate, including threats to environmental security and the dangers of widening access to weapons of nuclear, biological and chemical warfare, has persuaded many of new, and inescapable, pressures upon foreign and security policies.

Relating prevailing, or developing, circumstances to specific forms, or developments, in state policies encounters the kinds of difficulties that have been identified at a number of stages in this discussion of interdependence and globalisation. Superficial correlations and unwarranted rationalism both arise to beset sound judgements in this area. Bruce Moon's discussion of the relationship between the external dependence, particularly economic, and foreign policy compliance with the dictates of patron states addresses this issue frontally.[34] A combination of critical discussion and discriminating statistical analysis leads Moon to the conclusion that much of the apparent compliance, in the UN voting behaviour, of a range of 'dependent' states to the wishes of the United States of America is, in fact, primarily a product of past 'penetration' of such states by US interests with the consequence of 'the establishment of dominant elites whose interests and perspectives so resemble those of their American counterparts that a broad consensus on the major issues in international affairs develops between them'.[35] A broad structure of dependency is thus here seen to be more salient than any immediate dependencies that are open to manipulation by the dominant partner.

While direct dependencies can influence the foreign and security policies of the dependent parties, the general growth of interdependence and globalisation has also modified the general context within which all states have to determine their external policies. Sensitivity to a wide range of mutual dependencies and the consequences of complex patterns of interaction in the contemporary international system clearly bears in upon the deliberations of those charged with the formulation of state policy. Rich states, as well as their less advantaged neighbours, are highly attuned to the degree to which current prosperity is now dependent upon the continued vitality of the international trade system. The activities of Transnational Corporations, and developments within the international financial system, are monitored with notable concern and interest. Political or military developments that pose any serious threat to international economic and financial interactions are the objects of close attention and considerable caution.

Rationalistic analysis may, however, encourage an exaggeration of the nature and extent of the influences of contemporary interdependencies and tendencies towards globalisation upon state policies and behaviour. The proliferation of 'nationalistic' conflicts in many areas of the former communist bloc has compounded the prevalence of similarly lethal disputes within the African continent. The disruption, if not total destruction, of all forms of peaceful economic interaction amongst societies, exemplifies the weakness of economic interdependencies as constraints upon the 'external' behaviour of all groups, at all times and under all conditions.

Descent into intersocietal mayhem may mark the extreme of impotence of established interdependencies. However, 'national' security interests frequently persuade governments to reject the unrestrained influence of free-market processes and, in particular, to limit serious dependencies in areas of military and strategic concern. Restrictions to local suppliers, extensive subsidies for military research and development and widespread state support for the exports by armaments' industries all attest to the negative influence exerted by potential military dependencies upon the governments of those states that retain the capacity to preserve domestic production. Moreover, where purely 'national' production in areas of military and strategic sensitivity proves impossible, states are generally concerned to limit supplies to those states with whom they can collaborate in production, or in whom they feel able to place considerable political and strategic confidence.

A reluctance of response to the supposed imperatives of a world of increasing interdependence and globalisation is also evident in the behaviour of many states on the growing range of issues of supposed general 'interdependence'. Such reluctance reflects a number of considerations: the uneven consequences of some conditions or developments, particularly those of transmitted effects; the intrinsic intractability of some major issues, like those associated with rising population pressures; or the general need to qualify state sovereignty to deal effectively with a range of pressing global problems, such as possible 'global warming'.

Considerable discrimination, and caution, is thus required in dealing with the 'common' problems of the contemporary world. Not all problems are, or are perceived to be, equally serious for all states. Few, if any states, are enthusiastic about the substantial dilution of sovereignty and decisional authority, save where the new structure of authority is very carefully delimited and one in which considerable confidence can be invested. Continuing debates, and disputes, over relative patterns of authority within the European Community, however, attest to the political sensitivity of such issues.

The rhetorical richness, and substantive weakness, of the Rio Conference on the global environment, and its management, further attests to the problems besetting collective responses to 'common' problems of mankind. Rationalist and functionalist modes of thought sustain a belief that problems of such potential enormity *must* generate effective international collaboration. Experience of the realities of a world of states, however, cautions against false optimism. Here, as in all spheres of political activity, the conditions for effective joint action amongst states have to be constructed by persuasive argument and through determined political organisation. Indeed, the very modesty and slowness of progress in substantive forms of international co-operation attest to the strength of argument and determination that is often necessary.

Interdependence, globalisation and the prospects for peace and prosperity

The central proposition of 'liberal' views of the growth of international interdependence and globalisation was that it would establish the conditions for enhanced prosperity and harmony for all those exposed to such a benign experience. The growth of international trade encourages a new international division of labour which, by allowing all societies to specialise in the production of those goods and services in which they enjoy a comparative advantage, thus enriches participating economies, secures an optimal use of the world's productive resources and increases the general level of global prosperity and satisfaction. Constrained from war by new dependencies, and encouraged towards benign views of their neighbours by the experience of mutually advantageous trade, societies will turn away from the paths of confrontation and conflict.

Experience and sceptical reflection have, however, encouraged doubts about the robustness of the benign view of international interdependence and globalisation. The First World War dealt the first, great blow to the excessive optimism of nineteenth-century interdependence theorists. More recent experiences in the former Yugoslavia have reinforced the salutary lessons of 1914.

Moreover, many forms of interconnectedness and interdependence may actually stimulate frictions and potential conflicts. Where statistical studies are undertaken in a more discriminating manner, it has been found that, while non-costly forms of trade were associated with a decline in conflict amongst states, the more *costly* forms of interconnection and interdependence are associated with the increased incidence of international conflicts.[36]

Sceptical analysts have also developed sustained critiques of the presumptions and conclusions of benign interdependence theories. Views of the potentially misleading role of rationalist and functionalist thought have been reinforced by robust arguments about the continuing centrality of states, and their political durability.[37] Such arguments can all too readily dissolve into obdurate denials of the role and relevance of any actors upon the international scene other than states. Short of such intellectual extremities, however, the arguments of those who are sceptical about the extent and impact of interdependence and globalisation do serve to highlight the complexity of contemporary conditions, and their discriminating interpretation.

The central problem is that many interdependencies, and sources of globalisation, can have contrary implications and effects. A specific dependence may prompt compliance with its apparent imperatives or, in direct contrast, stimulate efforts to reverse the condition. Similarly, the advance of financial globalisation may prove irresistible or, eventually, generate strenuous efforts to contain, or even diminish, the level of international financial integration and the ease of international financial transactions. Such responses might follow from the intentional decisions of political authorities, or arise as consequences of other disruptive developments in the economic or politico-military spheres. All policies of significance have costs of one form or another. The costs of disrupting established conditions of interdependence or interconnectedness are merely one set of costly consequences amongst the many that bear upon policy-making deliberations. Their simple existence is no guarantor that choices will favour their avoidance.

If, therefore, the impact or durability of any form of dependence, interdependence or interconnectedness cannot be predicted with full confidence, it is impossible to chart the future course of interdependence or globalisation with full confidence. The advance of interdependence has not prevented the outbreak of war in the past. Specific instances of interdependence and interconnectedness have not had identical, or consistent, effects upon the societies involved. Possibilities, and even probabilities, in the course of human developments can be charted, but caution and scepticism always have to be exercised with the fruits of such speculations.

Conclusion

The consequences of international interdependencies, patterns of interconnectedness and globalising tendencies are varied and complex. The advance of such phenomena in the contemporary international system is often characterised as carrying a range of automatic implications. Indeed, the short-term impact of a number of established conditions is often relatively easy to chart. The difficulties arise, however, with the longer-term implications of many of the forms of interdependence, interconnectedness and sources of globalisation.

Many conditions in the international political economy are capable of stimulating a variety of reactions: some acquiescent; others adverse. Where the impact of conditions can be contrary, the ultimate significance cannot be predicted with any precision. Moreover, the motivating forces of states, their governments and their populations, are often such as to impel the disruption of patterns of interdependence and interconnectedness and, hence, to ignore or overturn their supposed imperatives. The complexities of the motivations and moving forces in political life are such as to exceed the embrace of rationalistic models based upon a necessarily simplified range of assumptions about human behaviour, or the confidence prompted by Functionalist approaches to political and economic developments.

The implications of various forms of interdependence, interconnectedness, or globalisation, are thus far from clear or consistent. Greater problems face the analyst, however, for neither the durability nor the orderly evolution of established patterns of international interaction can be taken for granted. There have been numerous suggestions of sources of disruption to established patterns of interdependence, interconnectedness and globalisation throughout this discussion, in general, and the current chapter, in particular. It is to the future of international interdependence, and globalisation, that the next, and final, chapter is addressed.

Notes and References

1. Richard N. Cooper, 'Economic interdependence and foreign policy in the seventies', in Richard N. Cooper, *Economic Policy in an Interdependent World: Essays in World Economics* (Cambridge, Mass.: MIT Press, 1986), pp. 1-22, p. 1 (originally published in *World Politics*, Vol. 24, No. 2 (1972), pp. 159-81).
2. Ibid., p. 5.
3. See Richard N. Cooper, *The Economics of Interdependence: Economic Policy in the Atlantic Community* (New York: McGraw-Hill, 1968), pp. 4-5.
4. Ibid.
5. Cooper, 'Interdependence and foreign policy', p. 6.
6. Ibid.
7. Ibid., p. 7.
8. Ibid., p. 7.
9. Ibid., pp. 7-9.
10. Ibid., p. 9.
11. Ibid., pp. 9-10.
12. Ibid., pp. 10-11.
13. Ibid., p. 11.
14. Ibid., pp. 11-12.
15. For a critique of the view that imports from low-wage countries are the major source of unemployment with the Advanced Industrial Countries see: 'Workers of the world, compete', *The Economist*, 2 April, 1994, pp. 82–3.
16. See, for example: Part 6 of, T. Forester (ed.), *The Microelectronics Revolution* (Oxford: Basil Blackwell, 1980); and S. Nora and A. Minc, *The Computerization of Society*, (Cambridge, Mass.: MIT Press, 1981).
17. For a brief discussion see: R.J. Barry Jones *Conflict and Control in the World Economy* (Brighton: Harvester/Wheatsheaf, 1986) esp. pp. 236-7.
18. For a general discussion of which see: P. Bailey, A. Parisotto and G. Renshaw *Multinationals and Employment: The Global Economy of the 1990s* (Geneva: International Labour Office, 1993).
19. For a summary of the OECD's study of problems and prospects of dealing with high unemployment levels amongst its member states see: 'Adapt and survive', *The Economist*, 11 June, 1994, p. 90.
20. For a discussion of institutional obstacles to labour mobility and flexibility in Germany see: 'The politics of work', *The Economist*, 7 March, 1994, pp. 43-4.
21. See, for example, John D. Macomber, 'East Asia's lessons for Latin America's resurgence', reprinted in J.A. Frieden and D.A. Lake, *International Political Economy: Perspectives on Global Power and Wealth* (London: Unwin, Hyman, (2nd edn.), 1991), pp. 386-95 (reprinted from *The World Economy*, Vol. 10, No. 4 (December, 1987).
22. See the argument in Robin Broad and John Cavanagh, 'No more NICs', in Frieden and Lake, *International Political Economy*, pp. 396-410, (reprinted from *Foreign Policy*,Vol. 72 (Fall 1988).)
23. See Mancur Olson Jr., *The Logic of Collective Action: Public Goods and the Theory of Groups* (Cambridge: Cambridge University Press, 1965), esp. Ch. 1.
24. On the problems of negotiating a New International Economic Order, see: E. Laszlo *et al.*, *The Obstacles to the New International Economic Order* (New York/Oxford: Pergamon Press, for UNITAR/CEESTEM, 1980); and Robert K. Olson, *U.S. Foreign Policy and the New International Economic Order: Negotiating Global Problems, 1974-1981* (Boulder, Colo.: Westview Press, and London: Frances Pinter, 1981), esp. Chs. 4 and 7. For a review of the issues involved in

these negotiations, see J.N. Bhagwati (ed.), *The New International Economic Order: the North-South Debate* (Cambridge, Mass.: MIT Press, 1977).

25. For early discussions of the general impact of non-state actors see: R.O. Keohane and J.S. Nye, Jr. (eds.), *Transnational Relations and World Politics* (Cambridge, Mass.: Harvard University Press, 1972); and Richard W. Mansbach, Yale H. Ferguson and Donald E. Lampert, *The Web of World Politics: Nonstate Actors in the Global System* (Englewood Cliffs, NJ: Prentice Hall, 1976).
26. On which see R. Murray, *Multinationals Beyond the Market* (Brighton: Harvester, 1981).
27. On which, in general, see: Evan Luard, *The Globalization of Politics: The Changed Focus of Political Action in the Modern World* (New York: New York University Press, 1990), esp. Ch. 1, 'The distribution of political power'.
28. David Held, 'Democracy and the global system', in David Held (ed.), *Political Theory Today* (Cambridge: Polity Press, 1991), pp. 196-235, pp. 207-8; and see also David Held, 'Democracy: from city-states to a cosmopolitan order?', *Political Studies,* special edition on Prospects for Democracy', Vol. XL (1992), pp. 10-19.
29. David Held, 'Democracy and the global system', pp. 225-6 and p. 234.
30. See, in particular, Larry Diamond, 'The globalization of democracy', in R.O. Slater, B.M. Schutz and S.R. Dorr, *Global Transformation and the Third World* (Boulder, Colo.: Lynne Rienner Publishers, 1993), pp. 31-69.
31. Ibid., esp. pp. 49-51, and pp. 54-7.
32. Ibid., pp. 51-4.
33. See, in particular, Neil Richardson, 'Political compliance and US trade dominance', *American Political Science Review,* Vol. 70, (1976), pp. 1098-1109; Neil Richardson, *Foreign Policy and Economic Dependence,* (Austin: University of Texas Press, 1978); N. Richardson and C. Kegley, 'Trade dependence and foreign policy: a longitudinal analysis', *International Studies Quarterly,* Vol. 24 (1980), pp. 191-222; A. Armstrong, 'The political consequences of economic dependence', *Journal of Conflict Resolution,* Vol. 25, No. 3 (1981), pp. 401-28; James Ray, 'Dependence, political compliance, and economic performance: Latin America and Eastern Europe', in C. Kegley and P.J. McGowan (eds.), *The Political Economy of Foreign Policy Behavior* (Beverly Hills: Sage, 1981).
34. Bruce E. Moon, 'Consensus or compliance? Foreign-policy change and external dependence', *International Organization,* Vol. 39, No. 2 (Spring 1985), pp. 297-329.
35. Ibid., pp. 304-5.
36. See Mark J. Gasiorowski, 'Economic interdependence and international conflict: some cross-national evidence', *International Studies Quarterly,* Vol. 30 (1986), pp. 23-38.
37. See, in particular, Kenneth Waltz, 'The myth of national interdependence', in Charles P. Kindleberger, *The International Corporation* (Cambridge, Mass.: MIT Press, 1970), pp. 205-23.

Section 4

INTERNATIONAL INTERDEPENDENCE AND GLOBALISATION: PROSPECTS

CHAPTER 10

The future of international interdependence and globalisation

Reflection upon the future of international interdependence and globalisation is a complex matter. The definitional nature, empirical character and ultimate significance of interdependence and globalisation are all matters of considerable controversy and potential confusion. These difficulties should not, however, detract from the central significance of the issues raised and the conditions suggested by notions of interdependence and globalisation.

The future of international interdependence, or globalisation, is partly a matter of the definitions applied to these terms. It is entirely possible that the interconnectedness of separate states could increase without any corresponding increase in real dependencies, interdependencies, or qualitative globalisation. Dependencies and interdependencies could, in their turn, intensify in the absence of any general increase in interconnectedness or globalisation. Central, here, is the distinction between sensitivity and vulnerability in relationships of dependence or interdependence and, within the realm of sensitivity, the distinction between 'objective' sensitivity (with its close connection to interconnectedness) and the more complex phenomenon of 'subjective' sensitivity. The definitional distinctions between interconnectedness and interdependence must, therefore, be maintained, as must the controversial, qualitative implications of many usages of the term globalisation.

Definitional issues aside, the empirical world is likely to exhibit complex patterns of association amongst developments in patterns of interconnectedness, interdependence and globalisation. These associations do not mean, however, that such developments are always closely correlated, or regular and irreversible. Considerable unevenness has been exhibited by all patterns of international economic association in the past and substantial reversals have occurred at times of major political and economic disturbances. Many interconnections have been broken by political decisions and developments. State policies have often been directed towards the modification, elimination or even reversal of existing external dependencies. Impersonal forces sometimes mould the longer-term development of patterns of interconnectedness and interdependence, but usually only within a framework of 'suitable' policies and institutions.

Interdependence, globalisation and regionalisation in the international political economy

A central question concerns the general shape of the evolving international political economy. Popular notions of progressive globalisation run counter to the possibilities of increasing regionalisation within the international system. A final judgement about the emergent dynamic of the international political economy is fraught with analytical difficulties. Moreover, the empirical evidence remains far from decisive, as was shown in Chapter 6. It is entirely possible that the international political economy will exhibit opposing patterns, of further globalisation in some respects and increasing regionalisation in others. The question remains as to the ultimate compatibility of an increasing regional pattern of organisation of productive industry with ever greater globalisation of movement and management in the international financial sector.

The tension between globalisation and regionalisation highlights the wider issue of deterministic versus voluntaristic perspectives upon human affairs. Much of the discussion of interdependence, complex interdependence and globalisation carried, whether intentionally or not, a sense of the inevitable consequences of irresistible, and often impersonal, forces. Globalisation thus suggests the remorseless advance of interests and pressures that will progressively undermine 'national' frontiers, the autonomy of states and the distinctiveness of different cultures. The hint of determinism, whether contextual or inherent, in such a vision is both unacceptable to a number of students of the human condition and a highly selective interpretation of highly complex processes.

First-order accounts of central developments within the international political economy often serve to reinforce interpretations in terms of the automatic consequences of prevailing conditions. A second-order analysis, however, opens up questions about the origins of apparently decisive conditions and influences. It is at this stage that the central significance of 'political' factors can often be identified. Militarily and politically dominant states can be seen to set the 'rules of the game' for the international system, globally or regionally . While theories of hegemonical influence may suffer from both ambiguities and controversies,[1] few dispute the central influence over the international political economy exerted by Great Britain in the late nineteenth century and the United States of America since the Second World War.

Carefully constructed bargains amongst political authorities can, as in the case of the European Community, establish a significantly 'new' reality within which other actors subsequently have to operate. Such politically constructed frameworks for economic activity establish new, distinctive sets of opportunities and constraints for all actors. Indeed, even the political actors that have exercised a dominant influence on the establishment of the new framework may find their subsequent room for manoeuvre constrained by the fruits of their own efforts.

The relative strengths of globalising and regionalising forces in the international political economy will thus reflect, in large part, the decisions of those charged with policy-making responsibilities within the most influential states and the forces that bear upon those decisions. Indeed, one of the fundamental features of the international political economy is the central role of 'self-fulfilling prophecy'. If advocates of further integration within Europe do so because of their perceptions of regionalising tendencies within the wider international political economy, then the resulting intensification of defensive European integration could provide a major stimulus to the regionalisation that was initially feared. Equally, political leaders who become convinced of the inevitability of greater globalisation in economic matters, may well mould national policies in the direction of greater openness, thereby encouraging actions by economic actors, such as Transnational Corporations and financial institutions, that reinforce tendencies towards globalisation.

Economic frictions can, however, be generated both by movement towards greater interdependence and globalisation and thereby stimulate divisive political reactions. In the extreme, conflicts can then emerge which alter the established patterns of interdependence and international association: severing some whilst stimulating other, and often new, dependencies. Such adverse reactions to rising international interdependence can add their weight to persisting political and ideological sources of international hostilities.

'Politics' thus plays a central role in the shaping of the future of the international political economy. It is at this stage, however, that the third-order level of analysis must be addressed, for it is possible that the 'political' actions of leading states will, themselves, be moulded by impersonal forces and/or the influence of other dominant interests. Traditional Marxism highlighted the role of the economic infrastructure as an impersonal force; an interpretation that continues to find diluted echoes in the World System of Capitalism and Dependency perspectives upon the international political economy. Modern Gramscian 'Marxists' adopt a more hybrid approach, that accords leading economic interests a central, though not strictly deterministic, role in the shaping of the prevailing ideologies that mould the basic perspectives and preferences of political decision-makers. Economic liberals generally believe in the steady pressures of economic opportunities, and competitive forces, that progressively ease the path towards greater economic globalisation and political liberalisation.

Interpretations derived from third-order levels of analysis cannot be discounted as possibly dominant influences over the political realm. Neither, however, can such meta-theoretical propositions be verified by any simple empirical tests. Just as any, or all, such interpretations may encompass elements of truth, so it is possible that they will be falsified by future developments.

Interdependence, globalisation, the global ecology and a New International Economic Order

A belief in the inevitable growth of international economic interdependence and globalisation can encourage an associated belief in the imminence of a new international economic order. Such sentiments seized the minds of many during the later 1970s, when the apparent growth of 'Northern' dependence upon 'Southern' primary commodities seemed to herald a new distribution of power and influence within the international political economy and, with it, the prospects of a new, more equitable, international economic order.

The experience of the 1980s was to dash many of the hopes in a new order in international economic affairs. The prevailing set of international economic 'interdependencies' proved to be far more complex than commonly imagined during the late 1970s. Moreover, the great majority of 'Southern' states were found to suffer from enduring dependencies upon their 'Northern' patrons, that were of considerable seriousness for both the well-being of their populations and their longer-term economic viability. The formal negotiation of a New International Economic Order, under the auspices of the United Nations, failed to disguise the quite different international economic realities of the 1980s: collapsing primary commodity prices; a burgeoning debt crisis; the economic contraction of many African and some Latin American countries; and an increase in the general susceptibility of much of the 'South' to policy prescriptions promulgated within the 'Northern' hemisphere.

A combination of empirical simplification and rationalistic thinking underpinned the false optimism that attached to the idea of a New International Economic Order. Similar influences underlie a number of the more recent visions of globalisation, particularly when inspired by functionalist notions of what *must* come to pass in the management and ordering of human affairs at an international level. The pro-Southern sentiments of the past have now been supplemented by arguments about the requirements of ecological protection. A new era of rational economic management, internationally, is now believed to be necessitated by the supposed imperatives for human and natural survival.[2]

As in the case of the earlier proposals for a New International Economic Order, the patterns of international economic interaction are neither so simple, nor so consistent in their development, as to generate clear imperatives for international decision-making, unilateral or multilateral. Such pressures are often clouded by uncertainty initially, only clarifying fully when the time has passed for optimal responses.

The fate of earlier environmental anxieties illustrates the problems posed by ecological concerns and their impact upon the international political economy. Alarmist studies, particularly those inspired by the Club of Rome,[3] were heavily criticised for their methodological simplicity.[4] Uneven patterns of supply and consumption of primary commodities contributed to the loss of Paul Erlich's infamous bet with the economist Paul Simon that the prices of a range of basic resources would have risen, substantially and unambiguously, by a stated date. The many real difficulties of resource management and ecological protection have rarely been fully captured by analyses based upon short-term statistical 'evidence' and simplistic computation.

Clear evidence of consistent, adverse developments in the natural ecology would, moreover, provide no guarantee of an appropriate response. The deliberations of political decision-makers, and the pressures generated by their populations, are rarely sufficiently orderly, or 'rational', to guarantee the development of optimal arrangements for the future governance of the international political economy. Hopes for a future New International Economic Order, to supplant the lost 'order' of the late 1980s, may thus warrant little optimism or complacency.

The ecological pressures confronting the world clearly constitute a form of mutually generated common fate. They may not, however, prove sufficient to stimulate the timely introduction of a new order for the management of the international political economy. It is not only the ambiguity of evidence at early stages of adverse developments, and the 'irrationality' of human beings, that jeopardise appropriate responses to challenges. The impact of many of the potentially threatening developments in the contemporary international political economy are not equally threatening to the populations or economies of all countries. Short of the 'total toxic overload' of popular fiction, many developments may remain localised in their primary effects. Others may actually bring benefits to some populations, at the same time as inflicting catastrophic damage on others. The differential impact of environmental change is likely to reinforce other sources of international disharmony and conflict.

The effects of any global warming are also likely to have differential effects upon populations. For some countries, climatic changes might bring agricultural ruin; for others new weather patterns may bring the possibilities of improved harvests, or new crops. The impact of growing population pressures will also be felt most acutely in those countries in which population growth is at its greatest. There, the strains on resources, development prospects and general social stability could prove disastrous. Elsewhere, there might be some unease at the sight of chaos in other societies, but little direct effect of any significance. 'Moral interdependence' is often more honoured in rhetoric than reality when costly, complex and 'distant' problems are confronted, as the sorry example of Bosnia in the early 1990s suggests. Real, and pressing, dependencies have tended to generate rather more decisive responses within the history of the modern states' system.

Interdependence, globalisation and the threats of mass destruction

Irreversible ecological damage is not the only major source of lethal common fate for mankind. The development and proliferation of a wide variety of weapons of mass destruction also pose a formidable challenge. Nuclear weapons have long held sway over the morbid side of human imaginations. The prospect of unrestrained nuclear war between the Soviet Union and the United States of America threatened the world with Armageddon. It was estimated that the release of their nuclear arsenals would not only poison the territories of the major protagonists and their near neighbours for generations, but would also precipitate a remorseless 'nuclear winter', threatening the survival of all humanity.

The threat of a major East-West nuclear conflagration has now given way to the somewhat lesser dangers of more limited nuclear actions by small, 'delinquent' states. The problem for such smaller nuclear states has remained that of the reliable delivery of their deadly ordnance. The range and reliability of delivery systems, available in any volume, will continue to confine the major nuclear threat posed by smaller states to their neighbours, for some time to come. Chemical and biological agents have, however, always provided smaller, and more distant, states with the prospects of lethal attack against the centres of population of the world's leading states. Such deadly agents, however, accentuate the problem of controllability that has increasingly beset modern forms of weaponry. Lethal retaliation in kind has added its danger to those of the possibly uncheckable spread of the effects of those agents that are first used: mass poisoning or infection with deadly plagues. Economically divisive forms of interdependence and globalisation may thus engender hostile reactions that reveal other, and equally acute, forms of human interdependence.

Modern weapons of mass destruction create three distinguishable kinds of difficulties and dangers. The first is that of the uncontainable consequences of their employment, as discussed in the preceding paragraph. The second, sometimes less obvious problem is that of the diversion of scarce resources from valuable, and often essential, developmental projects in both Advanced Industrial Countries and Less Developed Countries. The opportunity cost of military research, development and deployment is considerable, particularly where major scientific endeavours are involved. The third problem is, paradoxically, that not all nuclear, biological or chemical weapons will actually pose a threat to all the populations of the world, at the same time or to the same extent. Geographical proximity, technological sophistication and societal robustness all influence the extent to which any given state, and its population, is vulnerable to a specific threat of such a kind.

The problem of differential threat is that complacency is encouraged amongst those who feel themselves to be distant from any source of immediate danger and, hence, less inclined to take decisive action to contain the general danger posed by nuclear, biological or chemical weapons. It is for this reason that trenchant critics of the modern 'arms culture' can, in the final analysis, do little more than lament upon the situation with which they are confronted and caution constant vigilance against the further deterioration of the situation.[5] Such critiques, unfortunately, do little to resolve the paradox that it is the very states that constantly prepare for armed conflict against one another that must, apparently, be charged with the task of negotiating a new, and more peaceful, world order that better accommodates the persisting interdependencies of humanity.

Institutional responses to interdependence and globalisation

The pressures created by the level of integration within some aspects of the international political economy and the lack of sufficient co-ordination in others both invite an institutional response. International and transnational institutions offer obvious means for the control of the plethora of international financial transactions and the co-ordination of responses to the problems of international trade, economic growth and ecological management. Such institutional responses will not, however, be self-generating in the face of the emergent needs of the international political economy, particularly when many forms of international economic association have a differential, and sometimes divisive, impact upon different societies.

Appropriate institutions for the management of the developing international economy require construction by a number of agencies. States remain the dominant political actors globally. They continue to monopolise legitimate force and their representatives constitute the primary membership of the great majority of international institutions. The commitment of states and their representatives to the reinforcement of the institutional structure of the international political economy is thus essential for substantial progress.

The sources of a more internationalist outlook amongst the governments and representatives of states might be varied. Widespread popular pressures for environmentally responsible policy and behaviour provide an example of one, potential source of such persuasion. Popular pressures of this sort may also reflect, and reinforce, the work of the specialised 'epistemic communities' that can, in the view of some analysts, provide a critical catalyst to appropriate institutional developments at the international level: 'regimes' for the management of pressing issues within the international political economy.[6] Existing international institutions, which provide the framework within which commonalties of outlook can develop amongst potentially influential politicians and other representatives, can thus form a major source of future institutional developments.

Expectations of substantial future progress through international institutionalisation may, however, remain largely unfulfilled. Questions about the stability and effectiveness of popular pressure have to be asked in the light of the fragmentation of the 'Green' movements within many Western countries and the limited achievements of the Rio Conference on environmental protection. States remain centre stage and as much a part of the problem as they are a potential part of the solution. Publics continue to be fragmented by their separation into discrete political societies. Costs of many types, when confronted, dampen popular enthusiasm for all manner of otherwise desirable projects. Processes proceed and pressures accumulate, without timely recognition by governments or peoples. Automaticity does not prevail in the ordering of human affairs. Appropriate responses to pressing problems do not always emerge and, where they do, the process of their development is often fitful and imprecise. Doubts persist as to the ultimate fate, and certainly the functional effectiveness, of the World Trade Organisation, that is intended to replace and consolidate the position occupied by the General Agreement on Tariffs and Trade in the post-war international economy.

Conclusions

This discussion of international interdependence and globalisation has suggested, on a diversity of grounds, that the picture presented by the contemporary international system may be far more complex than is often suggested by simpler conceptions of interdependence and globalisation. Contemporary interdependencies exhibit considerable diversity, with imbalance and asymmetry the norm rather than the exception. Much of the disparity of power and influence within the international system derives from such asymmetries and imbalances.

Globalisation, too, is a concept that can mislead the unwary. The contemporary international political economy is actually multi-layered, with distinct 'levels' being characterised by differing patterns of action and interaction. Globalisation may provide an effective metaphor for developments at some levels of contemporary activity, but be seriously misleading at others. Moreover, the differences amongst the characteristics and dynamics of activity at the different 'levels' may well be a major source of future change in the international system and, under certain conditions, the actual reversal of current tendencies towards greater globalisation.

The greatest danger that continues to haunt observers of contemporary international interdependence and globalisation is to confuse conclusions derived from rationalist analysis with what will actually come to pass in the real world. Functionalism is controversial as a basis for explanation of past and present arrangements in human affairs. The survival of institutions and practices tells us only that they have not proved unacceptably dysfunctional in the past. Such a mode of analysis and interpretation is even more suspect as a basis for predictions about the future of the international political economy or the wider human condition. The complex processes and passions that direct collective human conduct hold no guarantees of sense or even survival.

Functionalist views also rest upon unduly optimistic interpretations of many contemporary developments in the international political economy. Friction is often a central feature of major changes. Many contemporary patterns of international association may thus have divisive, as well as cohesive, effects upon at least some sections of the world 'community'. The presence of such divisive influences then compounds the problems of constructing effective institutional responses to the general problems of managing an interconnected world.

A methodology capable of charting the complex sources and consequences of contemporary international interdependencies must incorporate an approach to analysis similar to, if not identical with, that of structuration 'theory'. This, however, remains a methodological starting-point for the analysis of complex arenas of behaviour. The constructed 'realities' that arise from structuration processes may be self-sustaining in the short, and even the medium, term, but they cannot avoid encounters with unexpected outcomes or contacts with wider behavioural spheres in which the intersubjectivities, that lie at the heart of structuration, have declining force and effect. The more complex the spheres of interaction and the more distant the entities with which interaction takes place, therefore, the weaker is the sway of structuration process amongst central participants and the more frequent the patterns of unintended and unexpected developments. This realm of larger-scale, and less 'personal', interaction requires a significant measure of rationalistic analysis to unearth its characteristics, consequences and dynamics of change, in a manageable and illuminating manner.

The argument thus comes full circle, from warnings against rationalist modes of thought and analysis to an acknowledgement of the inevitable role of rationalist intellectual procedures, at critical stages in the analysis of complex, and relatively impersonal, arenas of human interaction. Caution against excessive rationalism, or unduly optimistic functionalism, is, however, highly apposite as a final observation upon the nature and implications of interdependence and globalisation in the contemporary world.

Notes and references

1. See, in particular: Bruce Russett, 'The mysterious case of vanishing hegemony: or, Is Mark Twain really dead?', *International Organization*, Vol. 39, No. 2 (Spring 1985), pp. 207-31; Duncan Snidal, 'The limits of hegemonic stability theory', *International Organization*, Vol. 39, No. 4 (Autumn 1985), pp. 579-614; M.C. Webb and S.D. Krasner, 'Hegemonic stability theory: an empirical assessment', *Review of International Studies*, Vol. 15, No. 2, (April 1989), pp. 183-98; Andrew Walter, *World Power and World Money: The Role of Hegemony and International Monetary Order* (Hemel Hempstead: Harvester/Wheatsheaf, 1991), esp. Ch. 1; and P.K. O'Brien and G.A. Pigman, 'Free trade, British hegemony and the international economic order in the nineteenth century', *Review of International Studies*, Vol. 18, No. 2 (April 1992), pp. 89-113.
2. As is inherent in an additional Report to the Club of Rome: Jan Tinbergen (co-ordinator), *Reshaping the International Order* (London: Hutchinson, 1977 (In USA: New York: Dutton, 1976)).
3. See, in particular, the Club of Rome report: D.H. Meadows, D.L. Meadows, J. Randers and W.W. Behrens, *The Limits to Growth* (London: Pan Books, 1974).

A related, yet more ambitious study, was M. Mesarovic and E. Pestel, *Mankind at the Turning Point* (New York: Dutton/Readers Digest, 1974 and London: Hutchinson, 1975).

4. See, in particular, H.S.D. Cole, C. Freeman, M. Jahoda and K.L.R. Pavitt, *Thinking About the Future: A Critique of the Limits to Growth* (London: Chatto and Windus/Sussex University Press, 1974); and C. Freeman and M. Jahoda (eds.), *World Futures: The Great Debate* (Oxford: Martin Robertson, 1978).
5. See, for example, Mary Kaldor and Julian Perry Robinson, 'War', in Freeman and Jahoda, *World Futures*, Ch. 10, pp. 343-79.
6. See, for example, Peter M. Haas, 'Epistemic communities and the dynamics of international environmental co-operation', in V. Rittberger with P. Mayer, *Regime Theory and International Relations* (Oxford: Clarendon Press, 1993), pp. 168-201; and see also Christer Jonsson, 'Cognitive factors in explaining regime dynamics', in Rittberger and Mayer, *Regime Theory*, pp. 202-22.

Select bibliography

Aggarwal, M.R., *New International Economic Order: Interdependence and Southern Development* (London: Oriental University Press, 1987).

Alker, H.R., 'A methodology for design research on interdependence alternatives', *International Organization*, Vol. 31, No. 1 (1977), pp. 29-63.

Amin, Samir, *Accumulation on a World Scale: A Critique of the Theory of Underdevelopment*, Vols. 1 and 2 (New York: Monthly Review Press and Hassocks: Harvester Press, 1974).

Amin, S., Arrighi, G., Frank, A.G.and Wallerstein, I., *Dynamics of Global Crisis* (London: Macmillan, 1982).

Archer, Margaret S., *Culture and Agency: The Place of Culture in Social Theory* (Cambridge: Cambridge University Press, 1988).

Armstrong, A., 'The political consequences of economic dependence', *Journal of Conflict Resolution*, Vol. 25, No. 3 (1981), pp. 401-28.

Ashley, Richard K., *The Political Economy of War and Peace: The Sino-Soviet-American Triangle and the Modern Security Problematique* (London: Frances Pinter Ltd., 1980).

Bailey, P., Parisotto, A. and Renshaw, G., *Multinationals and Employment: The Global Economy of the 1990s* (Geneva: ILO, 1993).

Baldwin, D., 'Interdependence and power: a conceptual analysis', *International Organization*, Vol. 34, No. 4, (Autumn 1980) pp. 471-506.

Baldwin, D., *Economic Statecraft*, (Princeton, NJ: Princeton University Press, 1985).

Bank of Japan, *The Greater Role of Asian Economies in the World and Growing Interdependence among Asia, the United States and Japan* (Tokyo: Bank of Japan, 1988).

Barnett, Correlli, *The Collapse of British Power* (London: Eyre Methuen, 1972).

Bauer, P.T., *Equality, the Third World and Economic Delusion* (London: George Weidenfeld and Nicolson, 1981).

Beenstock, Michael, *The World Economy in Transition* (London: George Allen and Unwin, 1983).

Beer, F.A., *Peace Against War: The Ecology of International Violence* (San Francisco: W.H. Freeman and Co., 1981).

Bennett, A. Leroy, *International Organizations: Principles and Issues* (Englewood Cliffs, NJ: Prentice-Hall, 1977).

Bergsten, C.F., *Toward a New International Economic Order: Selected Papers of C. Fred Bergsten, 1972-1974* (Lexington: Lexington Books/D.C. Heath, 1975).

Bergsten, C.F., *The Globalization of Industry and National Economic Policies* (London: Longman/Institute for International Economics, 1993).

Bhagwati, J.N. (ed.), *The New International Economic Order: The North-South Debate* (Cambridge, Mass.: MIT Press, 1977).

Bhagwati, J.N., *Dependence and Interdependence* (Oxford: Basil Blackwell, 1985).

Bhagwati, J.N., 'Ideology and North-South relations', *World Development*, Vol. 14, No. 6 (1986), pp. 767-74.

Blake, D.H. and Walters, R.S., *The Politics of Global Economic Relations* (Englewood Cliffs, NJ: Prentice-Hall, 1976 and subsequent editions).

Brandt, W., *North-South: A Programme for Survival* (London: Pan Books, 1980).

Brandt, W., *Common Crisis: North-South: Cooperation for World Recovery* (London: Pan Books, 1983).

Brett, E.A., *The World Economy Since the War: The Politics of Uneven Development* (Basingstoke: Macmillan, 1985).

Brookfield, H., *Interdependent Development* (London: Methuen, 1975).

Brown, L.R., *World Without Borders; The Interdependence of Nations* (New York: Foreign Policy Association, 1972).

Bull, H., *The Anarchical Society: A Study of Order in World Politics* (London: Macmillan, 1977).

Bull, H. and Watson, A. (eds.), *The Expansion of International Society*, (Oxford: Clarendon Press, 1984).

Burton, J.W., *World Society* (Cambridge: Cambridge University Press, 1972).

Buzan, B., *People, States and Fear* (Brighton: Wheatsheaf/Harvester, 1983).

Buzan, B., 'Economic structure and international security: the limits of the liberal case', *International Organization*, Vol. 38, No. 4 (1984), pp. 597-624.

Buzan, B., 'Interdependence and Britain's external relations', in L. Freedman and M. Clarke (eds.), *Britain in the World* (Cambridge: Cambridge University Press, 1991), pp. 10-41.

Buzan, B. and Jones, R.J. Barry (eds.), *Change and the Study of International Relations: The Evaded Dimension* (London: Frances Pinter Ltd., 1981).

Buzan, B., Jones, C. and Little, R., *The Logic of Anarchy: Neorealism to Structural Realism* (New York: Columbia University Press, 1993).

Casson, Mark (ed.), *International Business and Global Integration: Empirical Studies* (Basingstoke: Macmillan for GSEIS (Reading), 1992).

Cerny, P.G. (ed.), *Finance and World Politics: Markets, Regimes and States in the Post-Hegemonic Era* (Aldershot: Edward Elgar, 1993).

Christopherson, Jon A., 'Structural analysis of transaction systems: vertical fusion or network complexity?', *Journal of Conflict Resolution*, Vol. 20, No. 4 (December 1976), pp. 637-62.

Clark, C. and Welch, S., 'Western European trade as a measure of integration: untangling the interpretations', *Journal of Conflict Resolution*, Vol. 16 (September 1972), pp. 363-82.

Cohen, Benjamin J., 'International debt and linkage strategies: some foreign-policy implications for the United States', *International Organization*, Vol. 39, no 4 (Autumn 1985) pp. 699-727.

College of Europe, *Europe and Global Economic Interdependence* (Bruges: College of Europe, 1991).

Cooper, Richard N., *The Economics of Interdependence: Economic Policy in the Atlantic Community* (New York: McGraw-Hill, 1968).

Cooper, Richard N., 'Economic interdependence and foreign policy in the seventies', *World Politics*, Vol. 24, No. 2 (1972), p. 159-81.

Cooper, Richard N., *Economic Policy in an Interdependent World: Essays in World Economics* (Cambridge, Mass.: MIT Press, 1986).

Cox, R.W., *Production, Power and World Order: Social Forces in the Making of History* (New York: Columbia University Press, 1978).

Cox, R.W., 'Multilateralism and world order', *Review of International Studies*, Vol. 18, No. 2 (April 1992), p. 161-80.

Dell, Edmund, *The Politics of Economic Interdependence* (Basingstoke: Macmillan, 1987).

Deutsch, K.,*.Nationalism and Social Communication* (Cambridge, Mass.: MIT Press, 1953).

Deutsch, K. *et al.*, *Political Community and the North Atlantic Area* (Princeton, NJ: Princeton University Press, 1957).

Dixon, W.J., 'Change and persistence in the world system: an analysis of global trade concentration, 1955-1975', *International Studies Quarterly*, Vol. 29 (1985), pp. 171-89.

Doran, C.F., 'Oil politics and the rise of co-dependence', in D.W. Orr and M.S. Soroos, *The Global Predicament* (Chapel Hill: University of North Carolina Press, 1979).

Dunning, J.H. and Robson, P., *Multinationals and the European Community* (Oxford: Basil Blackwell, 1988).

Edwards, Chris, *The Fragmented World: Competing Perspectives on Trade, Money and Crisis* (London: Methuen, 1985).

Emmanuel, Arghiri, *Unequal Exchange: A Study of the Imperialism of Trade* (trans. Brian Pearce; London: New Left Books, 1972).

Faber, Gerrit, *Trade Policy and Development: The Role of Europe in North-South Trade; a Multidisciplinary Approach* (The Hague: Universitaire Pers Rotterdam, 1990).

Ferguson, Yale H. and Mansbach, Richard W., *The Elusive Quest: Theory and International Politics* (Columbia, S. Carolina: University of South Carolina Press, 1988).

Frank, Andre Gunder, *On Capitalist Underdevelopment* (Bombay: Oxford University Press, 1975).

Frank, Andre Gunder, *Dependent Accumulation and Underdevelopment* (London: Macmillan, 1978).

Freeman, C. and Jahoda, M. (eds.), *World Futures: The Great Debate* (Oxford: Martin Robertson, 1978).

Friedman, J. Bladen, C. and Rosen, S. (eds.), *Alliance in International Politics* (Boston, Mass.: Allyn and Bacon, 1970).

Frohlich, N., and Oppenheimer, J.A., 'I get by with a little help from my friends', *World Politics*, Vol. 20 (1970), pp. 104-20.

Frohlich, N., Oppenheimer, J.A. and Young, Oran R., *Political Leadership and Collective Goods* (Englewood Cliffs, NJ: Prentice-Hall, 1971).

Fromkin, D., *The Interdependence of Nations* (New York: Praeger, 1981).

Galtung, Johan, 'A structural theory of imperialism', *Journal of Peace Research*, Vol. 8 (1966), pp. 81-117.

Garnett, J.C., 'States, state-centric perspectives, and interdependence', in J. Baylis and N.J. Rengger (eds.), *Dilemmas of World Politics* (Oxford: Clarendon Press, 1992).

Gasiorowski, Mark J., 'The structure of Third World economic interdependence', *International Organization*, Vol. 39, No. 2 (Spring 1985), pp. 331-42.

Gasiorowski, Mark J., 'Economic interdependence and international conflict: some cross-national evidence', *International Studies Quarterly*, Vol. 30 (1986), pp. 23-38.

Gasiorowski, Mark J., and Polacher, S.W., 'Conflict and interdependence: East-West trade and linkages in the era of détente', *Journal of Conflict Resolution*, Vol. 26, pp. 709-29.

Giddens, Anthony, *The Constitution of Society: Outline of the Theory of Structuration* (Cambridge: Polity Press, 1984).

Gill, Stephen, *American Hegemony and the Trilateral Commission* (Cambridge: Cambridge University Press, 1991).

Gill, Stephen, *Gramsci, Historical Materialism and International Relations* (Cambridge: Cambridge University Press, 1993).

Gill, Stephen and Law, David, *The Global Political Economy: Perspectives, Problems and Policies* (Hemel Hempstead: Harvester/Wheatsheaf, 1988).

Gilpin, Robert, *US Power and the Multinational Corporation: The Political Economy of Direct Investment* (New York: Basic Books, 1975; and London: Macmillan, 1975).

Gilpin, Robert, *War and Change in World Politics* (Cambridge: Cambridge University Press, 1981).

Gilpin, Robert, *The Political Economy of International Relations*, (Princeton, NJ: Princeton University Press, 1987).

Glastetter, W., 'The integration of the developing countries into the world economy', *Intereconomics* (November/December 1988), pp. 277-85.

Godet, M. and Ruyssen, *The Old World and the New Technologies* (Luxembourg: Office for Official Publications of the European Communities, 1981).

Goldmann, K. and Sjostedt, G. (eds.), *Power, Capabilities, Interdependence: Problems in the Study of International Influence* (Beverly Hills: Sage, 1979).

Goldmann, Kjell, *The Logic of Internationalism* (London: Routledge, 1994).

Gomes, L., *International Economic Problems* (London: Macmillan, 1978).

Green, F. and Nore, P., *Economics: An Anti-Text* (London: Macmillan, 1977).

Groom, A.J.R. and Taylor, P. (eds.), *Functionalism: Theory and Practice in International Relations* (London; University of London Press, 1975).

Grubel, H.G., 'The case against the New International Economic Order', *Review of World Economics,* Vol. 113 (1977), pp. 284-307.

Haas, Peter M., 'Knowledge, power and international policy coordination', *International Organization,* special edition, Vol. 46, No. 1 (Winter 1992).

Haggard, S. and Simmons, Beth A., 'Theories of international regimes', *International Organization,* Vol. 41, No. 3 (Summer 1987), pp. 491-517.

Hardy, Garthorne, *The International Anarchy, 1904-1914* (London: George Allen and Unwin, 1926).

Harle, V. (ed.), *The Political Economy of Food* (Westmead, Hants: Saxon House, 1978).

Harris, N., *Of Bread and Guns: The World Economy in Crisis* (Harmondsworth: Penguin Books, 1983).

Hartley, K., *Problems of Economic Policy* (London: George Allen and Unwin, 1977).

Harvey, D., *The Limits to Capital* (Oxford; Basil Blackwell, 1982).

Hall, John A., *Powers and Liberties: The Causes and Consequences of the Rise of the West* (Oxford: Basil Blackwell, 1985).

Hayter, Teresa, *Aid As Imperialism* (Harmondsworth: Penguin Books, 1971).

Hayter, Teresa, *The Creation of World Poverty* (London: Pluto Press, 1981).

Heiduk, Gunter and Yamamura, Kozo (eds.), *Technological Competition and Interdependence: The Search for Policy in the United States, West Germany, and Japan* (London: Washington University Press, 1990).

Heilbroner, R.L., *Between Capitalism and Socialism: Essays in Political Economics* (New York: Vintage Books, 1970).

Held, David, 'Democracy: from city-states to a cosmopolitan order?', *Political Studies*, Vol. XL, special issue (1992), pp. 10-19.

Held, David, *Democracy and the New International Order* (London: Institute for Public Policy Research, 1993).

Hensman, C.R., *Rich Against Poor: The Reality of Aid* (Harmondsworth: Allen Lane, 1971).

Hills, Jill, 'Dependency theory and its relevance today: international institutions in telecommunications and structural power', *Review of International Studies,* Vol. 20, No. 2 (April 1994) pp. 169-186.

Hine, Robert C., special edition of *Journal of Common Market Studies* on 'Regionalism in the international economy', Vol. XXX, No. 2 (June 1992).

Hine, Robert C., 'Regionalism and the integration of the world economy', *Journal of Common Market Studies*, Vol. XXX, No. 2 (June 1992), pp. 115-23.

Hirsch, Fred., *Social Limits to Growth* (London: Routledge and Kegan Paul, 1977).

Hirsch, Fred and Goldthorpe, J.H. (eds.), *The Political Economy of Inflation* (Oxford: Martin Robertson, 1978).

Hirschman, Albert O., *National Power and the Structure of Foreign Trade* (Berkeley: University of California Press, (1980 (expanded edn.)).

Holland, Stewart, *The Global Economy: From Meso to Macro Economics* (London: Weidenfeld and Nicolson, 1987).

Hollingsworth, J. Rogers (ed.), *Government and Economic Performance,* special edition of *The Annals* (Beverly Hills: Sage, 1982).

Hollis, M. and Smith, S., *Explaining and Understanding International Relations* (Oxford: Clarendon Press, 1991).

Holloway, J. and Picciotto, S. (eds.), *State and Capital: A Marxist Debate* (London: Edward Arnold, 1978).

Holsti, K.J., *Peace and War: Armed Conflicts and International Order 1648-1989* (Cambridge: Cambridge University Press, 1991).

Hopkins, R.F. and Puchala, D.J., *Global Food Interdependence: Challenge to United States' Policy* (New York: Columbia University Press, 1980).

Howard, M.C. and King, J.E. *The Political Economy of Marx* (Harlow: Longman, 1975).

Iida, Keisuke, 'Analytic uncertainty and international cooperation: theory and application to international economic policy coordination', *International Studies Quarterly*, Vol. 37, No. 4 (1993), pp. 431-57.

Ilchman W.F. and Uphoff, N.T., *The Political Economy of Change* (Berkeley: University of California Press, 1971).

Ilgen, T.L., *Autonomy and Interdependence: US-Western European Monetary and Trade Relations, 1958-1984* (Totowa, NJ: Rowman and Allanheld, 1985).

Inkles, Alex, 'The emerging social structure of the world', *World Politics*, Vol. 27 (1974), pp. 467-95.

Isaak, R.A., *International Political Economy: Managing World Economic Change* (Englewood Cliffs NJ: Prentice-Hall, 1991).

Jacobson, H.K., *Networks of Interdependence: International Organizations and the Global Political System,* (New York: Knopf, 1984).

Jacquemin, A.P. and de Jong, H.W. (eds.), *Markets, Corporate Behaviour and the State,* (The Hague: Martinus Nijhoff, 1976).

Jassawalla, M., Okum, T. and Araki, T. (eds.), *Information Technology and Global Interdependence* (New York and London: Greenwood, 1989).

Jenkins, R., *Exploitation: The World Power Structure and the Inequality of Nations* (London: MacGibbon and Kee, 1970).

Jessop, Bob., *The Capitalist State* (Oxford: Martin Robertson, 1982).

Johns, R.A., 'Transnational business, national friction structures and international exchange', *Review of International Studies*, Vol. 10, No. 2 (April 1984), pp. 125-42.

Johnson, Harry G., *Technology and Economic Interdependence* (London: Macmillan for the Trade Policy Research Centre, 1975).

Jones, R.J. Barry (ed.), *Perspectives on Political Economy: Alternatives to the Economics of Depression* (London: Pinter Publishers, 1983).

Jones, R.J. Barry, *Conflict and Control in the World Economy: Contemporary Economic Realism and Neo-Mercantilism* (Brighton: Harvester/Wheatsheaf, 1986).

Jones, R.J. Barry (ed.), *The Worlds of Political Economy: Alternative Approaches to the Study of Contemporary Political Economy* (London: Pinter Publishers, 1988).

Jones, R.J. Barry and Willetts, Peter (eds.), *Interdependence on Trial: Studies in the Theory and Reality of Contemporary Interdependence* (London: Pinter Publishers, 1984).

Jones, Roy E., 'The English School of international relations: a case for closure', *Review of International Studies*, Vol. 7, No. 1 (January 1981), pp. 1-13.

Katzenstein, P.J., 'International interdependence: some long-term trends and recent changes', *International Organization*, Vol. 29 (1975), pp. 1021-34.

Kegley, C.W. and McGowan, P.(eds.), *The Political Economy of Foreign Policy Behavior* (Beverly Hills: Sage, 1981).

Kelly, H.H. and Thibaut, J.W., *Interpersonal Relations: A Theory of Interdependence* (New York: John Wiley and Sons, 1978).

Kennedy, Paul, *The Rise and Fall of the Great Powers: Economic Change and Military Conflict from 1500 to 2000* (London: Unwin Hyman, 1988).

Kennet, W., Whittey, L. and Holland, S., *Sovereignty and Multinational Corporations* (London; Fabian Society, 1971).

Kenwood, A.G. and Lougheed, A.L., *The Growth of the International Economy, 1820-1980* (London: George Allen and Unwin, 1983).

Keohane, Robert O., *After Hegemony: Cooperation and Discord in the World Political Economy* (Princeton, NJ: Princeton University Press, 1984).

Keohane, Robert O. (ed.), *Neorealism and its Critics* (New York: Columbia University Press, 1986).

Keohane, Robert O., 'Reciprocity in international relations', *International Organization*, Vol. 40 (Winter 1986), pp. 1-27.

Keohane, Robert O., 'International institutions: two approaches', *International Studies Quarterly*, Vol. 32 (1988), pp. 379-96.

Keohane, Robert, O. and Hoffmann, Stanley (eds.), *The New European Community: Decisionmaking and Institutional Change* (Boulder, Colo.: Westview Press, 1991).

Keohane, Robert O. and Nye, Joseph S. Jr. (eds.) *Transnational Relations and World Politics* (Cambridge, Mass.: Harvard University Press, 1972).

Keohane, Robert O., and Nye, Joseph S., Jr., *Power and Interdependence: World Politics in Transition* (Boston: Little, Brown, 1977).

Keohane, Robert O., and Nye, Joseph S., Jr., 'Power and Interdependence revisited', *International Organization*, Vol. 41, No 4 (Autumn 1987), pp. 725-53.

Kindleberger, C.P., *Power and Money: The Politics of International Economics and the Economics of International Politics* (New York: Basic Books, 1970).

Knorr, Klaus, *Power and Wealth; The Political Economy of International Power* (New York: Basic Books, 1973).

Krasner, Stephen D., 'State power and the structure of international trade', *World Politics*, Vol. 28 (1976), pp. 317-47.

Krasner, Stephen D. (ed.), *International Regimes* (Ithaca: Cornell University Press, 1983).

Krasner, Stephen D., *Structural Conflict: The Third World Against Global Liberalism* (Berkeley: University of California Press, 1985).

Kratochwil, Friedrich V., *Rules, Norms, and Decisions: On the Conditions of Practical and Legal Reasoning in International Relations and Domestic Affairs* (Cambridge: Cambridge University Press, 1989)

Kroll, John A., 'The complexity of interdependence, *International Studies Quarterly*, Vol. 37 (1993), pp. 321-47.

Krugman, Paul, *Geography and Trade* (Leuven: Leuven University Press; and Cambridge, Mass.: MIT Press, 1991).

Lake, David A., 'Leadership, hegemony, and the international economy: naked emperor or tattered monarch with potential', *International Studies Quarterly*, Vol. 37, No. 4 (1993), pp. 459-89.

Langlois, R.N. (ed.), *Economics as a Process: Essays in the New Institutional Economics* (Cambridge: Cambridge University Press, 1986).

Lash, Scott and Ury, John, *The End of Organized Capitalism* (Cambridge, Mass.: Polity Press, 1987).

Laszlo, E. *et al.*, *The Obstacles to the New International Economic Order*, (New York: Pergamon Press, for UNITAR and CEESTEM, 1980).

Lean, G., *Rich World: Poor World* (London: George Allen and Unwin, 1978).

Leontiades, J.C., *Multinational Corporate Strategy*, (Aldershot: Gower, 1985).

Lewis, W. Arthur, *Evolution of the International Economic Order* (Princeton, NJ: Princeton University Press, 1978).

Lindber, L. *et al.* (eds.), *Stress and Contradiction in Modern Capitalism* (Lexington: D.C. Heath, 1975).

Lipton, Merle, *Capitalism and Apartheid: South Africa, 1910-84* (Aldershot: Gower, 1985).

List, Friedrich, *The National System of Political Economy* (1841) (trans. S.S. Lloyd; London: Longman Green, 1904).

Little, R. and McKinlay, R.D., 'Linkage responsiveness and the nation-state: an alternative conceptualization of interdependence', *British Journal of International Studies*, Vol. 4, No. 3 (October 1978), pp. 209-25.

Lowes Dickinson, G., *The International Anarchy, 1904-1914* (London: George Allen and Unwin, 1926).

Luard, Evan, *The Management of the World Economy* (London: Macmillan, 1983).

Luard, Evan, *The Globalization of Politics: The Changed Focus of Political Action in the Modern World* (New York: New York University Press, 1990).

McClellan, J. (ed.), *The Global Financial Structure in Transition: Consequences for International Finance and Trade* (Lexington, Mass.: Lexington Books, 1985).

McGrew, A.G. and Lewis, P.G. (eds.), *Global Politics: Globalization and the Nation-State* (Cambridge: Polity Press, 1992).

McKibbin, W.J. and Sachs, J., *Global Linkages: Macroeconomic Interdependence and Cooperation in the World Economy* (Washington, DC: Brookings Institution, 1991).

McKinlay, R.D. and Little, R., *Global Problems and World Order* (London: Pinter Publishers, 1986).

MacNeil, J., Winsemius, P. and Yakushiji, T., *Beyond Interdependence: The Meshing of the World's Economy and the Earth's Ecology* (New York: OUP, 1991).

Maghoori, Ray and Ramberg, Bennett (eds.), *Globalism Versus Realism: International Relations' Third Debate* (Boulder, Colo.: Westview Press, 1982).

Manning, C.A.W., *The Nature of International Society* (London: G. Bell and Sons Ltd., 1962).

Mansbach, R, Ferguson, Y, and Lampert, D., *The Web of World Politics: Nonstate Actors in the Global System* (Englewood Cliffs, NJ: Prentice-Hall, 1976).

Mesarovic, M. and Pestel, E., *Mankind at the Turning Point* (New York: Dutton/Readers Digest 1974 and London: Hutchinson, 1975).

Merlini Cesare, *Economic Summits and Western Decision-Making* (London: Croom Helm, 1984).

Michaely, Michael, *Concentration in International Trade* (Amsterdam: North Holland Publishing Co., 1962).

Minchinson, W.W. (ed.), *Mercantilism: System or Expediency* (Lexington: D.C. Heath, 1969).

Modelski, G. (ed.), *Multinational Corporations and World Order* (Beverly Hills: Sage, 1972).

Moon, Bruce E., 'Consensus or compliance? Foreign-policy change and external dependence', *International Organization*, Vol. 39, No. 2 (Spring 1985), pp, 297-329.

Moore, Lynden, *The Growth and Structure of International Trade Since the Second World War* (Brighton: Wheatsheaf, 1985).

Moran, M., 'The politics of international business', *British Journal of International Studies*, Vol. 8, No. 2 (April 1978), pp. 217-36.

Moran, M. and Wright, M. (ed.), *The Market and the State: Studies in Interdependence* (London: Macmillan, 1991).

Morgenthau, H.J., *Politics Among Nations: The Struggle for Power and Peace* (New York: Alfred Knopf, numerous editions).

Morse, E., 'Crisis diplomacy, interdependence and the politics of international economic relations', in R. Tanter and R. Ullman (eds.), *Theory and Policy in International Relations* (Princeton, NJ: Princeton University Press, 1972).

Morse, E., *Modernization and Transformation in International Relations* (New York: Free Press, 1976).

Morse, E., 'Interdependence in world politics', in J.N. Rosenau, K.W. Thompson and G. Boyd (eds.), *World Politics: An Introduction* (New York: Free Press, 1976).

Mueller, D.C. and Barnet, R.J., *Global Reach: The Power of Multinational Corporations* (New York: Simon and Schuster, 1974).

Mulroney, Brian, *Trade Outlook: Globalization or Regionalization* (Singapore: Institute of Southeast Asian Studies, 1990).

Murphy, Craig N. and Tooze, Roger, *The New International Political Economy* (Boulder, Colo.: Lynne Rienner, 1991)

Murray, R., *Multinational Companies and Nation States* (London: Spokesman Books, 1975).

Murray, R., *Multinationals Beyond the Market* (Brighton: Harvester, 1981).

Myrdal, Gunnar, *The Political Elements in the Development of Economic Theory* (trans. Paul Streeten; London: Routledge and Kegan Paul, 1953).

Nelson, J.M., *Aid, Influence and Foreign Policy* (New York: Macmillan, 1968).

Nkrumah, Kwame, *Neo-Colonialism: The Last Stage of Imperialism* (London: Heinemann, 1965).

Noelke, M., *Europe-Third World Interdependence: Facts and Figures* (Brussels: European Commission, 1979).

Northedge, F., 'Transnationalism: the American illusion', *Millennium*, Vol. 5 (1970).

O'Brien, P.K. and Pigman, G.A., 'Free trade, British hegemony and the international economic order in the nineteenth century', *Review of International Studies*, Vol. 18, No. 2 (April 1992), pp. 89-113.

O'Brien, R. Cruise (ed.), *Information, Economics and Power: The North-South Dimension* (London: Hodder and Stoughton, 1983).
O'Brien, R. Cruise, and Helleiner, G.K., 'The political economy of information in a changing international economic order', *International Organization*, Vol. 34, No. 4 (Autumn 1980), pp. 445-70.
OECD, *World Economic Interdependence and the Evolving North-South Relationship* (Paris: OECD, 1983).
Offe, C., *Disorganized Capitalism* (Cambridge: Polity Press, 1985).
Olson, Mancur, *The Logic of Collective Action: Public Goods and the Theory of Groups* (Cambridge: Cambridge University Press, 1965).
Olson, Mancur, *The Rise and Decline of Nations: Economic Growth, Stagflation, and Social Rigidities* (New Haven: Yale University Press, 1982).
Olson, R.K., *U.S. Foreign Policy and the New International Economic Order: Negotiating Global Problems, 1974-1981* (Frances Pinter, 1981).
Olson, W.C. and Groom, A.J.R., *International Relations Then and Now: Origins and Trends in Interpretation* (London: Harper Collins, 1991).
O'Meara, R.L., 'Regimes and their implications for international theory', *Millennium*, Vol. 13, No. 3 (Winter 1984), pp. 245-64.
O'Neill (ed.), *Modes of Individualism and Collectivism* (London: Heinemann, 1973).
Ostrey, Sylvia, *Interdependence: Vulnerability and Opportunity* (Washington, DC: George Washington University, 1987).
Owen, R. and Sutcliffe, B. (eds.), *Studies in the Theory of Imperialism* (London: Longman, 1972).

Parkin, M. and Zis, G. (eds.), *Inflation in Open Economies* (Manchester: Manchester University Press, 1976).
Payer, Cheryl, *Commodity Trade of the Third World* (London: Macmillan, 1975).
Payer, Cheryl, *The Debt Trap: The IMF and the Third World* (Harmondsworth: Penguin Books, 1974).
Pearce, R.D. and Singh, S., *Globalizing Research and Development* (Basingstoke: Macmillan for GSEIS, 1992).
Pearson, Lester B. *et al.*, *Partners in Development: Report of the Commission on International Development* (New York: Praeger, 1969).
Pierre, A.J. (ed.), *Unemployment and Growth in the Western Economies* (New York: Council on Foreign Relations, 1984).
Pijl, Kees van der, *The Making of an Atlantic Ruling Class* (London: Verso, 1984).
Pinder, J. (ed.), *National Industrial Strategies and the World Economy* (London: Croom Helm, 1981).
Piore, M.J. and Sabel, C.F., *The Second Industrial Divide* (New York: Basic Books, 1984).
Pirages, D. *Global Ecopolitics: The New Context for International Relations* (Belmont, Calif.: Duxbury, 1978).
Polanyi, Karl, *The Great Transformation: The Political and Economic Origins of Our Time* (Boston: Beacon Press, 1957).
Pollard, Sidney, *The Integration of the European Economy since 1815* (London: George Allen and Unwin, 1981).
Poulantzas, Nicos, *State, Power, Socialism*, (London: New Left Books, 1978).
Powelson, J.P., 'The LDCs and the terms of trade', *Economic Impact*, Vol. 22 (1978), pp. 33-7.
Prebisch, Raul, *Towards a New Trade Policy for Development* (New York: UN Publications, 1964).
Putnam, R.D. and Bayne, N., *Hanging Together: The Seven Power Summits* (Cambridge, Mass.: Harvard University Press, 1984).

Radice, H. (ed.), *International Firms and Modern Imperialism* (Harmondsworth: Penguin Books, 1975).

Rapoport, A., *Conflict in a Man-Made Environment* (Harmondsworth: Penguin Books, 1974).

Ray, J.L. and Webster, T., 'Dependency and economic growth in Latin America', *International Studies Quarterly*, Vol. 22, No. 3 (September 1978), pp. 409-34.

Reynolds, P.A., and McKinlay, R.D., 'The Concept of interdependence: its uses and misuses', in Kjell Goldmann and Gunnar Sjostedt, *Power, Capabilities, Interdependence* (Beverly Hills: Sage, 1979).

Richards, J.H., *International Economic Institutions* (London: Holt, Rinehart and Winston, 1970).

Richardson, Neil, *Foreign Policy and Economic Dependence* (Austin: University of Texas Press, 1978).

Richardson, N. and Kegley, C., 'Trade dependence and foreign policy: a longitudinal analysis', *International Studies Quarterly*, Vol. 24 (1980), pp. 191-222.

Riddell, A.R. (ed.), *Adjustment or Protectionism: The Challenge to Britain of Third World Industrialisation* (London: Catholic Institute for International Relations, 1980).

Rittberger, Volker (with Peter Mayer) (ed.), *Regime Theory and International Relations* (Oxford: Clarendon Press, 1993).

Robertson, Roland, *Globalization: Social Theory and Global Culture*, (London: Sage, 1992).

Robinson, Joan, *Economic Philosophy* (London: A.C. Watts, 1962)

Robinson, Joan, *Multinationals and Political Control* (Aldershot: Gower, 1983).

Robinson, Joan, and Eatwell, J., *An Introduction to Modern Economics* (rev. edn.; London: McGraw-Hill, 1973).

Robson, P., 'Europe 1992 and the developing countries' — special edition of *Journal of Common Market Studies*, Vol. XXIX, No. 2 (December 1990).

Rosecrance, R. and Gutowitz, W. 'Measuring interdependence: a rejoinder', *International Organization*, Vol. 35, No. 3 (Summer 1981), pp. 533-60.

Rosecrance, R. and Stein, A., 'Interdependence: myth or reality', *World Politics*, Vol. 26, No. 1 (October 1973), pp. 1-27.

Rosecrance, R. *et al.*, 'Whither interdependence', *International Organization*, Vol. 31, No. 3 (Summer 1977), pp. 425-71.

Rosenau, James N., *Linkage Politics* (New York: Free Press, 1969).

Rosenau, James N., *The Study of Global Interdependence* (London: Frances Pinter, 1980).

Rosenau, James N., *Turbulence in World Politics: A Theory of Change and Continuity* (Hemel Hempstead: Harvester/Wheatsheaf, 1990).

Rosenau, J.N. and Tromp, H. (eds.), *Interdependence and Conflict in World Politics* (Brookfield, Vt.: Avebury, 1989).

Ruggie, John Gerard, *The Antinomies of Interdependence: National Welfare and the International Division of Labor* (New York: Columbia University Press, 1983).

Russett, Bruce (ed.), *Economic Theories of International Politics* (Chicago: Markham, 1968).

Russett, Bruce, 'The mysterious case of vanishing hegemony; or, Is Mark Twain really dead?', *International Organization*, Vol. 39, No. 2 (Spring 1985) pp. 207-31.

Rustow, D.A., and Mugno, J.F., *OPEC: Success and Prospects* (Oxford: Martin Robertson, 1976).

Sampson, Anthony, *The Sovereign State: The Secret History of ITT* (London: Hodder and Stoughton, 1973).

Sampson, Anthony, *The Seven Sisters; the Great Oil Companies and the World They Made* (London: Hodder and Stoughton, 1975).

Sampson, Anthony, *The Arms Bazaar* (London: Hodder and Stoughton, 1977).

Sampson, Anthony, *The Money Lenders: Bankers in a Dangerous World* (London: Hodder and Stoughton, 1981).

Samuels, W.J. (ed.), *The Economy as a System of Power*, 2 vols. (New Brunswick, NJ: Transaction Books, 1979).

Sauvant, K.P. and Lavipour, F.G., *Controlling Multinational Enterprises: Problems, Strategies, Counterstrategies* (London: Wilton House Publications, 1976).

Schampel, James H., 'Change in material capabilities and the onset of war: a dyadic approach', *International Studies Quarterly*, Vol. 37, No. 4 (1993), pp. 395-408.

Schelling, T.C., *The Strategy of Conflict* (Oxford: Oxford University Press, 1963).

Schmidt, Hans O., 'Integration and conflict in the world economy', *Journal of Common Market Studies*, Vol. 7 (September 1969) pp. 1-18.

Schonfield, A., *Modern Capitalism: The Changing Balance of Public Power* (Oxford: Oxford University Press, 1965).

Schonfield, A., *International Economic Relations: Washington Paper No. 42* (Beverly Hills, Calif.: Sage, 1976)

Schumpeter, J.A., *Capitalism, Socialism and Democracy*, 5th. edn. (London: George Allen and Unwin, 1976).

Scibberas, E., *Multinational Electronics Companies and National Economic Policies* (Greenwich, Conn.: JAI Press, 1977).

Scott, A.M., *The Dynamics of Interdependence* (Chapel Hill: University of North Carolina Press, 1982).

Sen, Gautam, *The Military Origins of Industrialisation and International Trade Rivalry* (London: Frances Pinter Ltd., 1984).

Seers, Dudley, *The Political Economy of Nationalism* (Oxford: Oxford University Press, 1983).

Seers, D. and Joy, L., *Development in a Divided World* (Harmondsworth: Penguin Books, 1971).

Sharp, M. and Shearman, C., *European Technological Collaboration* (London: Routledge and Kegan Paul, for RIIA, 1987).

Singer, Hans and Ansari, Javed, *Rich and Poor Countries*, 2nd edn. (London: George Allen and Unwin, 1978).

Sivanandan, A., *Imperialism in the Silicon Age: Race and Class Pamphlet No. 8* (London: Institute of Race Relations, 1980).

Skolnikoff, E.B., *The International Imperatives of Technology: Technological Development and the International Political System* (Berkeley: Institute of International Studies, University of California, 1972).

Slater, R.O., Schutz, B.M. and Dorr, S.R., *Global Transformation and the Third World* (Boulder, Colo.: Lynne Rienner, 1993).

Smith, A., *The Geopolitics of Information* (London: Faber, 1980).

Smith, Adam, *An Inquiry into the Nature and Causes of the Wealth of Nations* (1776), numerous editions.

Smyth, Douglas C., 'The global economy and the Third World: coalition or cleavage', *World Politics*, Vol. 29, No. 4 (July 1977), pp. 584-609.

Snidal, Duncan, 'The limits of hegemonic stability theory', *International Organization*, Vol. 39, No 4 (Autumn 1985), pp. 579-614.

Snyder, Richard C., Bruck, H.W. and Sapun, Burbon (eds.), (New York: Free Press, 1962.

Spero, J.E., *The Politics of the International Economic Relations*, 2nd edn. (London: George Allen and Unwin, 1982).

Staniland, Martin, *What is Political Economy?: A Study in Social Theory and Underdevelopment* (New Haven, Conn.: Yale University Press, 1985).

Stauffer, R.B (ed.), *Transnational Corporations and the State* (Sydney: University of Sydney, Transnational Corporations Research Project, 1985).

Steele, D.B., 'The case for global economic management and UN system reform', *International Organization*, Vol. 39, No. 3 (Summer 1985), pp. 561-78.

Stewart, M., *The Age of Interdependence: Economic Policy in a Shrinking World* (Cambridge, Mass.: MIT Press, 1984).

Strange, Susan (ed.), *Paths to International Political Economy* (London: George Allen and Unwin, 1984).

Strange, Susan, *Casino Capitalism* (Oxford: Basil Blackwell, 1986).

Strange, Susan, *States and Markets: An Introduction to International Political Economy* (London: Pinter Publishers, 1988).

Tanzi, V. and Bovenberg, A.L., *Economic Interdependence and the International Implications of Supply-Side Economics* (Washington, DC: IMF papers, 1988).

Taylor, Michael, 'Structure, culture and action in the explanation of social change', *Politics and Society*, Vol. 17, No 2 (1989), pp. 115-62.

Taylor, P. and Groom, A.J.R. (eds.), *International Institutions at Work* (London: Pinter Publishers, 1988).

Tetreault, Mary Ann 'Measuring interdependence', *International Organization*, Vol. 34, No. 3 (Summer 1980), pp. 429-516.

Tetreault, Mary Ann 'Measuring interdependence: a response', *International Organization*, Vol. 35 (1981), pp. 557-60.

Tinbergen, Jan (ed.), *Reshaping the International Order: A Report to the Club of Rome* (London: Hutchinson, 1977 in USA: New York: E.P. Dutton, 1976).

Tollinson R. and Willett, T., 'International integration and the interdependence of economic variables', *International Organization*, Vol. 27 (Spring 1973), pp. 255-71.

Trebilcock, M., *The Political Economy of Economic Adjustment* (Toronto: University of Toronto Press, 1986).

Tucker, R.W., *The Inequality of Nations* (New York: Basic Books, 1977).

Tugendhat, C., *The Multinationals* (London: Eyre and Spottiswoode, 1971).

Turner, L., *Politics and the Multinational Corporation* (London: Fabian Society, 1969).

Turner, L., 'The oil majors in world politics', *International Affairs*, Vol. 52, No. 3 (July 1976), pp. 368-80.

Tussie, Diane, *Globalization, Regionalization and New Dilemmas in Trade Policy for Development* (Geneva: UNCTAD, 1992).

Vernon, Raymond, *Sovereignty at Bay: the Multinational Spread of US Enterprises* (London: Longman, 1971).

Viner, Jacob, 'Power versus plenty as objectives of foreign policy in the 17th and 18th Centuries', *World Politics*, Vol. 1 (1946), pp. 1-29.

Wall, David, *The Charity of Nations: The Political Economy of Foreign Aid* (New York: Basic Books, 1973).

Wallerstein, Immanuel (ed.), *World Inequality: Origins and Perspectives on the World System* (Montreal: Black Rose Books, 1975).

Wallerstein, Immanuel, *The Capitalist World-Economy* (Cambridge: Cambridge University Press, 1979).

Walter, Andrew, *World Power and World Money: The Role of Hegemony and International Monetary Order* (Hemel Hempstead: Harvester/Wheatsheaf, 1991).

Waltz, Kenneth, 'The myth of interdependence', in C. Kindleberger (ed.), *The International Corporation* (Cambridge, Mass.: MIT Press, 1970).

Waltz, Kenneth, *Theory of International Politics* (Reading, Mass.: Addison-Wesley, 1979).

Ward, Benjamin, *The Ideal Worlds of Economics: Liberal, Radical and Conservative Economic World Views* (New York: Basic Books, 1979).

Ward, Dwayne, *Toward a Critical Political Economics: A Critique of Liberal and Radical Economic Thought* (Santa Monica, Calif.: Goodyear Publishing Co., 1977).

Warren, Bill, *Imperialism: Pioneer of Capitalism* (London: Verso New Left Books, 1980).

Watson, A., *The Evolution of International Society: a Comparative Historical Analysis* (London: Routledge, 1992)

Webb, M.C. and Krasner, S.D., 'Hegemonic stability theory: an empirical assessment', *Review of International Studies*, Vol. 15, No. 2 (April 1989), pp. 183-98.

Webster, Allan and Dunning, John H. (eds.), *Structural Change in the World Economy* (London: Routledge, 1989).

Wilde, Jaap de, *Saved from Oblivion: Interdependence Theory in the First Half of the 20th Century: a Study on the Causality between War and Complex Interdependence* (Aldershot: Dartmouth Publications, 1991).

Woodis, Jack, *Introduction to Neo-Colonialism* (London: Lawrence and Wishart, 1967).

Yannopoulos, G.N. (ed.), *Europe and America, 1992* (Manchester: Manchester University Press, 1991).

Yarborough, B.V. and Yarborough, R.M., 'Cooperation in the liberalization of international trade: after hegemony, what?', *International Organization*, Vol. 41, No. 1 (Winter 1987), pp. 1-26.

Yergin, D. and Hillenbrand, M., *Global Insecurity: A Strategy for Energy and Economic Renewal* (New York: Houghton Mifflin, 1982).

Yoffie David B., 'The Newly Industrializing Countries and the political economy of protectionism', *International Studies Quarterly*, Vol. 25, No. 4 (December 1981), pp. 569-99.

Young, Oran R., 'Interdependencies in world politics', *International Journal*, Vol. 24 (Autumn 1969), pp. 726-50.

Young, Oran R., *International Cooperation: Building Regimes for Natural Resources and the Environment* (Ithaca, NY: Cornell University Press, 1989).

Young, Oran R., 'Political leadership and regime formation: on the development of institutions in international society', *International Organization*, Vol. 45, No. 3 (Summer 1991), pp. 281-308.

Index